SOCIAL WORK and SOCIAL CARE PRACTICE

SOCIAL WORK and SOCIAL CARE PRACTICE

Ian O'Conner, Mark Hughes, Danielle Turney,
Jill Wilson and Deborah Setterlund

S SAGE Publications

London ● Thousand Oaks ● New Delhi

© Pearson Education Australia

First published as Social Work and Welfare Practice, 1991, fourth
edition 2003
This edition first published 2006

 SAGE Publications Ltd
1 Oliver's Yard
55 City Road
London EC1Y 1SP

SAGE Publications Inc.
2455 Teller Road
Thousand Oaks, California 91320

SAGE Publications India Pvt Ltd
B-42, Panchsheel Enclave
Post Box 4109
New Delhi 110 017

British Library Cataloguing in Publication data

A catalogue record for this book is available from
the British Library

ISBN 0-7619-4062-6   ISBN 978-0-7619-4062-3
ISBN 0-7619-4063-4   ISBN 978-0-7619-4063-0 (pbk)

Library of Congress Control Number: 2005927513

Typeset by C&M Digitals (P) Ltd., Chennai, India
Printed in Great Britain by The Alden Press, Oxford
Printed on paper from sustainable resources

CONTENTS

PREFACE

Social work practice and education have undergone considerable change in recent years. The Care Councils, the Social Care Institute for Excellence, and the new framework for social work education and training are important developments that are still in their early stages of operation. While social work has long demonstrated a commitment to working alongside service users, a renewed emphasis on service user involvement in recent years offers possibilities as well as challenges. In these developments there is hope of a reinvigorated social work that strives for both professionalism and social justice.

However, difficulties remain. The challenge of social work practice lies in its complexity and diversity. On a daily basis social workers engage with people, groups and communities who are most damaged by social and economic structures and by the consequent ways of living and coping. Social workers often feel limited in their roles because of the particular policies of government or the organizations that employ them and many are overworked because of staff shortages or lack of funding. Some may feel let down by their professional education, which they believe has not equipped them to handle confidently the real day-to-day tasks of social work practice.

In this book we encourage social work students and practitioners to determine and control their own practice, rather than experience practice as being totally reactive to immediate demands or as being exclusively determined by external forces. We hope that through contextualizing social work and social care, by articulating the purpose of practice, by raising issues and by advocating a disciplined approach to practice, students and beginning practitioners will be able to locate themselves in practice, whatever the country, agency or field of practice may be. While we acknowledge that social work is influenced by its location within organizations and the wider legal, social welfare and social care systems, individual workers can put into practice their own social work purpose. We aim to encourage an active approach so that you are empowered to deal with, and enjoy, the challenges, diversities and complexities of practice.

In the book we introduce to Britain a practice framework that was originally developed in Australia. We provide a way of understanding human behaviour in interaction with social structures, in order to select interventions that produce improved social outcomes for the individuals, groups and communities with whom we work. Our practice framework encompasses a particular view of the world, a definition of purpose derived from that view, and a particular approach to assessment which guides the choice of interventions. While the framework draws broadly on critical, feminist and postmodern theories, we argue that different fields of practice require the application of a range of theories and knowledge and that the application of theory and knowledge needs to be guided by an explicit understanding of the purpose of social work. We have not written an encyclopaedia of practice, nor produced a series of recipes for practice. It is not our intention to provide the intricate details of specific forms of practice. You will need to go beyond this text for such an understanding and we suggest readings that are useful in this regard.

Throughout the book we acknowledge and respond to current issues in social work practice and education in Britain. In particular, each chapter of the book covers material that can assist in developing and ultimately demonstrating competence in relation to the Code of Practice for Social Care Workers, the National Occupational Standards (NOS), and the knowledge and skill requirements outlined in the Quality Assurance Agency for Higher Education's Benchmark Statement for Social Work (QAA, 2000). These documents outline the expectations of qualified workers as held by governments, regulatory bodies and employers (particularly social services departments). We will be returning to the National Occupational Standards (NOS) at various points in the text and will also be refering to the Scottish Standards in Social Work Education (SiSWE). The Standards in Social Work Education (SiSWE) draw on the NOS and key elements of the Quality Assurance Agency's Benchmark Statement and will be a key source of reference for students in Scotland. Throughout the book we also acknowledge the ongoing devolution of constitutional powers to each of the countries of the United Kingdom. While some of the implications of devolution are only just becoming apparent, we note where some differences lie, particularly in relation to social policy.

The changing nature of social work in Britain is apparent also in shifts in terminology. The language we adopt in this book reflects current terminology in social work practice. In general we speak of service users rather than clients, except where people are involuntary clients. However, in using the term 'service user' we are careful not to obscure the wide range of differences between different service user groups (Beresford, 2001). Students' practice placements are also referred to as 'practice learning opportunities', although we recognize that there are other forms of practice learning which may not take the form of a placement, such as skills labs and one-off observations of service users or workers. In this book we employ the current term 'practice assessor' to refer to the assessor of a student's work while on placement. The term 'practice teacher' is reserved for those who hold the Practice Teaching Award. Nevertheless we are mindful that practice teacher and supervisor continue to be used in a more general sense in line with past practice. In the book we use the term 'social welfare' to refer to the organized delivery of services by society to meet people's needs, including their health, social care and education needs. This term is similar to the concept 'the welfare state' and is much broader than 'individual welfare' or the provision of social security benefits.

While mainly concerned with the activities of social work practitioners and students, we also hope that the book will speak to those in social work-related occupations, such as community workers, youth workers, care managers, support workers, project workers, and Connexions Personal Advisors, among others. Some of these people may be qualified social workers, but some may not. Much is to be gained from an ongoing dialogue between social workers and their social care colleagues. We believe that these practitioners can make good use of social work knowledge and, in turn, social workers can benefit from learning more about these related fields of practice. Our conceptualization of social work in Britain is not limited to the, albeit important, role of the statutory local authority-based social worker. Nor is it limited to those who may become registered as social workers by the Care Councils. We see social work as a broad discipline, informing directly the work of those who can be officially called social workers but also informing the work of others. It is for this reason that we see our book as an introduction to social work *and social care* practice.

Many people have assisted us in this collaboration. Staff and students from the University of Queensland and Goldsmiths College, University of London, provided support and advice over the development of the book and the application of the practice framework to the UK context. We also acknowledge the ongoing support of colleagues from Griffith University (Ian O'Connor), the University of New South Wales (Mark Hughes), the Open University (Danielle Turney) and the University of Queensland (Jill Wilson and Deborah Setterlund). We are particularly indebted to Suzanne Mullally, Diane Aldridge, Michelle Rusterholz, Geoff Fitzgerald, Morrie O'Connor and Christine Kerneke for permission to use examples from their practice and we are confident that these illustrations of good practice speak to both students and practitioners. We would also like to acknowledge the support and encouragement provided by editorial staff at SAGE Publications, particularly Zoë Elliott and Anna Luker, as well the invaluable role of Pearson Education Australia in developing the Australian editions of the book.

This edition of *Social Work and Social Care Practice* is published by arrangement with Pearson Education Australia Pty Limited.

ACKNOWLEDGEMENTS

Every effort has been made to trace all the copyright holders, but if any have been inadvertently overlooked the publishers will be pleased to make the necessary arrangement at the first opportunity.

Chapter 4

Quotation on page 96 from B. Jordan (1979) *Helping in Social Work*. London: Routledge and Kegan Paul. pp. 22–3. Reproduced with permission of Thomson Publishing.

Chapter 5

Table 5.1 from P. Condliffe (1991) *Conflict Management: A Practical Guide*. Lexis Nexus, Butterworths. Reproduced with permission.

Chapter 8

Table 8.1 adapted from:
A. Gewirth (1978) *Reason and Morality*. Chicago, IL: University of Chicago Press. © The University of Chicago Press. Reproduced with permission;
Ethical Decisions for Social Work Practice, 5th edition by LOEWENBERG/ DOLGOFF © 1995. Reprinted with permission of Wadsworth, a division of Thomson Learning: www.thomsonrights.com Fax 800 730 2215; and
'Table: Bioethics Perspective – Unranked', from PRINCIPLES OF BIOMEDICAL ETHICS, FIFTH EDITION by Tom L. Beauchamp and James F. Childress, copyright © 1979, 1983, 1989, 1994, 2001 by Oxford University Press, Inc. Used by permission of Oxford University Press, Inc.

LIST OF ACRONYMS

BASW	British Association of Social Workers
CCETSW	Central Council for Education and Training in Social Work (now defunct)
CCW	Care Council for Wales/Cyngor Gofal Cymru
CMHT	Community Mental Health Team
CPN	Community Psychiatric Nurse
DfES	Department for Education and Skills
DoH	Department of Health
EU	European Union
GSCC	General Social Care Council (England)
IMF	International Monetary Fund
NHS	National Health Service
NHSCCA	National Health Service and Community Care Act 1990
NISCC	Northern Ireland Social Care Council
NOS	National Occupational Standards
NSPCC	National Society for the Prevention of Cruelty to Children
NVQ	National Vocational Qualification
ONS	Office for National Statistics
PCTs	Primary Care Trusts
PSSRU	Personal Social Services Research Unit
QAA	Quality Assurance Agency
SCIE	Social Care Institute for Excellence
SiSWE	Standards in Social Work Education (Scotland)
SSI	Social Services Inspectorate (now incorporated within the Commission for Social Care Inspection)
SSSC	Scottish Social Services Council

1 INTRODUCING THE PRACTICE FRAMEWORK

In this chapter we examine:

- The practice framework developed in this book;
- The contexts of social work, including social welfare policies and politics, and the social work organization;
- The importance of understanding people's social arrangements;
- The focus and purpose of social work practice;
- Our assumptions underpinning the practice framework;
- The book's structure and chapter contents.

WHAT IS SOCIAL WORK PRACTICE?

THE ACTIVITIES OF SOCIAL WORK PRACTITIONERS

Social work practice seeks to promote human well-being and to redress human suffering and injustice. Practitioners aim to mobilize the forces of the individual, community and state to address the processes by which individuals and groups are marginalized or diminished in their capacity to participate as citizens. Such practice maintains a particular concern for those who are most excluded from social, economic or cultural processes or structures. Consequently social work practice is a political activity and tensions between rights to care, control and self-determination are very much a professional concern. This agenda is expressed in a wide variety of practice contexts involving many different service user groups. It is practised in government settings, voluntary organizations, religious organizations, and the profit-making sector. In any one of these settings, social work practice embraces a huge variety of activities.

The authors asked a group of social work students from Goldsmiths College, London, about their first few days of placement. Their activities included:

- typing letters to service users about assessment interviews;
- arranging visits to outside agencies;
- checking resources in the borough;
- attending an information seminar on benefit entitlements;
- talking through an induction programme with a practice teacher;
- attending a large team meeting;
- reading through case notes;
- attending a ward round;
- visiting an older service user at home;
- participating in a case allocation meeting;
- having a supervision meeting.

Practitioners engage in all of these activities and more. Yet many find it hard to reconcile the image of the highly skilled professional with the apparently mundane activities undertaken in their day-to-day work. The mundane activities, such as filing or attending staff meetings, are often discounted as not being real professional practice. It is only when involved in a needs assessment interview or when facilitating a community meeting that they feel they are actually engaged in professional practice. Such a perspective reflects the divorce between the actuality of day-to-day social work practice and the way in which it is conceptualized and written about. In contrast, our text encompasses and embraces the diversity of practice and the myriad activities that social workers perform during the course of their work.

To understand social work practice one must take as a starting point the fact that social work exists only in contexts: personal, social, historical, organizational, economic and ideological, among others. It is socially constructed, not an ahistorical technological entity. By this we mean that social work and other forms of social care did not always exist and that they take different forms in different types of societies. The form that social work has taken in western societies reflects the particular issues associated with the later stages of capitalism. However, even within the western economies the characteristics and forms of social work vary between countries.

These variations in social work reflect aspects of the culture and the role of the state and social welfare in each country. The increasingly regulated form of social work that is developing in Britain is different from the social work practised in government agencies in Sweden, and different again from the social work of the voluntary sector in the United States. In New Zealand there are significant differences in how social work is conceptualized and practised because the profession has sought to respond to the bicultural nature of New Zealand society (Nash, 2001). For example, *Kaupapa* Maori research (where Maori self-determination and constructions of knowledge mark the starting point of the research) has the potential to inform western research and facilitate the development of Indigenous theories of social work and Indigenous interventions (Gibbs, 2001: 36). In the Asia-Pacific region the form that social work practice takes reflects the socio-economic reality that many Asian countries cannot afford extensive public welfare systems. In this context, Mehta and Vasoo (2001: 4) suggest that social work needs to focus more on family support and other development activities such as parenting, family lifestyle education, community care, and economic cooperatives to improve individual skills and capabilities.

In China, where cultural traditions are likely to inhibit some aspects of social work such as open sharing of problems, other traditions such as community rituals, and the value placed on individual qualities such as perseverance, may be utilized to develop innovative interventions that strengthen relationships within communities (Chan, 2000).

In this book, we are engaged in an exercise of transferring learning from the Australian context, itself based largely on British conceptualizations of social welfare, to the UK context. However, we are careful not to import without question the approaches and methodologies developed in different contexts to respond to the issues of our own context (Payne, 1997: 7–13). These historical and contextual issues are also important for the individual workers. We each bring to our practice our personal biographies, capabilities and desires as a product of and a participant in society.

THE PRACTICE FRAMEWORK

In the book we develop a practice framework to assist students and practitioners in understanding the purpose of social work and in considering how they may express this purpose through their own professional practice. While recognizing factors that constrain social work activities, we see individual social workers as active agents, capable of making decisions about how they use themselves and their power in their practice. The practice framework is presented as a concept map in Figure 1.1. This concept map is reintroduced at the beginning of each chapter with those dimensions of the practice framework covered in the chapter highlighted. Each chapter builds on the previous one so that by the end of the book the practice framework is fully explicated.

THE SOCIAL WELFARE CONTEXT

Social work developed as part of society's institutional responses to tensions of production and reproduction in the current social and economic arrangements (Berreen and Browne, 1986). These institutional responses are referred to as social welfare or the welfare state. Jordan argues that social work emerges where communities start breaking up under pressure from market forces:

> It arises where systems of reciprocity, sharing and redistribution (either informal, as in communities and networks, or formal, as in public welfare schemes) begin to break down and are replaced by contractual exchanges, leaving some individuals without protection. It substitutes 'professional friendship' (or 'targeted intervention' in present-day business-speak) for the inclusive membership rights provided by those disintegrating systems, thus seeking to shore up the social relations of disrupted communities, and shield the vulnerable and excluded. There is a contradiction at the heart of social work, because it is spawned by market-orientated economic individualism, yet its values are those of a caring, inclusive, reciprocal community that takes collective responsibility for its members. (1997: 9–10)

It follows therefore that social work practice is bound to, but not determined by, the domain of social welfare and the social, economic and culture structures in which it is embedded. This domain encompasses not just a wide range of formal and informal institutional

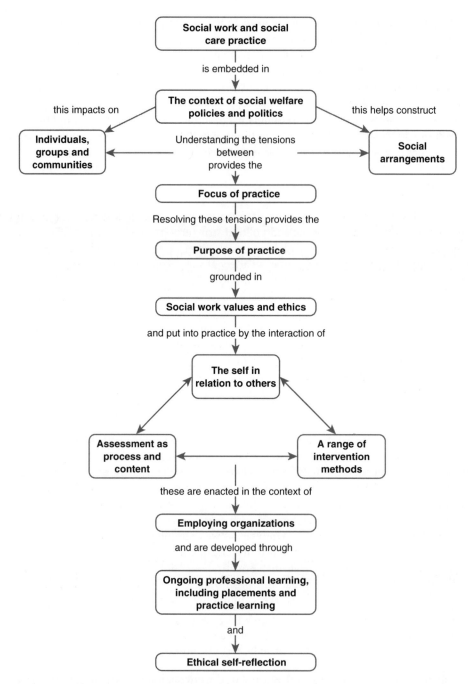

Figure 1.1   The practice framework

arrangements related to the distribution and redistribution of resources (e.g. the market, informal care, social security benefits, personal social services and so on), but also knowledge and ideology about social welfare and social processes. By this we mean that neither knowledge nor practice exists independently of its context. Social work practice is part of these welfare-related processes and social workers' understanding of and interventions in the world draw upon their arrangements, knowledge and ideology. This knowledge, technology and ideology do not exist independently of specific social processes or broader social conditions. See Payne (1991, 1997) for a discussion of the impact of the changes in social and economic circumstances and their corresponding impact on social work theory.

THE ORGANIZATIONAL CONTEXT

Most social work practice is carried out in organizations. These organizations are similarly influenced by the social, economic and political structures in which they exist and by prevailing knowledge and ideology. Organizations also develop their own culture, interpreting and reinterpreting external influences in a variety of ways. Throughout the 1980s and 1990s social work organizations were significantly influenced by New Right and managerialist ideas and practices largely instigated by the legislation, policies and funding measures of central government. And now, managerial language and frameworks of thinking have become so pervasive that it is hard to know how we talked about things before we had the words: cost-effectiveness, quality assurance, performance indicators and outcome measurement.

A concern for many social workers in the UK is the extent to which organizational and managerial issues impact on a sense of professional autonomy and an ability to respond to the complexity and ambiguity of the work. Sheppard (1995), drawing on Jamous and Peloile (1970), summarizes part of this tension as indetermination versus technicality. In responding to the complexities of practice, organizations tend to encourage workers to follow clearly articulated procedures and to stay focused on and improve their technical skill. Professional agendas, however, tend to highlight the need for workers to be more flexible, creative and independent so that they can engage with the indeterminacy and ambiguities of practice. In order to be effective, social work (as a profession) and individual social workers (in their organizations) need to find a balance between exercising technical skill within procedural frameworks and exercising a degree of autonomy which may at times be used to challenge the organization. However, as we examine in Chapter 6, it is important for social workers not to become trapped in a critique which simply pits social work (as a caring, value-based profession) against organizations and bureaucracies (as uncaring, monolithic structures). Professional and organizational agendas often coalesce and the authority and usefulness of social workers commonly arise from the role they play within organizational systems.

SOCIAL WORK AND SOCIAL ARRANGEMENTS

The domain of social work practice consists of the interaction between people and social arrangements. We have chosen the term 'social arrangements' to emphasize that the world with which the individual interacts is socially constructed. So in this book the term 'social arrangements' refers to the many processes and relationships by which people and the social structure are produced and reproduced. Thus it encompasses the relationships between individuals and others, such as their friends, families, employers, community and so on. Similarly, social arrangements also include those formal and informal institutions of the state: the judicial, health, economic, social care and education systems, the labour market and so on. Social arrangements express and reflect the distribution of power and the processes of domination and subordination in society, including those related to gender, disability, class, ethnicity, sexual identity, age and so on.

People's lives are not only affected by the apparently objective components of these factors, but also by the way we theorize about them. Thus it may seem a fact that a particular individual is a 10-year-old girl, but our understanding of what it means to be a 10-year-old girl and what capacities a 10-year-old girl has are heavily influenced by a whole range of theoretical formulations which are culturally, occupationally and historically specific. Thus the understanding that a teacher or social worker in a local authority in Wales has of the needs, wants, desires and rights of a 10-year-old girl may differ from the understanding of the child's parents, or from the parents and teachers of a similarly aged child living in a village in Bangladesh. Similarly for example, it is only in the recent past that we saw people with Down's Syndrome or other learning disabilities as lacking any capacity to live an independent life and assumed that they were most appropriately cared for in institutions. Now we are guided by an approach which seeks to maximize human potential, social inclusion and human rights, and to respond to service users' own definitions of their needs.

Factors such as class, 'race', gender and so on affect the nature and quality of people's interactions with their social arrangements. For individuals and groups these factors may be experienced singly or in combination. However, according to Vernon (1999) the way various factors intersect can multiply the effects on the individual and the oppression they experience. For example, where social constructions of age, gender and sexual identity intersect, it is possible to identify the combined impact that ageism, sexism and homophobia has on the invisibility of and discrimination against older lesbians (Fullmer et al., 1999). While such factors do not solely determine an individual's experience, when they are examined we can often gain a better understanding of why people are experiencing difficulties or tensions in their interactions with social arrangements.

ASSUMPTIONS UNDERPINNING THE PRACTICE FRAMEWORK

Our practice framework makes certain assumptions about the interactions between people and social arrangements and about the nature of social arrangements. We argue that people do not exist outside of social arrangements; they form social arrangements and are formed by them. These assumptions are important because they are central to our analysis of the purpose, roles and tasks of social work practice. They provide the lenses through which we understand and hence engage with social situations and engage with theory and knowledge. Practice involves choices – choices of how to understand and how to act, as well as value choices – choices of preferred ends and ways of being in the world. The assumptions underlying our approach to social work inform our choices and understanding.

Our first assumption is that there is no fixed and unchanging reality and that people are active participants in the construction of their world. People constantly engage in a process of making sense of (i.e. imposing some order on) their world as they interact with it and act in terms of the sense they make of particular aspects of the world. One implication of this assumption is that we cannot assume that our understanding of a particular aspect of the world is the same as another person's. In consequence, a basic task and process for social workers is endeavouring to understand the sense the other makes of the world. This position contrasts with the perspective that individuals are passive and are formed or 'determined' by a given objective external reality.

Our second assumption is that while people are active agents, they do not individually control the social, economic or personal circumstances in which they find themselves and make choices. So social arrangements and social structures are real constraining forces in people's lives. Thus, while an individual may express a problem as being solely located within themselves, that problem may have a social counterpart. For example, a young unemployed man living in a rural area who feels depressed and perhaps suicidal, is likely to experience his emotional pain and physical symptoms as a personal problem. He may not be aware of the range of socio-economic and cultural factors that are often associated with male suicide, such as lack of employment opportunities in economically depressed rural economies, male cultural norms that can constrain emotional development, and difficulties within family relationships. Such a perspective assumes that there is a dynamic relationship between people and social arrangements. This may be contrasted with the view that the relationship between people and the environment is a deterministic, linear one in which the individual is totally determined by external environmental forces or alternatively by internal psychic forces.

The third assumption of our practice framework is that social arrangements are the result of the actions of people, individually and collectively, and are reproduced and changed by such actions (Mullaly, 1997: 84). For example, people do not necessarily consciously intend to reproduce the existing economic system through engaging in paid labour, or the existing system of family relations through marrying, but it is nonetheless the unintended consequence of their activity and a prerequisite for it.

Our final assumption is that power is always present in human relationships. There are many sources and mechanisms of power: economic, sexual, ideological, professional, age, 'race' and so on. People may simultaneously exercise power and be governed by it. Power and the exercise of power are central to the dynamic interplay between people and social arrangements. Social workers should be concerned with how power is experienced by individuals, groups and communities, and the difficulties it causes for them and the potential it offers. Power is not simply an oppressive force, it also produces relationships, structures and knowledge that can be enriching and liberating (Cohen, 1985). Social work and social sciences discourses function as sources of power. So too do other discourses that reflect ideological assumptions about gender, class, 'race' and age. Social work service users may find their capacity to attribute meaning to their own experiences are undermined by such discourses. From our position, it is important that social workers understand their own power and the ways in which this can be used to advantage or disadvantage others.

SOCIAL WORK PURPOSE

In day-to-day practice and in developing services, social workers are frequently involved in situations where there is tension in the interaction between people and social arrangements. We are not arguing here that the purpose of practice is to fit the individual into the current social arrangements. Who identifies this tension and how it is defined can vary. People may themselves experience the interactions as uncomfortable and therefore seek assistance. Examples might include:

- a man with depression seeking assistance from a community mental health team;
- a teenager seeking assistance from a community-based families agency because she is subject to assault at home;
- a son seeking help from social services with caring for his disabled father;
- a community group seeking assistance to remedy the lack of after-hours public transport in its suburb.

In each of these situations the tension in the interaction between the individual(s) and social arrangements is identified by the people concerned. Alternatively, the request or requirement for intervention may come from a concerned other or from the state, as in the following examples:

- a worker from a youth centre approaching a group of young people who have been reported for being disruptive in a shopping centre;
- a social worker contacting a family to investigate an anonymous allegation of child abuse;
- a care manager visiting an older person awaiting discharge from hospital;
- a youth worker inviting groups of young people to be involved in developing local resources.

The identification of tension between people and social arrangements as the focus of social work activity does not define a purpose or a direction for practice. It is simply a way of describing the situations with which social workers become involved. The direction of practice will come from how a worker understands their professional purpose and their related analysis of a situation. For example, in the situation involving the supposedly disruptive young people, a social worker who sees her or his purpose as assisting young people to function better in society may attempt to involve them in mentoring or social skills group work to encourage more acceptable behaviour. The source of the tension is located in the young people (individually and as a group) and it is the young people who are engaged in change, rather than the social arrangements. The worker's change efforts do not consider the possibility of a collaborative partnership between the shopping centre management and the young people to generate broader solutions such as developing more appropriate spaces for young people.

One of our central assumptions about the nature of the interaction between people and social arrangements is that people act *intentionally*: 'They are agents of experiences rather than simply undergoers of experiences' (Bandura, 2001: 4). This applies just as much to social workers as it does to service users. In our capacity to shape our own and others' experiences, we need to be clear about the direction we want our practice to take. That is why a clear understanding of purpose is central to our practice framework.

We define the *focus and purpose of social work practice* as follows:

> The *focus* of social work practice is the interaction between people and social arrangements. The *purpose* of practice is to promote the development of equitable relationships and the development of people's power and control over their own lives, and hence to improve the interaction between people and social arrangements.

This definition identifies the focus for practice as: the interaction between people and social arrangements. It also provides a purpose and direction for practice: the development of equitable relationships and empowerment so as to enhance the interaction between people and social arrangements. By defining the focus and purpose in this manner we have provided:

1. a basis for assessment of practice situations;
2. a direction for any intervention; and
3. a benchmark for evaluating the outcomes of intervention. That is, the extent to which service user outcomes (e.g. increased information, enhanced social networks, receipt of community services) resulted in the development of equitable relationships and the service user's development of power and control over their life.

This formulation of the purpose of practice expresses a clear view of the preferred end state: of equitable relationships and power and control over one's life. The concern with equitable relationships reflects social work's mandate to express what Jordan refers to as the common interest: 'Social workers are not concerned exclusively with individual choices or social choices, they work on the borderlines between these, and are part of the process by which societies try to coordinate these two forms of decision making' (1990: 28). As such our definition of purpose recognizes the limits of empowerment: that the empowerment of one individual should only occur in a way that promotes equitable relationships. It also accepts that the abuse of a child in a family is a matter of public as well as individual concern. So too the assault of women, discrimination against black people and so on. Each is legitimately a public matter and merits a publicly sanctioned response. Our purpose thus acknowledges and accommodates the fact that much social work practice in the United Kingdom, as elsewhere, is conducted within statutory or quasi-statutory organizations.

SOCIAL WORK KNOWLEDGE

The practice framework presented in this book draws broadly on ideas from critical, feminist and postmodern theories. Critical theories focus on the relationship between private troubles and public issues by providing an analysis of the ways in which societal structures and processes advantage some groups and marginalize and disadvantage others. Feminist theories have developed this analysis and show how different factors such as gender, socio-economic status, 'race', age, disability and sexual identity interact to shape individual human experience. Postmodern theories help us understand the complexity of power relations and the ways in which power can be exercised through language and dominant discourse. We encourage you to investigate these theoretical ideas and their application to social work in more depth. Critical reviews of theory for social work can be found in Fook (1993), Payne (1997) and Healy (2005).

While we acknowledge these theoretical influences in our practice framework, we believe that no single theory guarantees empowering, liberating, radical or conservative practice processes and outcomes. No one theory applies to all situations or all levels of practice (Mattaini, 1995: 80); different theories have their strengths and limitations (Mendes, 1997: 482) and different levels of usefulness at different points in the helping process (Sheafor et al., 2000: 84). The application of specific theories should be guided by what we know about what works for which service users under what circumstances and our sense of the purpose of professional practice.

From our position it is important that social workers understand their purpose and that they can engage with theoretical and professional knowledge so as to implement purposeful interventions. The professional challenge is therefore to develop a critical reflective practice that articulates purpose, establishes preferred outcomes with service users, systematically employs values, skills, knowledge and theories and incorporates strategies to evaluate with service users the effectiveness of the work undertaken in achieving outcomes. Equally important is the professional challenge for practitioners of working in a critically reflective manner within the constraints and opportunities posed by the parameters of their employing organization.

THE VALUE OF THE PRACTICE FRAMEWORK

Our framework for social work practice focuses on the dynamics of power in interactions between people and social arrangements, and hence draws attention to the interactions between workers and service users, and workers and social arrangements. In this it does not differ from other approaches to practice in attending to the relational aspects of practice. However, the approach has specific implications for how that relation may be characterized. Within the many approaches to practice there is a continuum along which the relational aspects are characterized: at one pole there is a top-down approach where the professional is the expert, controlling the interaction and in control of the requisite knowledge; at the other pole, the practitioner is a co-learner with the service user, seeking mutuality in the relationship. Our approach strives towards mutuality in that it directs the practitioner to seek to understand the world of the other and locate the practitioner as part of the social arrangements with which the other interacts. In so locating the practitioner (and their agency) in the analysis, it does not ignore the knowledge and expertise of the practitioner and in many cases their capacity to assert their interpretation of situations. The appropriateness or otherwise of such an assertion is judged against the explicit statement of purpose.

This formulation of social work practice has significant benefits:

- it is a frame of reference which can be grounded in daily practice;
- it provides a clear statement about the purpose of social work practice;
- it recognizes that social work and social care are part of the social arrangements that may impact positively or negatively on people's lives;
- it values subjective definitions of experience;
- people are viewed as active subjects, not passive objects;
- process is valued as well as product;
- the development of equitable relationships relates to every level of practice, whether working with an individual or a group, or trying to transform the nature of social arrangements.

This framework is not method-specific and does not discount mundane everyday activities. Rather, it provides a focus which will facilitate practice in many settings. Nor does it discount the potential for a critical informed practice in any setting, though different strategies need to be worked through for different contexts. In the UK, where the relevance, standards and professionalism of social work are sometimes questioned, the approach encourages workers to reflect on and critique their practice, eventually taking more personal control in their professional lives.

THE STRUCTURE OF THIS BOOK

The task of this book, and hence the content of the text, logically flow from this conceptualization of social work practice. Particular dimensions of the practice framework are elaborated and built on in each chapter. In **Chapter 2** we examine the context of social welfare policies and politics in Britain. In particular we focus on the assumptions underpinning New Right and Third Way ideologies and their impact on the practices of Conservative and New Labour governments. We examine the role of social work in the delivery of personal social services, including child welfare and community care services.

Chapter 3 examines self, processes, communications and the relational aspects of practice. The disciplined use of self is basic to practice. The issues of 'Who I am', 'How I have come to be who I am' and 'How I seek to control my own life' are central to our reasons for becoming social workers and to the way in which we practise. Thus we commence with an examination of self and move to a consideration of the use of self in relationships. An understanding of our relationships and our self in relation to others enhances our ability to help others to develop equitable relationships, to take control and exercise power in aspects of their lives.

Making sense of and assessing situations is the focus of **Chapter 4**. Our practice framework seeks to locate people in their social arrangements, analyse the sources and experiences of power and powerlessness and work with service users towards outcomes that will enhance equitable relationships and their power and control over their lives. In assessing, we draw on knowledge from many sources, including statutory and organizational knowledge. But we draw on other knowledge as well, including an understanding of local resources and supports and how to mobilize these when needed. An inevitable part of the assessment task involves locating self as practitioner in the social arrangements, both at an interpersonal and an organizational/agency level.

In **Chapter 5** we examine some of the ways social workers put their purpose into practice through the use of different intervention strategies. Some of the strategies discussed are generic, such as building relationships and the purposeful use of self, problem solving and empowerment; while others relate to specific methods such as working with groups and building communities and networks. We also consider some of the ways intervention is structured in terms of long-term care, and working with involuntary clients.

The organizational context of social work practice is considered in detail in **Chapter 6**. Invariably interventions are shaped by the nature of the organization and the power and resources available to social workers in that organization. In social work practice, organizations may be the target of or allies in intervention. The National Occupational Standards (NOS) and Scottish Standards in Social Work Education (SiSWE) highlight the importance of social workers being effective organizational operators, and such skills have direct implications for the delivery of resources to service users. Approaches to working in organizations (teamwork) and influencing organizations (advocacy), as well as case management and care management, and recording are discussed.

In **Chapter 7** we turn to practice learning and placements. We briefly examine the policy surrounding practice learning on the social work honours degree and the implications for practice assessment in line with the NOS and SiSWE. Consideration is given to the countervailing pressures of learning and doing, of maximizing opportunities for learning and for taking control of one's own learning. We also reflect on the dynamics of the practice assessor–student relationship and consider issues of power and negotiating across difference.

Finally, in **Chapter 8**, we return to a focus on self and argue that effective practice requires ongoing critical self-reflection. Social workers need to develop an understanding of how they use themselves and their power in practice. This should be informed by a critical awareness of their personal and professional moral and ethical base. Of particular concern are those circumstances where social workers must negotiate ethical dilemmas and we consider strategies for facilitating this process.

In this book we hope to introduce you to some of the basic tasks of practice, to the conflicts and dilemmas that we face now and in the future. We examine the various dimensions of our practice framework in each of the chapters, beginning with understanding the policies and politics of social welfare in Britain.

FURTHER READING

Jordan, B. (1997) 'Social work and society', in M. Davies (ed.), *The Blackwell Companion to Social Work*. Oxford: Blackwell, pp. 8–24.

In this first edition of the Blackwell Companion, Jordan maps out social work's relationship to society and reflects on the paradox that, while social work is closely related to ideas of community and reciprocity, it expands in times of economic individualism, albeit with an increased role as an enforcer of social policy. Other articles in this and the second edition of the Blackwell Companion (Davies, 2002) provide comprehensive coverage of social work issues, knowledge and perspectives.

Adams, R., Dominelli, L. and Payne, M. (eds) (2002) *Critical Practice in Social Work*. Houndmills: Palgrave.

This book examines the potential of a critical approach to practice in a wide range of social work settings and with different user groups. It locates social work within its value base and engages with the tensions and dilemmas of working within organizational and management constraints. It is a valuable resource in developing a critical and reflective practice style.

USEFUL WEBSITES

PROFESSIONAL ASSOCIATIONS

An indication of the breadth and differences of social work and social care practice internationally is available by visiting the websites of professional and related associations. We list sites with English pages, but details of professional associations where English is not the first language can be found via the International Federation of Social Workers site.

Aotearoa New Zealand Association of Social Workers: www.anzasw.org.nz.
Australian Association of Social Workers: www.aasw.asn.au.
British Association of Social Workers: www.basw.co.uk.
Canadian Association of Social Workers: www.casw-acts.ca.
Danish Association of Social Workers: www.socialrdg.dk.
International Council on Welfare: www.icsw.org.
International Federation of Social Workers: www.ifsw.org.
Korean Association of Social Workers: www.kasw.or.kr/eng/kasw.htm.
National Association of Social Workers (US): www.naswdc.org.
Singapore Association of Social Workers: www.sasw.org.sg.

SOCIAL CARE MEDIA

Care and Health: www.careandhealth.com.
Community Care: www.communitycare.co.uk.
Society Guardian: http://society.guardian.co.uk.

REFLECTIVE QUESTIONS

1. Reflect on why you have chosen social work as your occupation. What factors have influenced this career choice for you at this stage of your life?
2. How do you understand the place of social work in society? What has influenced you to think this way? How do you think others might agree or disagree with you?

2 SOCIAL WELFARE POLICIES AND POLITICS

In this chapter we examine:

- The nature and conceptualization of social welfare in Britain;
- Changing approaches to citizenship, poverty and social exclusion;
- Ideological influences of the main political parties and their approach to social welfare;
- Policies and politics involved in the delivery of personal social services;
- Child welfare policies, community care policies and health/social care partnerships;
- Some changes facing social welfare in Britain: demographic and family changes, and increased involvement by service users.

The development of Britain's social welfare system has shaped the social work profession and provided a changing context for social work and social care practice. Understanding and being able to critique the social welfare and social care systems in which social work is located is an important activity for social workers. In our practice framework, as outlined in Figure 2.1, we note that social work is embedded in the context of Britain's social welfare policies and politics. This context directly impacts on individuals, groups and communities and helps construct the social arrangements in which they find themselves. Thus, the social welfare context facilitates people's access to many of the resources and opportunities that help them live independent and meaningful lives. It may also be seen as restricting people's access to resources and opportunities and, in implementing social welfare policies, social workers may sometimes act as 'gatekeepers' to much needed resources. For social workers to use the resources provided by social welfare systems effectively or to engage in strategies to help change social policies, they need a good knowledge of the nature of the policies, their historical development and the ideological assumptions underpinning them.

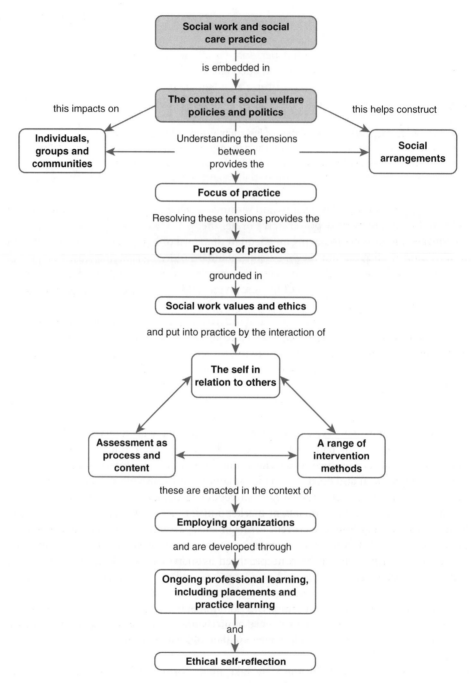

Figure 2.1   The context of social welfare policies and politics in the practice framework

WHAT IS SOCIAL WELFARE?

Our systems of health, welfare and personal social services seek to ensure not just the maintenance of physical life, but also an adequate standard and mode of living. Although there is disagreement over what constitutes an adequate standard of living, dimensions of such a standard could include:

- access to the material necessities of life such as food, shelter, health care;
- relationships which meet our social and emotional needs in a non-oppressive manner;
- an environment within which our needs to be cared for, and to care, are met; and
- opportunities to participate in the social life and decision making of the community.

Access to opportunities, relationships and resources such as these facilitate the individual's ability to live and to exercise power in his or her life.

Pathways and barriers to having an adequate standard of living vary across societies. In western industrialized economies, a person's standard of living is mainly based on participation in the labour market or access to privately owned capital. Paid employment facilitates access to the necessities of life and to participation in the social life of the community, but factors such as age, gender, disability or citizenship status may make it harder to get satisfactory employment. Living standards significantly depend on the overall health of the economy and how wealth is distributed. A healthy economy does not necessarily result in an improved standard of living for all citizens in society, nor is the surplus generated by the economy necessarily shared equitably, or reinvested to ensure future economic well-being.

The political right has typically characterized welfare measures as distorting the market, reducing individual motivation, such as the will to work, and creating a culture of dependency. Yet governments – even Conservative governments – do intervene. The types of policies governments pursue tend to reflect their ideological positions, as well as those of international institutions such as the European Union and the International Monetary Fund. Through social and economic policies, governments provide a structure of opportunities and barriers that enable or hinder successful participation in the market economy. Examples include education and labour market policies. Governments also seek to manage the tensions resulting from the current forms of social arrangements, particularly in relation to those excluded from or on the margins of the economy. These economic and social arrangements form what can be conceptualized as social welfare. Graycar and Jamrozik define social welfare as:

> A form of political organisation comprising both the public and private sectors of the economy. Its functions include the maintenance of social order and control, ensuring the physical survival of its citizens and the enhancement of their social functioning. (1993: 71)

Social welfare interventions by the state take many forms, including macro-economic policy decisions such as restructuring certain industries or introducing tax incentives to influence the availability and location of employment. Though macro-economic policy directly and indirectly impacts on the well-being of the population, it is rarely seen as welfare-related by the public. Macro-economic policy decisions are also very difficult for an individual worker to influence directly. From the viewpoint of the individual, social welfare interventions are instead experienced directly – for example, as direct cash transfers such as JobSeeker's Allowance – or indirectly through the provision of education, health care and personal social services. Such services are not delivered by the state only, but also by voluntary agencies, profit-making companies and by individuals within informal helping networks, such as family and friends, providing care.

Government welfare interventions affect the standard of living of the advantaged as well as the disadvantaged in the community. The gradual move away from direct taxation towards indirect taxation marks a shift in the redistribution of resources so that the wealthy bear less of the tax 'burden'. For example, the top rate of income tax was reduced in 1988 from 60 per cent to 40 per cent, benefiting a relatively small number of high earners while in 1991 the main rate of value added tax (VAT) – which we *all* pay on designated goods and services – was increased from 15 per cent to 17.5 per cent. Policies and expenditure by government on education – a key economic intervention – advantage and disadvantage different groups in the community. Indeed, many readers of this text (and the authors) receive substantial benefits from the welfare state: access to a subsidized higher education and an almost guaranteed place in the labour market on graduation. There are three social welfare systems operating in parallel: the visible system which provides support to those in poverty and who are socially excluded; the less visible system which provides access to high-quality education and health care to the middle classes; and finally, the hidden welfare system which provides benefits and subsidies to the very wealthy (Graycar and Jamrozik, 1993).

Such a conceptualization of social welfare directs our attention to the breadth of government policies. This way of thinking about social welfare also recognizes that all citizens benefit from welfare arrangements, not just social security claimants or those receiving personal social services. In addition, it is important to note that social welfare comprises both the private and public sectors of the economy. Welfare services are thus commonly organized and delivered by a range of agencies: central government, local government, the profit-making sector and the non-profit-making or voluntary sector. This aspect of social welfare delivery is referred to as the mixed economy of welfare.

Social welfare policy and service delivery vary to some degree between the different countries of the UK. The Blair government's devolution of constitutional powers to a Scottish parliament and executive, Welsh National Assembly and Northern Ireland Assembly (which was suspended in 2002) impacts upon social welfare provision. The system of devolved power provides more localized control over policy direction and service delivery, and gives recognition to long-standing claims of unique identity and nationhood in these countries. The potential for distinct expressions of social policy and social welfare – based on the particular histories and politics in these countries – has emerged. In Wales the statutory equality responsibilities of the Assembly – for example the human resource strategy of the civil service in Wales – were influenced not just by New Labour politics but also by the past campaigning of Welsh-language pressure groups and the women's movement in Wales (Chaney, 2004).

The impact of devolution is even more keenly felt in Scotland, which has its own legal system and has arguably had more of a social democratic tradition in social welfare, education and health policy than England (especially the south of England). Since devolution important differences have emerged in Scotland, notably a commitment by the state to pay student tuition fees, an improvement in teachers' pay, an agreement that the state should pay for the personal care of people in long-term care, and the rejection of the idea of Foundation Hospitals. However, according to Mooney and Poole (2004), such differences between Scotland and England are not necessarily as important as the differences within both Scotland and England, and Scotland is a long way yet from evolving its own unique welfare state.

Historically, social work and social care practice developed in the welfare arenas that are most visible: in aspects of social welfare concerned with the 'disadvantaged', the 'unfortunate' and the 'wayward'. These social welfare spheres encompass policies, programmes and actions intended to ensure physical survival, basic social functioning, and social care and control. In this context, social welfare can be seen as the organized response of the government, voluntary and profit-making sectors to mitigate the worst effects of the free market on individuals. Social welfare provision aims to guarantee a minimum standard of living. In some cases, social welfare also enforces a mode of living on people who are considered dependent, such as children, older people and disabled people, or people whose behaviour is seen as unacceptable. While Beresford acknowledges that most people benefit from social welfare policies, he claims that 'long-term, regulatory, intimate and segregating contact with welfare services *is* different and is associated with stigma, discrimination, poverty and exclusion' (2001: 507).

According to our practice framework, initially outlined in Chapter 1, the focus of social work should be about understanding the interactions and tensions between people and their social arrangements. As the social welfare system helps construct these arrangements it is particularly important that social workers examine the negative effects of this system on individuals, groups and communities. This involves being sensitive to and trying to mitigate the effects of stigma that people may experience when benefiting from services. In the next section we look at the ideas underpinning the main political parties' approaches to the welfare state.

IDEOLOGY AND SOCIAL WELFARE

When people refer to 'the welfare state' in Britain they are often referring to a particular set of policy and service arrangements instituted following the Second World War. This was the welfare state of William Beveridge: universal provision of health care, child allowances and employment. The Beveridge Plan was based on Keynesian economics that advocated the active involvement of government in the economy to manage the demand for goods and services and maintain full employment (Sullivan, 1996). Under the 'New Right' Conservative Thatcher and Major governments, Britain saw a considerable retreat from post-war welfare arrangements. Although ideologically opposed to many of these changes, Blair's New Labour has continued to withdraw from central government involvement in the delivery – if not the regulation – of social welfare services. We will now look at the implications for social welfare of New Right and Blair's 'Third Way' politics.

THE NEW RIGHT AND NEO-LIBERALISM

The role of the welfare state in the liberal society is minimal: it forces individuals to meet their needs through the economy except in extreme cases of poverty where intervention would be aimed at getting individuals to a point where they could participate economically. The fusing of neo-liberalism and conservatism in British politics was apparent in the emergence of the New Right in the 1970s and 1980s. Although this mixture also emerged in other countries, such as in the United States under Reagan, the New Right in Britain is most commonly associated with the policies of the Thatcher and Major governments.

According to Giddens (1998), the New Right links a commitment to an unrestrained market with the promotion of institutions such as the family and the nation. While individuals should act freely in the economy, they are bound to moral codes in other spheres of life. In articulating their neo-liberal ideological position Thatcher's governments did not simply reduce the welfare state to a minimal safety net, but '*reorganised* methods of welfare delivery in ways that reflected their broad commitment to market solutions, significantly altering the state's role as a direct welfare provider' (Ellison, 1998: 33). Correspondingly, the existing welfare state's emphasis on self-help and the role of the family in providing support was extended. The Thatcher governments' focus on individualism was aimed at restricting the power of collectives, such as trade unions and local authorities, in order to facilitate individual autonomy and freedom of choice (Jordan, 2000). Their antagonism to the structures of the welfare state resulted in significant cutbacks to funding of the NHS, education, housing and the personal social services. However, as Sullivan (1996) notes, this was undermined by a 300 per cent increase in social security expenditure from 1979 to 1982 because of rising unemployment.

As well as reflecting a neo-liberal agenda, the ascendance of the 'quasi-market' as a means of organizing welfare activities represented the influence of a managerialist agenda in government circles (Pierson, 1998). In the 1980s and 1990s, former Managing Director of Sainsbury's Roy Griffiths carried out major policy reviews in health and community care. The 1983 *Griffiths Report* on the NHS led to a government review that recommended the development of an internal market in which hospitals would be required to compete with each other in order to gain the business of newly created health authorities (Sullivan, 1996). This policy was shortly followed by the introduction of quasi-markets in the community care sector, through the NHS and Community Care Act 1990, in which social services departments were expected to stimulate and purchase services from the voluntary and profit-making sectors (the so called purchaser/provider split).

NEW LABOUR AND THE THIRD WAY

New Labour is most obviously 'new' in that it broke with the socialist traditions of the Labour Party and set itself on a course of 'modernization'. This break involved the abandonment of Keynesian economics, a rejection of the principle of nationalization, decreased reliance on the unions and an increased emphasis on individual rights and personal choice (Giddens, 1998). Tony Blair famously sought a 'Third Way' supporting globalized free markets while strengthening the connections between individuals and communities.

Giddens (1998) argues that Third Way politics involve not a shift toward the New Right, but a reinvigoration of social democracy. This involves being committed to generating wealth by engaging in the global economy, expanding democratic processes (e.g. devolution of power to the countries of the UK), increasing partnerships between government and the community, and modernizing government through improving accountability, efficiency and competitiveness.

Blair's approach to Third Way politics is also influenced by communitarian ideas (Driver and Martell, 2002). In Blair's words, he has 'a simple belief that people are not separate economic actors competing in the marketplace of life. They are citizens of a community' (cited in Driver and Martell, 1997: 34–5). According to Jordan (2000), New Labour's communitarianism focuses on instilling in community members a responsibility for caring for each other, as well as providing a form of social control and discipline, for example, via the surveillance of neighbourhood watch groups. New Labour has advocated for individuals in the community to challenge the inappropriate behaviour of others. For example, in 1999 former Home Secretary, Jack Straw, called on adults to tell young people acting up in public that what they are doing is wrong (Travis, 1999). Driver and Martell (1997) conclude that New Labour policies emphasize a form of communitarianism that is:

- conditional (e.g. jobseekers must accept one of the options presented);
- morally prescriptive (values are defined in legislation);
- conservative (e.g. stable – that is, two-parent – families are emphasized); and
- individualized (e.g. individuals rather than corporations take responsibility).

New Labour's plans to democratize and decentralize the public sector is part of an attempt to refashion relationships between individuals, communities and the state. These policies impact significantly on social workers and their implications will be considered further later in this chapter. These strategies do not exist in isolation, but instead reflect shifting global and regional politics, particularly in terms of the globalization of trade and human rights codes and the changing nature of citizenship throughout western nations.

CITIZENSHIP AND GLOBALIZATION

Citizenship is one way of thinking about the relationship between people and the state – and a way that has been employed by different ideological perspectives. The touchstone of modern constructions of citizenship is Marshall's (1950) conceptualization of citizenship as civil, political and social rights. Civil rights relate to individual freedom and are partly achieved through individuals' rights to own property and to legal justice. Political rights refer to the exercise of political power, such as through participation in democratic processes, like voting. Social rights are characterized by individuals' rights to participate in society and in the economy in order to maintain a certain standard of living. Our conceptualization of the purpose of social work as promoting equitable social relationships and enabling people to take more control of their lives can also be seen to enhance their citizenship and participation in society.

In the late 20th century, the citizenship discourse shifted towards defining citizenship less in terms of rights and more in terms of obligations. This emphasis can be seen in both Conservative and New Labour governments, particularly in their approaches to employment policy. For example, New Labour's 'welfare to work' programme emphasizes the obligations of unemployed people through its requirement that they participate in some form of valued community activity (Finn, 2003). The communitarian tradition has particularly sought to restrict the framing of new individual rights and to redress the perceived imbalance between rights and responsibilities (Etzioni, 1993).

There are other conditions of the late 20th and early 21st centuries that also affect citizenship. The period is characterized by the shift from industrial to service and information modes of production, by the development of global capitalism and by the changing and some would argue reducing role of the nation state in influencing the welfare of its citizens. According to Roy (1997: 2117) '[g]lobalisation is centred on the integration of international markets for goods, services, technology, finance and labour'. Consequently, international trade and finance increasingly exert more influence over national economic policies, while nation states exert less.

Lister (1997) argues that the globalization thesis can be overstated and that nation states do continue to retain sovereignty within limits, such as the power to make and enforce laws in their own territory. However, she concedes that their autonomy has been reduced by the exposure of economies to international markets and by the ceding of powers to supranational organizations and through international law. Organizations like the International Monetary Fund have been instrumental in requiring governments to cut their national debts, often through drastically reducing government expenditure and the privatization of welfare services (Mishra, 1998). Contributing to the construction of global citizenship, supranational organizations have also become central in the codification of human rights 'as a world-level organising principle in legal, scientific and popular conventions' (Soysal, 2001: 67).

Importantly, all EU member states are signatories to the European Convention on Human Rights, a treaty of the European Council. The Convention was agreed in 1950 in order to guarantee rights and freedoms under the UN Declaration on Human Rights 1948. The Convention affords protection in a wide range of areas, prohibiting, for example, torture and slavery, as well as guaranteeing rights and freedoms such as the right to a fair trial and to liberty and security, and freedom of thought, conscience and religion.

The Human Rights Act 1998 enshrines in UK law the rights and freedoms of the European Convention and means that people can make their claims to UK courts rather than having to go through the lengthy process leading to the European Court in Strasbourg. The Act makes it unlawful for any UK public authority, which may include a private company carrying out public functions, to act in a manner incompatible with the European Convention (Home Office, 2000). While Human Rights Act compliance has initiated change within social work and social care agencies, British courts have not been overwhelmed by human rights cases (Lord Chancellor's Department, 2001) and greater use could be made of the Act in improving services (Lammy, 2003).

The idea that everyone may have global rights and responsibilities raises an important issue. One of the defining aspects of citizenship is the exclusion of non-citizens. The sense of solidarity that emerges from being a citizen is shaped by the knowledge of who are not citizens. There are many different bases on which citizenship rights have been restricted within a society. Lister (1997) and Bussemaker and Voet (1998) note that exclusion on the basis of gender has been a common dimension of citizenship; and immigration policy explicitly seeks to exclude certain types of people from participating and remaining in a society, such as those seen as not meeting employability criteria. Asylum seekers, in particular, are subject to the exclusionary practices of supranational organizations such as the EU and of nation states. For example, in 2001 it was reported that British immigration officials were sent to Prague's airport to screen passengers heading for London in an attempt to block any potential asylum seekers. The screening process reportedly targeted all Czechs of Roma or Gypsy origin, while allowing other Czechs unhindered passage (Hall, 2001). Other groups that have been excluded from exercising full citizenship rights in nation states include: ethnic minorities, gay and lesbian people and disabled people.

The internal exclusionary processes of the nation state were most publicly highlighted during the Stephen Lawrence Inquiry, which concluded that the London Metropolitan Police Force was institutionally racist. The claim that an arm of the nation state could be inherently and structurally racist has had widespread ramifications, not least the introduction of the Race Relations (Amendment) Act 2002 which set out for public authorities (including educational institutions) a series of general and specific duties to promote race equality. The issues expected to be covered by the Act are wide ranging and include unemployment, school exclusions, racist attitudes, health outcomes and police treatment (Commission for Racial Equality, 2003).

Social movements and activist groups, such as the disability rights movement, have commonly adopted the concept of citizenship as a way of highlighting marginalization and of mobilizing support. However, as social workers it is important to be aware that there is a flip-side to citizenship's inclusionary force in that it may well serve to exclude some people at the same time as others are drawn within its boundaries. This exclusionary tendency may diminish the power of political mobilization across groups such as feminist, gay and trade union activists, providing a source of conflict in their political activities. Lister (1997), in outlining a feminist citizenship project, argues for social movements to be grounded in solidarity in diversity, articulating a citizenship which values difference. However, solidarity is difficult to achieve in part due to the multilayered and subjective nature of identities and experiences. There may be aspects of one's identity that connect with experiences of being oppressed, such as being a woman and a lesbian, while other aspects have involved experiences of being oppressive, such as being white, middle class and able-bodied. As social workers it is important to be aware of the interconnections between different sources of oppression and the way in which these can shift over time and be mutually reinforcing or contradictory (Lister, 1997). We now turn our attention to one important contributor to oppression which social welfare attempts to address: poverty.

POVERTY AND SOCIAL EXCLUSION

While social welfare benefits the advantaged in society as well as the disadvantaged, the focus of much welfare planning is towards those in poverty. According to Davis and Garrett (2004) progressive social work must continue to be concerned with poverty and its effects on people and their life opportunities. Throughout the 1980s and 1990s there were shifting discourses on poverty and inequality in Britain, which have directly influenced successive British governments' economic and social welfare policies as well as media and public perceptions of 'deserving' and 'undeserving' welfare recipients. The focus on social exclusion in Britain at the beginning of the new century reflects the ideological position of New Labour, the influence of EU social policy and theorizing, and a view that poverty and inequality are complex and multi-dimensional, affecting the basic connections between an individual and society.

Traditionally, UK policy makers and researchers have conceptualized poverty and inequality in terms of income. This approach is evident in the focus of the British social welfare system on income maintenance, while European nations, such as France, have mainly emphasized social solidarity. Income is a reasonably simple and effective indicator for measuring poverty and inequality and for comparing changes over time and with other nations. A common measure of poverty employed by the government is income below 60 per cent of the median. In 2000 15 per cent of people in the UK were below this level, while across the EU the figures ranged from 49 per cent in Portugal and 41 per cent in Greece to 1 per cent in Luxembourg and 5 per cent in Austria. The EU average was 17 per cent. (Office for National Statistics, 2004). The Office for National Statistics (ONS) provides valuable data in their Social Trends series on earnings and income distribution in the UK. The following is a snapshot of recent patterns:

- Averaged over 1997–9, the lowest levels of disposable income were found in Wales (87% of UK average) and Northern Ireland (as low as 72% in some parts), while the highest levels were recorded in inner-west London (64% above UK average);
- In 2002 women's average hourly earnings when in full-time employment were 82 per cent of men's and 88 per cent of men's when in part-time employment;
- In 2000–1 58 per cent of Bangladeshi or Pakistani people lived in households with incomes below 60 per cent of the median (before housing costs), compared to 29 per cent of black non-Caribbean people, 25 per cent of Indian people, 21 per cent of black Caribbean people and 16 per cent of white people.
- Based on 1993–2001 data from the Labour Force Survey it appears that both men and women experience a 50 per cent wage increase if they leave full-time education at 21 rather than at 16.
- In 2001–2 21 per cent of children (2.7 million) were living in households with below 60 per cent of the median income (before housing costs).

A key concern has been the widening of the gap between the poorest and the richest groups in society. In 1978 the bottom fifth of income earners accounted for 10 per cent of the post-tax national income, compared to the top fifth who earned 36 per cent of post-tax national income. By 1998–9 the gap had widened considerably: the bottom fifth by then earned 6 per cent of post-tax national income, while the top fifth earned 45 per cent (Harris, 2000). Work carried out by the OECD has highlighted factors in this shifting pattern of inequality: trade globalization pushing wages down, technological changes not benefiting unskilled workers, and the impact of the deregulation of labour markets (Harris, 2000).

Although measures of income inequality are still important in the UK, the Blair government has championed the concept of 'social exclusion' (e.g. by setting up the Social Exclusion Unit) for examining the complexities of poverty and social inequality and implementing a programme of social reform. For New Labour, social exclusion is an alternative to the more Thatcherite concept of the 'underclass' which, according to Jordan (2000), stereotyped a disadvantaged social group as dependent, dangerous and morally degenerate.

Room (1999) argues that the adoption of the concept of social exclusion into mainstream policy debate in Britain represents a fundamental reconfiguration of how we see hardship and disadvantage. The new construct recognizes disadvantage as:

- multi-dimensional, with intersecting factors such as low income, poor housing and mental health needs;
- dynamic, with shifting patterns and duration;
- grounded in communities and neighbourhoods, not in individuals or households; and
- connected to individuals' relationships with others: their participation in social networks.

Room argues that the concept of social exclusion can move analysis away from seeing inequality as a continuum with an arbitrary poverty line. Rather, a central concern is that at some point the extent and multi-dimensionality of the inequality experienced is so severe that it causes a 'catastrophic rupture' in the relationship between the individual and the rest of society.

While the concept adds depth to our understanding of disadvantage, as social workers we need to pay attention to tensions inherent in the idea of social exclusion and difficulties facing government and policy makers trying to combat exclusion. Part of the problem is that while seeking to reduce exclusion it is not automatically apparent what should be increased: inclusion, involvement, citizenship, participation, integration? These concepts seem fairly neutral, but have different implications when interpreted in a political context and formulated as policy or practice. So when inclusion or integration policies are put in place, where does this leave people who are different to the mainstream and/or who do not want to be included or integrated?

New Labour's self-imposed test of its ability to redress poverty and social exclusion is its commitment to end child poverty by 2020. The scope and effects of child poverty are enormous:

Four million children – one in three – live in poverty in Britain; this is the highest child poverty rate of any major industrialised country apart from the United States. Fifty thousand children aged 8–10 have nothing to eat or drink before going to school in the morning. Many leave school illiterate, innumerate, alienated and a danger to society. (Piachaud, 2001: 446)

Researchers have emphasized the effects of child poverty on child development, educational performance and general health and well-being, as well as stigma attached, for example, to receiving free school meals (Goldson, 2002). The government's response has thus been characteristically wide ranging: from Health Action Zones to address health inequalities to Sure Start to improve the quality of services for children living in the most disadvantaged communities.

But for New Labour the main answer to poverty and social exclusion, including child poverty, is paid work. The government's strategy is to get working-age adults off welfare and into work. The key elements of this 'work first agenda' are:

- the Jobseeker's Allowance making benefit entitlement dependent on active jobseeking;
- compulsory 'work-focused' interviews with benefit recipients;
- the New Deals; and
- the modernization of employment and benefit services through Jobcentre Plus (Department for Work and Pensions, 2003).

From 1997 to 2003 New Deals were implemented to assist and obligate people to find paid work, or obtain skills and education to that end. Separate 'deals' targeted young people who had been unemployed for six months or more, long-term unemployed adults, lone parents, and people with long-term illness or disability. The New Deal for Communities (targeting social exclusion in small urban neighbourhoods) is a key plank of New Labour's regeneration policy, which emphasizes the need not just for quality public housing but also for economic revitalization and improved job prospects (Hall and Nevin, 1999). Reflecting the government's communitarian influences, the New Deals focus on responsibilities as well as rights. For example, young people who have not found work after assistance from a professional advisor are required to participate in full-time education or training or work with a subsidised employer, an environmental taskforce or a voluntary sector agency (Finn, 2003).

Despite the Blair government's best intentions and its public rejection of Thatcher's individualism, it seems that New Labour's approach to poverty emphasizes individual agency over structure. Colley and Hodkinson (2001) maintain that the Social Exclusion Unit's *Bridging the Gap* Report locates the causes of young people's non-participation in education, training or employment within individuals in terms of personal deficits. The report largely ignores any form of structural disadvantage that might underpin non-participation. Beresford and Wilson (1998) argue that New Labour's social exclusion policies are reminiscent of the old notion of the underclass and serve mainly to reinforce social divisions. They suggest that the debate about social exclusion policies and service delivery needs to become more inclusive, giving centre stage to the perspectives, knowledge and analyses of those identified as being socially excluded. We now focus on the personal social services and the role played by social work in their delivery.

PERSONAL SOCIAL SERVICES

The personal social services in the UK are unique because of their location within an integrated local authority-based public sector and the significant contribution made by a unified social work profession (Jordan and Jones, 1995). However, while the personal social services are delivered mainly by local government, the national governments in Westminster, Edinburgh and Cardiff remain important (and will do so in Belfast when it is reinstated) in the direction of social services policy and the regulation of social care and social work practice. Government legislation can place duties on authorities, forcing them to carry out certain activities; legislation can also give authorities powers to use their discretion (Mandelstam, 1995). An important development unique to Scotland was an agreement to accept the recommendation of the Royal Commission on Long Term Care (1999), contrary to the Blair government's response (DoH, 2000a), that all personal care provided to older people in residential and nursing homes should be funded by the state, leaving service users to pay only accommodation fees. However, considerable power continues to rest with the Westminster Parliament through the Sewell Convention – by which Westminster can develop and implement legislation in an area designated as devolved – and the fiscal and political constraints imposed by the UK treasury and government (Mooney and Poole, 2004).

In the late 1980s and 1990s social services reforms contributed to a withdrawal of social work activity from direct service user contact, private and voluntary sector expansion, and increasing reliance on informal care provided by families (mainly women). Much social work activity was redesignated as 'care management'. This emphasis and a concern for demonstrating service outcomes influenced the development of a series of competencies which formed the basis for assessing practice on the Diploma in Social Work. According to Dominelli (1996), these competencies separated out the complexities of professional interaction and denied the qualitative nature of the social work relationship. Jordan (2000) maintains that the development (or restriction) of public sector social work in the 1990s meant that social workers were becoming increasingly preoccupied with the management of resources and risk and less concerned with the interpersonal qualities of the service user/social worker relationship. A commonly expressed concern was that social work, under the influence of managerial and New Right reforms, adopted 'a style of practice that was legalistic, formal, procedural and arm's length' (p. 8). There is a wider sense that the welfare state generally has been shifting from being needs-led to risk-led with a greater role for personal insurance and more emphasis on personal responsibility (Kemshall, 2002).

According to Jordan (2000), this changing context for social work was consolidated by New Labour in its white paper *Modernizing Social Services* (DoH, 1998). This document and the subsequent White Paper, *A Quality Strategy for Social Care* (DoH, 2000c), heralded a major restructuring of the regulation and education of social workers and social care workers. The modernizing agenda is continuing and aims to: improve collaboration between health, education and housing departments to ensure a seamless service; increase the involvement of citizens (taxpayers, service users and carers) in service planning and delivery; and restructure the social work and social care workforce (Humphrey, 2003). The main features of the plan include the introduction of:

- National Care Councils to develop codes of practice, implement registration of social workers and social care workers, and (replacing CCETSW) regulate social work education and training;
- A national qualifications framework for the social work and social care workforce based on national occupational standards. It was recommended that the Diploma in Social Work be transformed into an honours degree;

- The Quality Protects Initiative (including a new assessment framework) for child welfare services and the development of new inspection standards for childcare services;
- The setting and monitoring of standards in services such as long-term care homes, children's homes, domiciliary care agencies, voluntary sector adoption and fostering agencies, day centres and nursing agencies;
- Improved partnerships between social services and health (e.g. via Care Trusts) and education (e.g. via Children's Trusts);
- The Social Care Institute for Excellence to consolidate a knowledge base of what works in social work and social care and promote best practice;
- Targets for quality and efficiency improvements by local authorities and strategies to address 'failing' authorities (e.g. strategies outlined in the Best Value initiative).

Some of the changes as they affect social work education – the introduction of the Care Councils, the National Occupational Standards and the honours degree in social work – have the potential to reshape social work as a profession. The Care Councils now register social workers, ensuring individual social workers will be held to account for their professional behaviour in a way that was not previously possible. This change should improve standards, prevent or identify and address poor and dangerous practice, and protect the reputation of social work. Generally, despite the stress of bidding for and putting the new programmes into place, social work educators seem pleased with the framework of the new degree (e.g. Community Care, 2003). Moreover, the consolidation and dissemination of knowledge through the Social Care Institute for Excellence has great potential to inform professional practice.

However, other changes instigated by the government may undermine the potential of attempts to improve the status and standards of social work outlined earlier. The rigorous and wide-ranging inspection regime may overburden the profession with regulation, and reduce social work's professional autonomy and capacity to challenge the systems that shape social work practice (Orme, 2001). For Butler and Drakeford (2001), the problem is that New Labour is increasingly aligning social work with authoritarian rather than libertarian policies and the profession is losing its radical potential. This argument is well illustrated by the new role of social workers in implementing immigration policy. Under the Nationality, Immigration and Asylum Act 2002, staff employed in local authority social services departments are required to investigate and report to the Home Office anyone trying to obtain services who appears to be in the country illegally (Humphries, 2004). Discussion of the tensions between the controlling dimensions of social work and its empowering potential has a long history and we will examine these tensions later in the book.

In the next section, we look at two broad areas of social welfare that define much of social work practice: child welfare and community care. We then consider strategies for facilitating partnerships between health and social services.

CHILD WELFARE

Child welfare policy has the difficult task of addressing the overlap between the domains of the personal and the public, with social work practice mediating between individuals (children and parents) and the state. Child welfare policies express views about the relationship between state, family and child (e.g. whether the state should legislate to stop parents smacking their children) and reflect dominant ideas about the nature, role and responsibilities of the family. For social workers, whose interventions can have a major – and not always positive – impact on the lives of children and their families, childcare work is invariably fraught with emotional, ethical and practical complexity.

The 1948 Children Act was one of many changes to social welfare following the Second World War. This Act drew on the recommendations of the Curtis Report (1946) and established local authority Children's Departments to address childcare and welfare issues. Corby (2000: 32–3) suggests that after the war and until the early 1970s 'family policy in general and the response to neglectful families in particular was relatively benign', with an 'unequivocally family-oriented and family-sympathetic' approach. But the public mood changed following the death of seven-year-old Maria Colwell at the hands of her stepfather in 1973. The public inquiry into her death received considerable media attention and put social work in general, and specifically the role of Maria's social worker, under the spotlight. While the media response largely focused on the failings of the individual workers involved, the government response also drew attention to systemic failures, highlighting poor communication and inter-agency coordination (Gibbons, 1997) – themes which have recurred consistently in inquiries in the 30 years since then. The implication that better systems could have saved Maria resulted in a shift towards a more procedurally based practice, supported by a succession of government circulars and guidance. However, the social work response to child abuse may have been tougher in theory than practice. Reder and colleagues suggest that practitioners were still motivated by the 'rule of optimism' (Dingwall et al., 1983 cited in Reder et al., 1993: 90) which encouraged them to think the best of parents (Reder et al., 1993) and militated against assertive intervention in situations of potential or suspected abuse.

Between 1948 and the 1980s, different pieces of legislation had been passed that addressed a variety of social welfare issues including family support and preventive work, delinquency and youth offending, and adoption. But this left the legislative framework fragmented and complicated, so that by the early 1980s practitioners and others were struggling to interpret and make effective use of it. A Parliamentary Select Committee was therefore set up to examine the situation and recommend action for change. The 1970s and 1980s also saw an increase in public and media scrutiny of social work following several high-profile child deaths where social workers were held to account for apparently doing too little to protect children from physical violence and abuse. At the same time, a high level of disquiet was expressed (notably in the popular press) about what was perceived as overzealous action to remove children from their families in cases of suspected sexual abuse, as happened in Cleveland. The furore surrounding events in Cleveland and the subsequent *Report of the Inquiry into Child Abuse in Cleveland 1987* (the Butler-Sloss Report) (DHSS, 1988) provided further impetus for changes to the law. The legislation that resulted – the Children Act 1989 – brought various provisions for children's welfare established in previous legislation into one more coherent structure and placed the child very centrally as 'the primary focus of the law's concern' (Johns, 2003: 10). (See Parton (1991) for a detailed history of the Children Act 1989.) In Scotland, legislation and policy took a different path with the passing of the 1995 Children (Scotland) Act.

The Children Act 1989 started from the assumption that children are usually best looked after within their own family, and provided a framework for addressing the needs of *all* children: those deemed to be 'at risk' and therefore requiring protection but also prioritizing support for children seen as 'in need' and their families. Events in Cleveland had highlighted the tension in childcare work between the privacy and autonomy of the family and the responsibility of the state to protect children. In practice terms, in the early 1990s, this tension was evident as social workers attempted to negotiate between an assertive (and potentially intrusive) approach to child protection and a more family supportive approach. As part of the government response to the problems raised by Cleveland and other inquiries, the Department of Health commissioned a series of research studies into different aspects of child abuse and protection. These studies, summarized in *Child Protection: Messages from Research* (DoH, 1995), suggested that the child protection system was not working effectively for many families. Subsequent 'refocusing' saw a shift back towards family support, underpinned by a broader understanding of child welfare.

The 1990s also saw a massive growth of concern about the abuse of children in residential care (highlighted by cases in Staffordshire in 1991 and Leicestershire in 1993), and care services for children were subjected to a series of reviews. The Utting Report *People Like Us* (1997) recommended a range of safeguards designed to protect children living away from home from abuse or harm.

As noted, successive Conservative governments had reduced expenditure on social welfare services, curtailed the role of local authorities, and introduced a mixed economy of welfare which brought public services under market principles. The effects on children and families were marked: 'in the 1980s child poverty doubled, inequalities widened significantly and resources were transferred away from families with children to those without' (Berridge, 1999: 290). So when New Labour came to power in 1997: '[t]he child welfare legacy it inherited then was a mixed picture. The economic and social climate was unfavourable for the most disadvantaged children' (p. 293).

Part of the Blair government's agenda for reform of the personal social services, the White Paper *Modernizing Social Services* (DoH, 1998) set out an ambitious programme to improve the quality of services for children. The 'Quality Protects' initiative aimed to deliver protection, quality of care and improved life chances for children (DoH, 1998). It identified 11 objectives for children's services and for the first time set out clear outcomes for children, with precise and measurable targets, for example in relation to placement stability.

In the early years of the government's first term, three further significant cross-government initiatives were launched:

- *Supporting Families*, a consultation document setting out the government's approach to family support and outlining wide-ranging proposals for action;
- *Sure Start*, a multi-million pound programme 'which aims to achieve better outcomes for children, parents and communities by: increasing the availability of childcare for all children; improving health and emotional development for young children; supporting parents as parents and in their aspirations towards employment' (www.surestart.gov.uk).

This involves a process of service development in disadvantaged areas alongside financial help for parents to enable them to access childcare and hence, employment opportunities. The government aims to extend the principles underpinning the Sure Start approach to all services for children and families (www.surestart.gov.uk);

- The Social Exclusion Unit, which developed a number of strategies targeting children and young people (Berridge, 1999).

These initiatives reflect a commitment to improving outcomes for all children and supporting parents and families (though see Gillies (2005) for a more critical response to New Labour's approach). At the same time, the initiatives reflect a practical and ideological commitment to helping people currently outside the labour market join the workforce. Measures include different strategies aimed at offering better financial support for families, the national strategy to increase the provision of affordable quality childcare, and strategies to develop out-of-school childcare and increase the number of free nursery places for three- and four-year olds. Thus, childcare is one of many areas in which Blair government policy involves 'strategies to support, encourage or direct all those who can into work' (Scott et al., 2002: 227).

In recent years, perhaps the most significant changes to child welfare policy have been those arising from the inquiry into the death of Victoria Climbié (Laming, 2003). Victoria was an eight-year-old West African child brought to Britain by her aunt, ostensibly for 'a better life'. She died in 2000 as a consequence of extreme maltreatment and neglect from her aunt and her aunt's boyfriend. A number of agencies were aware of Victoria (the family had been involved with four local authority social service departments, health and housing services and two Police Child Protection Teams) but did not intervene effectively or consistently, with the result that she died in 'exceptionally cruel and degrading circumstances' (Cooper, 2005: 1). A public inquiry into the circumstances of her death, chaired by Lord Laming, revealed serious failings in the statutory services and made a series of recommendations for change (Laming, 2003).

The government responded with *Keeping Children Safe* (DfES, DoH and Home Office, 2003) and the Green Paper *Every Child Matters*, published for consultation in September 2003. This was followed in March 2004 by *Every Child Matters: Next Steps* (DfES, 2004), and a Children Bill was drafted to provide the legal framework for the programme of reform; the Bill became law in November 2004. As part of the Every Child Matters initiative, five outcomes were indentified as key to well-being in childhood and later life: being healthy, staying safe, enjoying and achieving, making a positive contribution, and achieving economic well-being. *Every Child Matters: Change for Children* (HM Government, 2004) brought together the government's range of strategies for improving those outcomes for all children and young people, based on a national framework for 150 'change programmes' led by local authorities and their partners.

Every Child Matters set out four areas for action:

- supporting parents and carers;
- early intervention and effective protection;
- accountability and integration – local, regional and national; and
- workforce reform.

A new emphasis on education runs through *Every Child Matters*; Williams suggests that:

Just as social security and taxation policies have emphasized getting people into paid work as central to an anti-poverty strategy, so, as far as children are concerned, educational qualifications are seen to play a similar role. (2004: 414)

The Government identified a critical and increased role for schools, putting them at the centre of a network of services for children and families in a new system of Children's Trusts. Other examples that illustrate this emphasis on education are the location of the new Ministry for Children, Young People and Families in the Department for Education and Skills (DfES) and the transfer of various responsibilities previously held within the Department of Health or the Home Office to the DfES. These developments represent a major shift in the locus of child welfare provision, away from local authority social service departments and a significant move towards the development of more 'joined up' frontline services for children, young people and families. The emphasis on joined up services is underlined in developments such as the Integrated Children's System and the Children's National Service Framework (DoH and DfES, 2004; Welsh Assembly Government, 2005) and proposals such as those relating to the reform of youth services (DfES, 2005). It is likely that services for children and young people will continue to be a focus for change for some time to come, but through the expansion of Children's Trusts, the emphasis for the future will be on integrated services, delivered by multi-professional teams operating within a robust framework of inter-agency accountability.

COMMUNITY CARE

The term 'community' is a slippery one, imbued with hidden and often contestable meanings (see Mayo, 1994). Victor (1997) makes the important distinction between care *in* the community: support at home or in community centres funded or provided by the state; and care *by* the community: the mobilization of informal supports and voluntary agencies in the provision of care. Policies have been shaped by changing views on whether some people are best cared for at home in the 'community' or in a form of institution. Community care policies have also been influenced by professional agendas and by attempts of those variously referred to as patients, clients or service users to challenge prevailing attitudes and practices. Although such issues affect people of any age group, in the UK personal social services, community care policies generally apply to work with adults.

In the post-war period many people with long-term needs, including older people and those with mental health and learning difficulties, were being cared for in acute hospitals. A series of scandals over the quality of care provided in long-stay hospitals led to White Papers in 1971 and 1977 which argued for the development of community alternatives for people with mental health needs (Victor, 1997). However, the impetus for investing in community care mostly came in the 1980s with concerns about the ageing population and the increasing number of older people, funded via social security, moving into private residential and nursing homes. A series of reports (Audit Commission, 1986; Griffiths, 1988) and White Papers – notably *Caring for People* (DoH, 1989) – highlighted these problems and mapped a strategy for dealing with them, leading to the introduction of the NHS and Community Care Act 1990 (NHSCCA). Central features of the reform programme included the development of:

- the purchaser/provider split and quasi-markets;
- a framework for assessment for community care services;
- the role of the care manager to assess needs, develop care plans and costs, purchase and review the package of services;
- annual community care plans by local authorities mapping community need for services and setting targets for development (e.g. setting eligibility criteria); and
- complaints procedures within local authorities and the increased role of the Social Services Inspectorate in monitoring standards and promoting best practice.

This legislation applied everywhere in the UK. Generally the guidance from the Scottish Office followed that of the Department of Health, although there was less support for the development of quasi-markets in Scotland (Mooney and Poole, 2004). While community care reforms accompanying the introduction of the NHSCCA were presented as a means of providing needs-led services and greater consumer choice, these principles were under-mined by a major shortfall in resources and the subsequent targeting of only the most needy (Ellis et al., 1999). Another criticism is that reconstructing the social work role as care management has contributed to the deprofessionalization of social work in the com-munity care sector (Langan, 1998).

Although the NHSCCA is the centrepiece of community care policy, it co-exists with other legislation. For example, the National Assistance Act 1948 and Chronically Sick and Disabled Persons Act 1970 help determine what services local authorities have duties and powers to pro-vide (Mandelstam, 1995). According to Mandelstam (1995), uncertainty is built into the com-munity care system through lack of definitions (e.g. of need and disability) and through the degree of discretion available to local authorities. Subsequently, much community care policy is shaped by case law and the setting of legal precedent. For example, after Gloucestershire County Council withdrew home care from 1,000 people, a case was brought to the House of Lords which decided in favour of the local authority (*R v Gloucestershire CC ex parte Barry* 1997). This case established that a local authority could not only take resources into consider-ation when setting eligibility criteria, it could also change these criteria in order to manage their budget. However, the ruling does not allow local authorities to change criteria in relation to specific cases: adjustments should only be made as part of a longer-term planning process.

According to Phillipson (1994), the community care reforms of the 1990s represented an implicit shift in citizenship, namely that people have a greater obligation to care for dis-abled or older relatives. The construction and intersection of 'disability' and 'caring' have taken on considerable importance and can be seen from different perspectives, including gendered, social psychological and disability rights perspectives. Gendered perspectives (see Finch and Groves, 1983) highlight the large number of women who act as informal carers (non-paid and commonly in the role of mother, wife, daughter or daughter-in-law) and as formal carers (paid and in both professional and non-professional roles). Ungerson (1997, 2000) has consistently highlighted the marginalization of women in the formal care market, particularly in non-professional roles such as home help, support worker, care assistant and nurse assistant. This work is noted for being fragmented, poorly paid, part-time and with minimal entitlements to sick leave, holiday pay and occupational pensions.

Social psychological perspectives have been influential in constructing caring as an additional dimension of human relationships. A considerable amount of research, particularly in the United States, has highlighted the stress or burden associated with being the primary care giver for disabled older relatives (Zarit et al., 1980). Although the notion of carer stress has entered public consciousness, social psychological researchers in the 1990s increasingly pointed out that stress is only one dimension of care giving (Kahana and Young, 1990) and emphasized patterns of communication and reciprocity in caring relationships, as well as the wider networks in which caring takes place. The origins of the Carers (Recognition and Services) Act 1995 can be found in both the social-psychological construction of caring relationships, as well as in recognition of the work provided by women as informal carers.

Disability rights perspectives are aligned to the social model of disability which considers disability to emerge not from individual impairment, but from physical and social barriers that exclude those seen as different (Oliver, 1996). Similarly to gendered perspectives, disability rights perspectives see the disadvantage facing disabled people as the responsibility of the state and argue for the needs of disabled people to be met directly by the state rather than informal care. Morris (1997) argues that the construction of caring has increasingly assumed a dependence or passivity on the part of the care receiver, reinforced by the notion that such dependence causes burden or stress in care givers. Society, through community care policies, should not enforce a person's dependence on another, resulting in damaged relationships and reduced life opportunities for both parties. Rather, individuals with disabilities should be able to lead independent lives, exercising control over how their needs might be met. The disability rights movement has been central in the campaign to introduce the Community Care (Direct Payments) Act 1996 through which disabled people are provided with funds to purchase their own care. The disability rights movement is also increasingly influenced by emerging emancipatory or affirmative models of disability. Swain and French (2000) argue that rather than seeing disability as a problem, either of the individual or of society, it should be celebrated as part of the diversity of human experience.

The ongoing development and simplification of the direct payments scheme is a major feature of New Labour's Green Paper *Independence, Well-being and Choice* (DoH, 2005). The programme of reform suggested in this paper is in line with the government's modernization strategy and centres around service users and carers taking more control in managing the services they receive. However, the programme attracts no new funding; it should be resourced through better use of existing funds and reducing bureaucracy. Importantly for social work, the Green Paper suggests that where possible service users and carers should conduct their own self-assessments (for example, over the internet), while social workers would be involved in assessing, for example, complex situations, where long-term therapeutic relationships are needed or where risk is a central issue (DoH, 2005). This indicates a reorientation of the role of care manager away from resource gatekeeper and towards a more traditional social work role. The proposed reforms also include preventative and early intervention strategies (for example, health promotion) to reduce social exclusion and promote quality of life. These and other strategies rely on the continued development of effective partnerships across health and social care organizations.

HEALTH AND SOCIAL CARE PARTNERSHIP

Concerns have been increasingly expressed about the split between health and social care services in Britain; the split was famously referred to by former New Labour Health Minister Frank Dobson as a 'Berlin wall'. In an analysis of the provision of home bathing services for disabled and older people, Twigg (1997) argues that a series of institutional and ideological factors influence where the boundary is drawn between medical and social care. Whether a service is considered medical or social might depend on the site of provision, the prognosis and the models of practice informing professionals' work. According to Twigg, medical care is afforded special legitimacy: in the main it is free via the NHS, medical staff are generally paid more than social care staff, and for many people there is something more real about medical needs. Twigg's analysis of the social bath reminds us that despite the territorial debates of what is medical and what is social care, services are not simply delivered or provided but also *experienced* by people. Invariably then, medical and social care tasks are imbued with complex meanings: for home bathing this involves the negotiation of intimacy in relation to cultural and social norms regarding the body, washing, touching and nakedness.

Successive governments have identified the separation of health and social care roles and subsequent communication and procedural breakdowns as a key problem. Public inquiries into the care of people with acute mental health needs have highlighted a series of communication failures between agencies. In some well-publicized cases this led to deaths of members of the public, such as the 1992 murder of Jonathan Zito by Christopher Clunis, who had been diagnosed with paranoid schizophrenia. Lack of communication between health and social services is also identified as contributing to the difficulty of moving older people from hospital back home or into residential or nursing home care (Health Advisory Service 2000, 1998). This issue becomes particularly acute in winter when many older people are susceptible to respiratory illnesses and hospitals complain of delayed discharges or 'bed blocking'.

For both major political parties there is a recognition that multi-disciplinary work across several agencies is necessary to provide the 'seamless service' needed for community care to work. Joint commissioning and joint purchasing strategies have sought to provide coordinated responses to local need. Although health authorities were able to provide funding for social services to purchase services under s.28a NHS Act 1977 for many years, the management and resourcing of joint initiatives remained separate. The Health Act 1999 radically changed this situation and provides for:

- *Pooled budgets:* local health and social services put money into a single dedicated budget to fund a wide range of care services;
- *Lead commissioning:* either the local authority or the health authority/primary care group takes the lead in commissioning services on behalf of both bodies;
- *Integrated providers:* local authorities and health authorities merge their services to deliver a one-stop package of care (DoH, 2000b: 70).

The Health and Social Care Act 2001 provides for the establishment of Care Trusts as a vehicle for developing integrated rather than joint services. The Trusts are empowered to commission and provide social care, in addition to community and primary health care, for a range of service user groups (DoH, 2000b). Local government is able to delegate statutory social service functions to Care Trusts and government retains the right to establish a Care Trust where existing health and social care organizations are seen to have failed (p. 73).

Many social workers are concerned that the identity and role of the profession, which for so long have been associated with local authority social services departments, will be threatened by social care under joint and integrated partnerships like Care Trust partnerships. Whether or not these partnerships are positive, it is certain that social workers are now working in more diverse and flexible ways than before and will increasingly do so. In the next section, we look more closely at key changes that social workers are facing.

CHANGE AND SOCIAL WELFARE IN BRITAIN

British social welfare policy and practice are changing, in part due to the impact of two broad influences. First, the intersection of political ideology and political expediency in the practices of central government is a key factor. While much of the past century was dominated by a Left–Right political discourse, the reality is that the blueprint for the modern welfare state was developed under Churchill's coalition government and then implemented by Labour. More recently, the Thatcher and Major governments' economic reforms have been consolidated by New Labour, despite the latter's emphasis on partnership and community. Second, the globalization of trade, and to a lesser extent social policy, is beginning to impact on Britain's social welfare systems, notably through restrictions on spending enforced by supranational organizations such as the International Monetary Fund and the promotion of human rights by the United Nations and European Union. In this section, we will examine two other important areas of change in social welfare: service user and carer involvement, and demographic and family changes.

SERVICE USER AND CARER INVOLVEMENT

There appears to be an increasing recognition of the role of service users and carers in policy development, management, implementation and evaluation. The NHS and Community Care Act 1990, introduced by a Conservative government, represented an attempt to provide consumers with purchasing power and consultation and complaints mechanisms. The Children Act 1989 advocated the importance of social services officers working in partnership with parents while maintaining a focus on the needs of the child. The Act also placed a duty on social services and the courts to determine the wishes of a child and to take these into consideration when making decisions. The Blair government has embraced the concept of partnership and frequently employs it when talking about relationships between the statutory, voluntary and profit-making sectors. Learning Disability Partnership Boards aim to bring these sectors together with people with disabilities and carers as 'full members' in order to develop integrated local services (DoH, 2001a: 108). For New Labour, such developments are part of their commitment to democratizing and devolving public services so that local communities – including a range of stakeholders – are involved in service planning, management and delivery. The emphasis on service user and carer involvement is also notably expressed in the requirements for the honours degree in social work that users and carers be involved in all aspects of programme design and delivery (DoH, 2002a).

However, the push for service user involvement has come less from the consumerist policies of past Conservative governments or the communitarian ideas of New Labour than from the empowerment movement of service users themselves. Grounded particularly in the politics of disability rights activists and mental health system survivors, the empowerment movement is concerned not just with increased involvement in service planning and delivery, but also with greater participation in social and community life. Summarizing Beresford and Croft's (2004) arguments, the movement has:

- challenged social work from a progressive and liberatory position;
- focused on the human and civil rights of service users rather than solely on their needs as constructed by 'experts';
- developed social models of service users' experiences and highlighted citizenship issues, discrimination and oppression;
- pioneered new approaches to service delivery, particularly user-controlled approaches, such as direct payments schemes;
- used democratic grassroots organizations for local, national and international campaigns; and
- worked for the inclusion of service users in a wide range of service and education systems.

Activists have often criticized government- and professional-led user involvement strategies as tokenistic and poorly resourced. According to Lindow, the three main priorities for mental health service users are poverty, homelessness and unemployment 'yet they consult us about the colour of the curtains in the day centre' (1993: 183). Service users are often concerned more about their participation in society (or citizenship) than their participation in services. As Beresford (1993) suggests, since many people have had unpleasant and frightening experiences in the service system, the thought of greater involvement may not always be welcome. And while arguing that user groups need to shape new forms of welfare, Barnes asks how feasible it is 'to talk of a real "partnership" with agencies which not only have substantially more power in terms of both resources and influence, but also power to control access to the services needed by group members?' (1999: 87).

User involvement poses real dilemmas for social work, particularly the statutory form of social work in which professionals need to make judgements that might restrict individual behaviour. Healy (1998) argues that the participatory discourse that has become popular in child protection work could lead to a retreat from making professional judgements, and to a denial of authority. An alternative participatory approach would instead bring greater clarity and openness in decision making so that 'our judgements are accessible and accountable to those with whom we work' (p. 911). The extension of not just user involvement strategies but also user control strategies, such as direct payments, will be an important feature of social policy and social work practice in the years ahead. Social work should have a key role in facilitating user involvement and addressing challenges in supporting people's rights to self-determination and safety.

Table 2.1   Life expectancy by gender 1841 to 1998

	1841	1901	1931	1961	1981	1991	1998
Males	41.0	45.7	58.1	67.8	70.9	73.2	74.9
Females	43.0	49.6	62.1	73.7	76.8	78.8	79.8

Source: ONS (2001).

DEMOGRAPHIC AND FAMILY CHANGES

The nature of social welfare in Britain is changing not just due to the different priorities of central government, but because the population is also changing. Like most western nations, Britain's population is ageing. This is mainly due to improved infant mortality rates, reduced fertility rates, people living longer and the impact of high birth cohorts reaching older age. As Table 2.1 indicates, throughout the previous century women have been increasingly living longer than men and thus the proportion of women in the older age groups has been much greater. However, the degree of difference between the proportion of men and women in the older age groups is decreasing slowly, mainly due to improvements in men's mortality (Arber and Ginn, 2004).

While a cause for celebration since it reflects improved population health and wellbeing, population ageing is often seen as a mixed blessing, particularly in terms of its implications for health and social welfare policy (Arber and Ginn, 2004). The growing very old (85 years +) population will see increases in age-related illnesses, such as coronary heart disease and dementia, and a correspondingly greater demand for services. The National Beds Inquiry (DoH, 2000a) identified that although in 1998–9 older people comprised about 16 per cent of the population, they accounted for 37 per cent of all general and acute hospital admissions and, because of longer than average stays, occupied 63 per cent of general and acute bed days.

However, an alternative reading of the data suggests that health expenditure is related not so much to increased age as to impending death; expenditure is greatest in the last year of a person's life, whenever this occurs (Arber and Ginn, 2004). Population ageing is often proclaimed to be a demographic time bomb and a cause of intergenerational conflict. This conflict is said to arise from the resentment of middle-aged taxpayers funding high levels of health and social security services. But such an analysis often conceals the resources supplied by older people, including care giving for partners, siblings, children and grandchildren and volunteering in local communities. Also ignored are resources the middle-aged generation have consumed while being cared for in childhood, adolescence and early adulthood. The composition of the older population suggests that social workers should pay close attention to gender and ensure that discriminatory assumptions are not placed on the older population because of gender stereotypes, such as the expectation that women should provide informal care-giving work.

Britain's population is also characterized by ethnic diversity, although compared to the white population the overall number of people from minority ethnic backgrounds is small. Based partly on data from the 2001 Census the ONS (2004) records 52.4 million people as white, just under 1.2 million as black or black British, about 2.3 million as Asian or Asian British and 674,000 as mixed race. In general, the age distribution of ethnic minority populations is younger than that of the white population; for example, in 2001 38 per cent of UK Bangladeshis were under 16, compared to 19 per cent of white people (ONS, 2004). However, over the next few decades a gradual ageing of ethnic minority populations is expected and social welfare policies will need to reflect the consequent shifts in need. A review of research over a 15-year period by Butt and Mizra (1996) indicated that as black people get older they tend to experience ill health and difficulties in daily living activities at a younger age than white people.

As with other service user groups, it is essential to recognize differences within and between groups of ethnic minority older people. Askham and colleagues (1995) identified in their study that older service users from African-Caribbean backgrounds preferred to use mainstream services, while those from Asian backgrounds preferred more specialist services. One explanation was a lower level of English-language skills in the older Asian communities and a related lack of confidence in accessing general services. Changes in family composition and changing attitudes of younger generations of migrant populations have considerable implications for the care of older people. Butt and Mizra (1996) argue that while many black families are multi-generational, it is wrong to assume that such families should or are necessarily able to meet care needs of older people.

Changes in family composition have been significant for the population as a whole. While the UK population increased by 6 per cent from 1971 to 2002, the number of households increased by 31 per cent (ONS, 2004). This was mainly due to the breakdown of extended family households, increased longevity, and increases in single-person households. In 2003 one in eight people lived alone, three times as many as in 1971 (ONS, 2004). The proportion of children living in lone-parent families has also increased considerably (from 7% in 1971 to 23% in 2003) (ONS, 2004). Lone-parent households are over-represented in the lower-income groups and face numerous difficulties in accessing work and childcare. About half of children living in lone-parent families where the parent was not working were living in a household with an income less than 60 per cent below the median (ONS, 2004). The proportion of people in non-marriage partnerships living together is also increasing (ONS, 2004). These changes highlight the need for social work practice to incorporate diversity of family arrangements and therefore different needs and problems faced by members of the community.

Social statistics also point to the increased visibility of groups that have previously largely been ignored or excluded by governments and services. Although it seems that the number of same-sex partners living together has increased, there is no data to support this trend, as national research has only recently included same-sex relationships. Although same-sex partnerships were identifiable through the 2001 Census and the Labour Force Survey, figures remain highly questionable due to a high rate of error (ONS, 2004) and the reliance on same-sex couples identifying as such (United Kingdom Parliament, 2004). With the advent of civil partnerships it seems likely that increasingly more people will feel able to disclose a same-sex partnership and therefore the recorded number of such relationships will increase. Moreover, people's household arrangements will probably continue to change to reflect greater acceptance of same-sex relationships and non-'traditional' relationships generally.

Social statistics regarding demographics and families indicate that Britain has changed enormously since the end of the Second World War and the institution of the modern welfare state. And it continues to change – population ageing, changes in ethnic minority populations, household and partnership changes – in ways similar to other western industrialized nations. The challenge for governments and other organizations involved in the planning and delivery of social welfare is to prepare for demographic changes, diversity and changing community attitudes. It is essential that responses do not scapegoat or stereotype particular groups of people. Older people won't be prepared to be scapegoated for the failure to deliver quality hospital and long-term care. Gays and lesbians won't put up with services that ignore their identities and partnerships. Lone parents won't take the blame if they can't enter employment or education because there is no affordable childcare. Black and ethnic minority people won't accept simplistic assumptions about the nature of their families and caring obligations. From our perspective, it is important that governments and other social welfare providers listen carefully to population and attitude shifts and respond to changes already taking place.

CONTINUITY AND CHANGE

Social policy analysts often reflect on points of both continuity and change in relation to the development of British social welfare (e.g. Ellison and Pierson, 1998). Some of the institutions of Beveridge's welfare state have proved remarkably resilient. Despite a tumultuous ride, the NHS emerged from the Thatcher era reasonably intact, and remains a universal health care system. However, currently the NHS is considerably underfunded in comparison with the health services of other European nations, resulting in ritualistic public criticism of waiting lists, overcrowded hospitals and the inevitable 'winter beds crisis'. The development of the personal social services and its fledgling profession, social work, has been similarly rocky. Social workers who see their identity as inextricably tied to local authority social service departments may perceive threats from efforts to better integrate health and social services and the increasing role played by the Department for Education and Skills in child welfare. However, the development of the honours degree in social work, as well as the consolidation of knowledge and expertise through the Social Care Institute for Excellence, may provide an opportunity to expand the base and horizons of the profession.

While the profession is currently undergoing considerable change, a continuing concern of social work is for those who have been badly affected by their social arrangements and their experience of the social welfare and social care systems. Thus, in the practice framework presented in this book, we highlight the focus of social work as understanding the tensions between people and their social arrangements, and the purpose of social work as intervening to redress these tensions. We argue that the best way of achieving this is by facilitating equitable social relationships and helping people take more control over their own lives (where this does not adversely affect others). Social welfare policies and politics may both assist and restrict social work in enacting this purpose. In implementing and sometimes challenging social policies, social workers can draw on important concepts such as citizenship, empowerment, social exclusion and service user involvement, although they should not do so uncritically. In the next chapter the potential of social work will be explored in more detail as we focus on social workers' use of self and communication skills in their professional practice, central features of our practice framework.

CHAPTER SUMMARY

Social welfare in Britain involves the provision of services and benefits to a wide range of people, including but not limited to those traditionally seen as poor or socially excluded. The public, private, voluntary and informal sectors of the community are all mobilized to provide this support. In this chapter we have argued that globalization and increased responsibilities of nation states within Europe have reconfigured the relationship between the individual and society. A related theme is the impact of neo-liberal economic reform, which is evident in many countries and is furthered by globalized economic conditions and international financial institutions. In Britain, the impacts of the reforms were felt most during the Thatcher/Major era, for example when people accessing community care services were forced to rely much more heavily on the private sector than before. While increased participation in community life is promoted, a neo-liberal economic agenda continues to influence social welfare policy in Tony Blair's Britain. New Labour's modernization agenda is mostly concerned with competition, enterprise and public/private partnerships. As a consequence, the personal social services, including child welfare and community care services, now rely less on the public delivery of services, although the government still takes an active role in monitoring and regulating service provision. Other changes in social welfare include moves towards partnerships across health, education and social care, as well as government partnerships with service users and carers. The ageing of the population and shifts in the nature and visibility of family relationships mean that social welfare delivery will continue to change.

FURTHER READING

Ellison, N. and Pierson, C. (eds) (2003) *Developments in British Social Policy*, 2nd edn. Basingstoke: Macmillan.

There are many books available that overview British social policy and the development of the welfare state. This book by Ellison and Pierson is a useful edited collection that examines themes and debates in social policy, including globalization and social exclusion, evaluates New Labour's social policies, and considers the implications of current developments, such as increasing reliance on information and communication technology.

Barry, M. and Hallett, C. (eds) (1998) *Social Exclusion and Social Work: Issues of Theory, Policy and Practice*. Lyme Regis: Russell House.

This is another valuable edited collection that moves beyond conventional definitions of poverty to explore the multi-faceted experience of social exclusion. Contributing authors cover a wide range of issues relating to social exclusion, including citizenship, disability, service user experiences, and the experiences of ethnic minority communities.

Jordan, B. (2000) *Social Work and the Third Way: Tough Love as Social Policy.* London: Sage. Jordan critiques the implementation of 'Third Way' policies and argues for a reconceptualization of the role of social work within the welfare state. The challenges of working within managerialist organizations are brought to life through case studies.

USEFUL WEBSITES

Centre for Social Work and Social Policy: www.swap.ac.uk.
Commission for Racial Equality: www.cre.gov.uk.
Department for Education and Skills: www.dfes.gov.uk.
Department of Health: www.dh.gov.uk.
European Court of Human Rights: www.echr.coe.int.
The New Deal: www.newdeal.gov.uk.
Office for National Statistics: www.statistics.gov.uk.
Social Exclusion Unit: www.socialexclusionunit.gov.uk.
Sure Start: www.surestart.gov.uk.

REFLECTIVE QUESTIONS

1. How do the values informing the practices of the Conservative and New Labour governments converge or conflict with your own values?
2. How is the relationship between the individual and the state changing and what are some implications for the knowledge, skills and values needed to work in the current context?
3. Consider an area of service provision of interest to you (e.g. child welfare), what would you most like to see changed in this area? Identify two ways in which you might pursue this.

3 SELF, RELATIONSHIPS, PROCESS AND PRACTICE

In this chapter we examine:

- The importance of self-awareness (including our motivations in doing social work) in facilitating our use of self in practice;
- Practice as a process that is influenced by our understanding of social work's purpose;
- Service users' experiences and expectations of social work;
- Issues in communication, such as the process of sending and receiving messages and communicating across difference;
- Verbal and non-verbal communication skills;
- Key stages of social work interviews;
- Core elements of social work relationships.

A distinguishing feature of social work that we emphasize in our practice framework is the skilful, disciplined use of self. Of particular concern is how we use ourselves in our professional relationships. Our use of self is often comprised of small-scale, humble interactions between social workers, social care workers and others – be they community groups, individuals or families. These interchanges form 'blocks' upon and with which practice is constructed, so the ability to make disciplined and constructive use of yourself in relationships is a prerequisite to all the activities that constitute social work practice. This is necessary whether you are in a situation of helping, of monitoring, of forming and maintaining a community group, of liaising with other professionals, of lobbying, or of acting as an administrator.

Within our practice framework so far we have highlighted the social welfare context of social work and social care practice, emphasizing the policies and politics that contribute to the social arrangements social workers and service users must deal with. In Chapter 1 we argued that the focus of social work practice is understanding the tensions between people and their social arrangements. The purpose of social work practice is to intervene to remedy these tensions by promoting equitable relationships and encouraging people to take more control over their own lives where this does not impinge on the rights of others. This purpose is grounded within social work values and its ethical and moral base. We believe that the purpose should be central to all social work activity and should direct the way we use ourselves in different interactions, most importantly in how we use ourselves when assessing and intervening in service users' lives. Thus in this chapter we examine in more depth the use of self in professional relationships, and the skills required for effective use of self, such as communication skills and skills in forming and maintaining relationships. In Figure 3.1, building on the focus and purpose of social work, we incorporate the dimension of the self and relationships into our practice framework.

SELF

WHY SOCIAL WORK?

A starting point to consider our self in relation to social work is to reflect on why we chose social work or social care as a career and what motivates us to continue on this path. While not everyone may feel they had many choices available to them, most of us chose social work in preference to doing something else, such as nursing or journalism or teaching. When students are asked why they entered social work they tend to respond in the following ways:

- 'I want to help people';
- 'I want to make a difference to someone's life';
- 'I want to change the system that keeps people poor or oppressed';
- 'I want a university degree and a secure job';
- 'I want to avoid a boring and meaningless life';
- 'I want to upgrade my qualification. I'm sick of being bossed around by social workers';
- 'I want to be paid for the work I'm already doing for nothing'.

For those who are already practitioners it would be interesting to reflect on whether the factors that keep you in social work are the same as those which motivated you in the beginning. Our reasons for entering and staying in social work are important because they are a statement of our own personal purpose: of who we are and what we seek to achieve through our work. They reflect our understanding of the world and our place and the place of others in it. It goes without saying that our purpose and our understanding of our place in the world and how the world operates will impact on the way in which we practise as social workers. In relation to interpersonal helping, Rowe expressed the importance of understanding one's purpose thus:

Each of us needs to be very clear as to just why we go into this business of helping, for, unless we are, we are in danger of being no help at all. We know, but we need to know that we know, whether we are helping so as to make people love us because they need us, or admire us because we are powerful and have secrets, or because we want to prove that the world really is a just and fair place, or that ignorance can be overcome or virtue triumph, whether we are seeking clarity and understanding, or salvation, or the right to exist or a happy rebirth. (1983: 56)

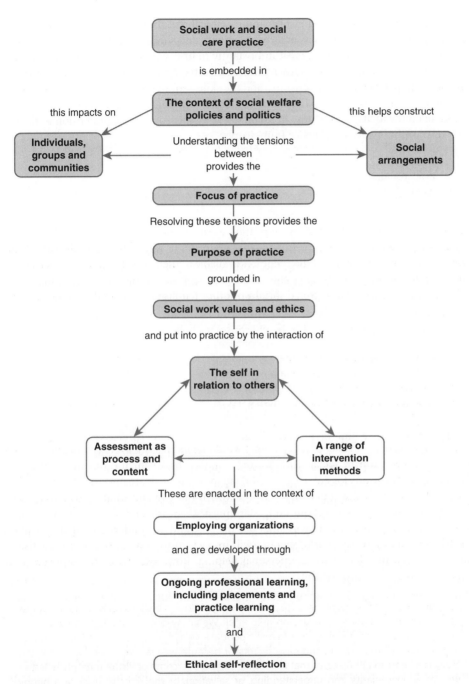

Figure 3.1   The self in relation to others in the practice framework

It is important to spend time reviewing your own biography, exploring how and why you came to the point where you entered social care or social work (rather than some other occupation). How did the processes and issues in your life come together so that you now find yourself a social care worker, social worker or aspiring to be one of these? Many factors will have influenced this:

- the role you played in your own family;
- the expectations of significant others;
- personal life issues (experiences of dependency, of oppression, of being helped or being a helper);
- available job opportunities;
- where you lived, and so on.

WHAT DO I BRING TO SOCIAL WORK?

Each of us comes to social work with our own biography, our own history, life issues and beliefs, and way of understanding the world and its perceived meaning. We have constructed this meaning through a lifetime of interacting and relating to the material, spiritual and social world. Some of the understandings that we have of different aspects of the world we are able to articulate clearly, while others we are much less sure about. In some situations we bring half-formed or barely conscious beliefs, such as:

- nothing is done properly unless I do it myself;
- there is no learning without suffering;
- middle-aged male bureaucrats can't be trusted;
- children are always better off with their family.

Such ideas influence how we perceive events and how we interpret and respond to them. Sometimes the ideas we have (our personal knowledge) may coincide with public knowledge and at other times they conflict. When our personal knowledge and feelings are inconsistent much uncertainty and confusion can result.

The conflicts between public and private knowledge and the implications for practice are increasingly coming to the attention of researchers. For example, research has revealed that the past practice of police, health and social care personnel often failed to address domestic violence. Despite recognition (mandated in criminal law) that violence is not appropriate in human relations, historically the assault of women within the home has been accepted and responded to quite differently from assault outside of the home. Workers have brought ideas about what is normal family life and applied these to the situations they have encountered – to the detriment of the women and children involved (O'Connor, 1992; O'Hagan and Dillenberger, 1995; Humphreys and Thiara, 2003).

The ideas that we bring to practice are developed through our interactions with the world: these interactions include reading, personal experience and education. Because we don't start each interaction as a blank sheet we make connections between new situations and other experiences we have had. As a social worker, this experienced similarity may relate to previously acquired knowledge and skill, such as: 'This is another community group having difficulty with the local council. My knowledge of council processes, local politics and my lobbying and advocacy skills should be useful again'. In other situations, the experienced similarity may also relate to the feelings associated with past events. For example, encountering a young person who has nowhere to live because of a violent family situation may touch on your own past family experiences, including exposure to conflict and violence.

Our understandings, including both their cognitive and emotional aspects, influence our perceptions of and reactions to a situation. In practising social work, our aim is not to eliminate our pre-existing ideas and feelings, but rather to subject them to critical scrutiny, so our use of self is conscious and disciplined.

USE OF SELF

But what does this term 'use of self' mean? Put simply it refers to our understanding, intentions and behaviour in a particular situation. By arguing that we should consciously use our self in practice we are saying that we are a resource for practice, and that who we are – and how we are perceived – will have an impact on the situation. As Thompson notes: 'much of what we have to offer comes from our own personality or our own personal resources' (2005: 89), and is affected by our values and experiences. We can use our self without being physically there; we can write strident letters, passionate letters, boring or fascinating memoranda. We can not turn up for appointments, or cancel them or fail to carry through on what we have promised. Use of self is stimulated by gaining more knowledge about ourselves.

The idea of self relates to a sense of identity. If we try to describe ourselves we often refer to our gender, our age, our 'race' or ethnicity, our religion, our sexual identity, our marital/parental status, our occupation. When we think about ourselves we probably also include some idea of our sense of direction in life, perhaps our body image, our sense of how we see ourselves and how others see us. Generally these words describe our public sense of ourselves. Some may refer to a private self we know quite well, the one we have private conversations with but keep out of sight from most others.

Goldstein (1973) extends the notion of self by referring to: self-conception (being), perceiving self (knowing) and intentional self (becoming). In Goldstein's terms, feeling good about ourselves depends on these three aspects being in harmony. It is probably more likely that there is always some tension between our view of our real and ideal selves. Once understood, this tension provides us with our motivation and direction for learning. A postmodern view suggests that what we experience as a sense of self changes depending on the context (work, family, marriage and so on), and in each context we may have different experiences of self, which may be contradictory and informed by both dominant and subordinate discourses (Epston and White, 1992: 41). Thus it is possible, for example, to experience ourselves in the role of a parent as both rejecting and nurturing.

The idea of self used in this book includes a concept of 'me' which we use to make comparisons with things that are perceived as 'not like me' but which, however uncomfortable it might be to acknowledge, do indeed reflect a way in which we operate in the world.

We are struck by the strength of the boundaries that we draw around ourselves when our concept of 'me-ness' is threatened, for example by a diagnosis of diabetes or by the loss of a job, which can produce such a challenge to our sense of self that we are unable to cope either with the medication regime or with deciding about further employment. We say to others and ourselves, 'It's just not like me', as we struggle to come to terms with not only the new situation, but also a new understanding of ourselves.

As Jordan notes: '[I]f we don't understand how much of our assessment comes from our own fears, hopes and needs we are unlikely to be able to understand what it might be like to stand in the other person's place' (1979: 12). The importance of self-knowledge is highlighted in the following reflective account by a then student social worker, Michelle Rusterholtz. The situation involved an assessment by the student and two social workers of a young mother and her three children, for suspected child abuse and neglect. Self-knowledge, gained by examining emerging feelings and proposed actions regarding the mother's behaviour allowed the student to make intentional choices about how best to respond in keeping with social work purpose.

Tina's situation

My supervisor was encouraging Tina to discuss the difficulties she was having in caring for her three children (aged three and two years and nine months). My emotions were constantly jarred by the intensity of Tina's verbal and emotional abuse of her children: 'I only left the baby alone for four hours – nothing wrong with that … it's them (children) that's to blame … I threw him … get away from me'. Her harsh words rang in my ears. I desperately wanted to pick up those children and comfort them as they dejectedly backed away from their mother. I stopped myself, and thought about my reasons for wanting to respond this way and how such a response would be received by Tina. At this point in the assessment process, professionals in authority were clearly questioning Tina's lack of empathy for and tolerance of her children's needs. In this context, I felt my desire to protect and comfort the children would serve largely to alleviate my own feelings of powerlessness and perhaps anger, and would do little to help Tina. My response could convey to Tina in an unhelpful way that I, 'the expert', was capable of responding to her children whereas she was not. Modelling of appropriate parenting behaviours (e.g. pro-social modelling as described by Trotter (1999)) could well be useful once it was clear what outcomes Tina would be willing to pursue with the Department.

As Tina began to recount her own abusive childhood, assaults, and eventual abandonment, I saw her as desperate as her children for the love and empathy she craved yet never received. Drawing on theories related to the importance of establishing a relationship of trust as the basis for change of abusive behaviour, I felt it was more important to express empathy towards Tina in spite of her treatment of her children. The other workers left the room to confer. I could have left, but felt that there was potential in this moment to make a deeper connection with Tina. I was drawn out of my seat to sit by her side. I didn't really know what to say but I wanted to enter her world and communicate my unconditional acceptance and support for her apart from her behaviour, even if she was not yet ready to fully receive it. This was a consciously directed use of self in keeping with the purpose of assessment. She turned to me saying, 'Could you turn your back on these children? Tell me, if you were their father could you turn your back on them and leave them and forget them like he did?' 'No' I said, 'I couldn't.' Her words had taken on a meaning for me far beyond what was said.

In coming to understand our sense of self in different situations and the way that our hopes, fears and needs impact on our interactions with others, it is useful to explore our experiences of gender socialization, particularly the influences that different discourses have had about what it means to be a man or a woman. This, of course, is culturally determined and can vary within and between cultures.

For a long time in western societies the dominant message for women has been that they should be good, whereas for men the dominant message has been that a good man is a strong man (Rowe, 1988: 275; Bepko and Krestan, 1991). There has been a tendency to devalue women and traits thought to be innately female, such as being highly emotional and nurturing, and to value and reward so-called male traits of autonomy, competitiveness, strength and acquisition (Bepko and Krestan, 1991: 44). While such stereotypes are changing, many women and men may still feel constrained by them.

For both women and men, these long-standing ideals about female goodness and male strength are contradictory and impossible to achieve. They may lead to stereotyped behaviour in both sexes and can create enormous difficulties in relationships. In social work practice, the relationships that we make with service users and colleagues are likely to evoke these aspects of our sense of self and our resolution of the images of man and woman. Bepko and Krestan (1991) describe this process for women. Being helpful to others, taking on their suffering, feeling responsible for them may serve as proof of our goodness, to shore up our feelings of self-worth, while warding off feelings of worthlessness.

More is also becoming known about how men's socialization experiences influence their work as practitioners (see Cree, 1996; Christie, 1998; Pringle, 1998). One possibility is that for some men, having to face chaotic and highly emotional situations may evoke needs to prove their sense of self as a competent male by imposing their control over situations and implementing solutions. This approach may serve to repress fears at a deeper level. Engaging with people around emotions is messy and unpredictable, and brings us in contact with our own psychic pain whereby our feelings of fear, sorrow and abandonment may surface unexpectedly. These are feelings traditionally associated with femininity and weakness, and thus for some men to acknowledge and express such feelings would call into question their masculinity.

As long as our behaviour confirms our sense of what it means to be a competent man or woman and our inner needs to avoid feelings of inadequacy are met, we are able to reassure ourselves of our innate goodness or strength. However, other people will inevitably fail to play their part in this process. They may fail to show appropriate gratitude for the efforts that we make and blame us and the organizations for which we work for not being helpful enough, or worse still, for ruining their lives. The difficulty that these issues around self create for both men and women in social work practice is that we are locating part of our sense of worth and competence in the behaviour of others and repressing our deeper feelings of shame and doubt. When people do well through our interventions we temporarily feel good, but since the source that created the feeling is external, we will need constant repetition to satisfy our needs. If our work is not going well and we are blamed or criticized by others, our sense of competence and goodness is threatened and we may react with self-punishment and increased efforts to do better, exert pressure on others to continue to confirm our image of us as helpful, and perhaps admonish and reject those who do not appear to benefit from our efforts (Rowe, 1988: 277). How many service users are deemed difficult, manipulative, untreatable, unworthy, because their behaviour sparks our own feelings of self-doubt and inadequacy?

As Bepko and Krestan (1991: 99) suggest, when we develop a mantle of pride in our goodness, we often manipulate others to confirm this sense of self, and do not take responsibility for our own feelings. Such reactions distort power, equality, honesty and openness in relationships and leave us and others feeling cut off, unsatisfied and misunderstood. Our interactions with others will always touch something in us. We need to acknowledge that and take responsibility for our own responses, our own sense of self-worth and, in doing so, allow others to take responsibility for theirs. This applies to work with a wide range of people, including service users and colleagues. How we deal with the issues that arise for us in the interactive process will depend on how well we understand our socialization experiences, our intentions in social work, our inner processes, our needs and our ways of operating in different contexts. We express our understanding of the world by our interventions in it, through our use of self. Our action will provoke a reaction and we may react to that as part of a process of interaction. It is not simply a matter of the individual acting in a void, but of people interacting with each other and with the issues that they bring with them. It is to this process of interaction and its implications for practice that we now turn.

UNDERSTANDING PRACTICE AS A PROCESS

Initially as students we may feel that interactions just happen. Sometimes the outcomes are as we hoped, sometimes not. After some of these experiences we may realize that there were points at which we made choices about how to direct the interaction (or vice versa). In any interaction there are points at which you may choose to follow something further, let it drop or perhaps introduce a new topic. These are the critical incidents or choice points which punctuate the interactive process.

When you can identify the choices, why you made them and how you presented these choices to the other person, you have a description of the overall process of the interaction. Our understanding of our self in process develops when we are able to describe the patterns in our interactions with another and shift our understanding from the description of a specific situation to concepts which link and explain what we saw, did or felt. It is a skill to be able to observe yourself in interaction and to be able to put words around what is happening. Initially it is often easier to see what happened after the event than at the time. Once you have acquired this skill in the situation, it enables you to be much more creative and purposeful in how you use your self.

It is clear in our practice framework that social work's processes should be derived from its purpose and values. Social work processes are put into effect by persons who are enough in tune with themselves to be able to lend energy to others to enable them to organize, to obtain information, to develop skills or to find some solution to what may trouble them. Methods in social work therefore should not be conceptualized as rigid programmes applied to others. Because social work involves interactive processes, it is the meaning of the transaction to the other person which is ultimately important, not the method itself.

From our perspective, service users should be fully involved in establishing outcomes and choosing interventions. Additionally, the processes of how things are done with other people must support the intended outcomes and both process and outcome must be given equal importance in practice.

In line with our practice framework, we argue that social work is intended to help people reclaim power in their lives as long as this does not result in inequitable relationships with others. Thus work is done 'with' rather than 'to' or 'for' people. Social work assumes that people have the capacity to change and that people can, with support, encouragement and information, make sense of what is happening to them. However, this understanding cannot be handed to the other person like a medical diagnosis. The process in practice, then, is to encourage the other to talk about and to review what they already know but perhaps haven't pulled together. We try to communicate that we really are interested in their situation and to establish a climate where the other person can present their story 'warts and all' and make sense of it. When, as interviewers, we become too pressed, for whatever reason, we may distance ourselves from the other person and their situation. As a result, our ability to see things with the other person, and hence our capacity to understand, breaks down. In these circumstances we move from doing 'with' to directing people and doing 'for' or 'to' them. Research on service user experiences of social workers or other social care workers indicates that service users' expectations and preferences relate to the process, content and outcome of intervention.

SERVICE USER EXPECTATIONS

To understand the service user's experience it is useful to reflect on our own experiences of being helped when we have felt vulnerable, powerless, lacking direction or short of necessary resources. Jordan (1979) reports that, for him, a 'true helper' has the capacity to listen to the whole person, to hear the mixed feelings associated with seeking help and to feel what it might be like to be in the grip of such mixed feelings.

Research on service user perspectives (Polansky, 1971; Rees and Wallace, 1982) has identified certain personal attributes, skills and knowledge as being helpful in social workers. However, these attributes, such as warmth, and knowledge of both the service users' particular problems and relevant resources, must be considered in the context of different expectations of different service user groups and the different expectations of service users and the organization as to the services offered. For the service user, where the social worker aligns himself or herself (i.e. with the organization or the service user) influences how the service is evaluated.

In an Australian study conducted by one of the authors, homeless young people tended to value open, non-controlling relationships accompanied by the actual transfer of power and resources (O'Connor, 1989). Often they believed that social workers were willing to talk, but rarely prepared to get involved and follow through. Research into how service users view social workers suggests that when the power differential is ignored, or where the relationship is neglected and social workers do things 'at' and 'to' people rather than with them, they are viewed negatively. If they are voluntary clients, people are likely to discontinue contact in these circumstances, even if the worker is perceived as an expert. Where the worker's emphasis is not so much on helping but facilitating (e.g. self-help group), service users regard positively the worker's capacity to assist people in developing their confidence, to find out information and to be able to move from a position of leadership to one of membership or consultant. These points were reinforced during a recent consultation exercise carried out by the General Social Care Council (GSCC). As part of the development of the new honours degree in social work, the GSCC organized a number of focus groups to find out what characteristics key stakeholders wanted in social workers. As Horner notes:

> What matters to service users is summarised in two short statements in their report. The need for social workers to understand what a person's life is really like, and not to make assumptions and judgements about what they think the person wants or needs. The importance of the quality of the relationships that the social worker has with the service user. (2003: 124)

He goes on to provide a more detailed list of characteristics that service users identified as important; they wanted social workers to be:

- physically and emotionally available;
- supportive, encouraging and reassuring;
- respectful;
- patient and attentive to the service users' problems;
- committed to the independence of the individual;
- punctual;
- trustworthy;
- reliable;
- friendly but not frightened to tell people how they see things;
- empathic and warm.

Again, it is clear that workers are valued if they can convey sensitivity to the needs of others, have a grasp of the whole, and can adapt the use they make of themselves to the changed needs of the people with whom they work. To do this, workers need to be sensitive to difference and to develop skills in working across difference.

THE CHALLENGE OF WORKING ACROSS DIFFERENCE

In any situation the relationship between people is the medium or the vehicle through which events are interpreted, decisions are made and work is done. This is true of social care work in all its forms. All relationships involve working across difference. Differences may be emphasized by cultural factors, by class, by gender, by age, by sexual identity, and by other power differentials such as needing to use services, or having a disability. In working across difference in relation to sexual identity, heterosexual social work practitioners may need to understand for example, that treating lesbians as no different to non-lesbians is not necessarily helpful and that there is a need for workers to be sensitive to lesbian and gay lifestyles and to questions which may be perceived as heterosexist (Langley, 2001: 928). For example, it is preferable to ask 'Please describe all relationships that are important to you' rather than inquire about 'marital status' (p. 928). Similarly when white social workers are working with black people or those from ethnic minority backgrounds it is important not to make assumptions about personal and family relationships based on stereotypes such as 'they prefer look after their own'. The dimension of class is also clearly important. Sometimes workers are either born to or achieve higher-class status than the service users they work with. Class affects our life chances, our health, our housing, our employment, and a whole range of distinctions which also includes greater or lesser facility with language and different ways of expressing ourselves. If we are not tuned in sharply enough to these differences and similarities, the potential for distortion in communication increases (Kadushin, 1972).

Part of the requirement for effective work across a range of difference is to develop an appropriate knowledge about a specific culture, or of the social arrangements in which the individual's life is embedded. This may mean adopting a position of not knowing, of trying to work in partnership with the other so that their expertise in their own situation is respected and our power is not used in an abusive manner. However, when we are faced with someone from the same broad cultural grouping as ourselves, we tend to take culture and class for granted. When white students are asked to comment on cultural issues involved in their practice with a white service user, they will frequently note that culture is not an issue – this person is also white and has lived in the UK all his or her life. Of course, though, white British people do have a culture and different subcultures. In the UK, moves towards devolution in Scotland and Wales are predicated on particular assumptions about national identity; even within England, we talk about the North/South divide, and claims for distinctive regional (e.g. Cornish) identities have highlighted significant issues around culture and sense of 'belonging'. But if we happen to be a member of the same group, we are often not very perceptive in identifying and describing the cultural norms. We may even say 'there is no culture'. But if we manage to behave in a reasonably predictable way, there must be a set of culturally defined norms and roles that enable such prediction to take place.

Ethnic-sensitive and anti-oppressive practice, which promotes an awareness of service users' values, social class, and the effects of oppression on racial and ethnic groups (Zastrow and Kirst-Ashman, 2001: 232), should be incorporated into all social work and social care practice. Empowerment and strengths perspectives are two important frameworks for anti-oppressive practice (p. 232).

The types of questions that social workers could ask include finding out how people view asking for help from a social care agency; what values individuals and groups hold and where members of this group are most likely to turn to when they need help – relatives, friends, neighbours, religious leaders, social agencies, school system, or local government? For example, in traditional Chinese culture self-reliance and self-control are important in maintaining group harmony (Rudowicz and Au, 2001: 89), whereas self-disclosure and expression of strong emotions may be viewed as a loss of face for individuals and their families (Ow and Katz, 1999: 620). When intervening in collectivist communities it is important to acknowledge that help seeking must not undermine the priority given to maintaining group harmony and protecting group members (p. 625).

Social workers should also be aware of their own values, prejudices, and stereotypes and focus on the unique attributes of each individual and question whether they are viewing people in terms of their own prejudices and stereotypes (Zastrow and Kirst-Ashman, 2001: 234). Lack of sensitivity to these differences when we are operating from a position of relative power, can lead to discriminatory practice. That is, we fail to take account of structural disadvantage (Thomas and Pierson, 1995: 16), and consequently run the risk of perpetuating it through our actions. There is a further dimension to working across difference: asking what can we learn from other cultures that could inform and enrich current social work and social care knowledge, theory and skills so that such knowledge becomes a part of professional discourse. The growing use of Family Group Conferences in cases involving children and young people shows how some traditional approaches to problem solving can be translated into the British context. Drawing on ideas from Maori traditions, Family Group Conferences represent a move away from an 'expert' model where the various professionals are the ones accorded expert status. This alternative approach shifts the locus of decision making away from the professionals and acknowledges the role and expertise of the broader family (and in some cases, community) in finding workable solutions to particular problems. While it can clearly be helpful to 'borrow' ideas and approaches from different cultural traditions, we must also be aware that some dominant techniques may not have much relevance for particular minority ethnic/cultural communities; these techniques may include set skills, detachment, neutrality, self-fulfilment, respect for each individual, confidentiality and self-determination (Lynn, 2001: 911).

Often a culture's literature will illustrate its expectations of different groups of people. From close reading of contemporary literature we can obtain insights into situations we normally take for granted. An understanding of a person's culture is essential to the development of an understanding of the hopes and fears of those with whom we work.

The main barrier to a truly equal exchange of ideas and practices across difference is perhaps the inability of those whose backgrounds reflect the dominant culture to embrace both the discomfort and rewards involved in looking outside of their frames of reference. Professional training needs to provide experiences for students to engage with other cultures in a more meaningful way. The relevant chapters in Munford and Nash (1994) provide useful insights into working across difference and there are a range of texts that explore issues of anti-racist and broader anti-oppressive practice in more detail, for example Dominelli (1997, 2002), Graham (2004) and Thompson (2001).

Establishing meaningful helping relationships across difference requires a capacity to communicate effectively. Effective communication is the basic starting point for building relationships and structuring interventions.

ISSUES IN COMMUNICATION

Communication is defined as the giving and getting of information. It is a complicated process. Each person involved in communication has:

- a transmitting system for encoding the message they want to send and then actually sending it;
- a receiving system composed of the interaction of the five senses (touch, taste, sight, hearing, smell); and
- a processing system constituted by our conceptual abilities, our knowledge, desires and attitudes to make sense of the message received.

The processes of transmitting, receiving and translating messages all take place within an environment, which both contributes a message of its own and distorts the meaning of the message. The distortion may be a result of the way the speech is produced, noise and other distractions, our gender and our cultural biases. Extra messages may be conveyed by the physical appearance of the place – for example, your office or someone's home. So a dark and gloomy sitting-room cluttered with knick-knacks may reduce your capacity to concentrate on what is being said. An office that reflects barely contained chaos may distract a person. They may wonder (among other things) whether you will have time for them.

In conversation, we generally assume that 'you are like me', although we may also be aware of differences between ourselves and our 'conversation partner' in terms, for example, of 'race', culture, class, gender or age. We talk to establish common ground, to diminish the differences between us so that 'you can understand me'. Difficulties arise when differences are not recognized – communication processes may then become distorted, contributing to a service user's feeling of being misunderstood, oppressed, or not taken seriously. Later in this chapter, under the heading 'Relationships in social work practice', we explore some of the implications of working across difference.

There are a number of dimensions along which we can analyse our efforts to communicate with another (see Figure 3.2). First, there is the 'taken-for-granted' background of our class, culture and gender. We are not usually conscious of this unless we experience one or another of these an issue in our attempts to communicate; for example: 'I don't understand West African culture'; or 'This person seems to be using a different language'; or 'I'm worried by this man or woman'. Although we are not constantly conscious of them, these factors affect the context, processing and style of our communication. It is helpful to spend some time understanding these 'taken-for-granted' dimensions so we can improve our capacity to communicate (see Combs et al., 1978). The actual sending and receiving of information in the here and now occurs against this background. This communication has verbal and non-verbal elements.

MESSAGE SENT

To communicate a message we need to decide on the right words to 'carry' the information. This process is called 'encoding'. It may involve an internal dialogue where we debate whether or not to say something and then, having decided to communicate a thought, it is necessary to decide on the right words and the right structure for those words – for example, should we ask a question, offer information and so on. This requires a vocabulary which can fine-tune thoughts and describe feelings precisely, and which is flexible enough to be adapted to the vocabulary of a wide range of people.

Our occupation and its jargon, our class, gender, education and culture, and perhaps our age and our history influence the meaning we attach to words. It is important to be aware of the extent of shared meaning attached to important words in an interaction. When one of the authors explored the understandings that a group of Australian children have of court, he found that the words and meanings attached to court officials and procedures were not shared by the young offenders. One young person identified the Clerk of the Court as the 'prostitute'. Others believed they had been 'abolished and discharged', 'given a

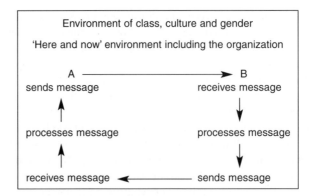

Figure 3.2   Environment of communication

dishonourable discharge', 'placed under superstition' and so on. One young person who pleaded 'guilty' believed he pleaded 'not guilty' (O'Connor and Sweetapple, 1988: 81). We must never assume a shared language. Practitioners (and other professionals) may use expressions which totally mislead the service user. Given that the service user is less able than the worker to check out meanings, it is important for the worker to consider the range of ways in which his or her message might be interpreted and to try to be as unambiguous as possible. One way of achieving this is by using the language of the other.

Though we are usually fairly conscious of the words we choose to use, we may not be as aware of the other messages we are sending through the use we make of our face and hands and through the way we sit and move. The onus is on the worker to ensure that the whole message is as congruent as possible. Nevertheless, once we have sent the message, we lose control over it. The sender never knows precisely how his or her message is received, just as the receiver never knows how the idea that is communicated was originally conceptualized. As communicators we make assessments of whether or not our message is 'getting through' from the verbal and non-verbal behaviour of the other person, and from reflecting on how skilled we were in finding the right words and the right structure for our ideas.

MESSAGE RECEIVED

Communication has not taken place until the other person has heard and processed what was said. We hear what we expect to hear and what we choose to listen to. Sometimes we hear what was not said and sometimes we totally shut out what was said. We can hear with our ears but not with our minds. We may subconsciously refuse to process the information if we do not expect to hear it or if it makes us anxious or uncomfortable.

The receiver's belief systems raise expectations about what they think they will hear. Our sense of the other person's identity influences how we hear their message: we expect a doctor to behave like a doctor and a teacher to act like a teacher. Stereotyping helps us to make sense of a wealth of data. However, it can also be a threat to accurate communication and to forming relationships if we do not explore how well the typical picture fits this particular person. As workers, the onus is on us to be aware of how we categorize our information and characterize people. With this awareness, we are more open to having our views challenged and hence are better able to listen accurately.

Social workers attempt to be active listeners in interactions. By active listeners, we mean that they expend considerable energy in processing what they see, hear and feel about the messages received. In everyday communication we do not usually think about and question what we hear. What does this person mean? How can I understand it? How does it fit with what I already know? Do I need to modify what I am doing or is this all right? It is almost impossible for anyone to be listening in this manner to another person and thinking about anything else – including what they will say next – at the same time. It follows that when a person is working hard at listening to someone else, the pace of their responses is slower than in their everyday 'chat'. You may be aware yourself of how luxurious it is to have someone sit and really listen to what you want to say. You may also be aware that such listening is an exhausting business, since it demands total concentration.

SOME AXIOMS ABOUT COMMUNICATION

In a seminal text Watzlawick et al. (1967) described what they termed 'axioms' of communication. The first of these is that all behaviour in an interactive situation has a message value; hence you cannot not communicate. You can, of course, seek to avoid communication but sometimes the impossibility of not communicating creates a dilemma. For example, behaviour that says 'I don't want to communicate' is a communication which may precipitate a response calling for further communication.

A second rule described by Watzlawick et al. (1967) is that all communication has a report aspect, or literal content, and a command aspect which refers to the sort of message it is to be taken as, as well as to the relationship between those communicating. Communication conveys information and at the same time it imposes behaviour. Relationships are not often defined deliberately in this way. Watzlawick and colleagues point out that the more spontaneous a relationship, the less attention is paid to it in conversation, while in relationships where there are difficulties a large amount of time and effort goes into deciding what sort of a relationship it ought to be, with what is talked about being of much less importance (p. 52).

Relationships are often described in terms of who seems to be exerting influence and how the other reacts to these attempts. Watzlawick et al. (1967) called the different types of relationships: complementary, symmetrical and meta-complementary. Complementary relationships are characterized by one person going 'one-up', and the other person accepting that definition and going 'one-down'. The person who is seen to have control or authority defines the relationship, and hence reality, for the other person. In symmetrical relationships, both strive to maintain equal shares in the authority to influence outcomes. Generally, healthy relationships need elements of both symmetry and complementarity. Meta-complementary relationships are marked by one person letting the other go 'one-up', so that the person who appears to be in control is in fact being controlled by the other. In all communication there is a relationship message that needs to be attended to both in understanding situations and in understanding the process of interactions in the here and now.

The relationship aspect of communication is a form of meta-communication – that is, communication about the communication. Its other aspects include the tone of voice, the use of special language, gestures and the style of delivery of speech. The purpose of meta-communication is to set the wider context in which the literal content is to be understood. It qualifies the relationship between sender and receiver, and this relationship provides the specific context in which the communication occurs. In healthy relationships, disagreement can generally be resolved. However, it can also be deflected or not resolved through behaviours called disqualifications. This occurs where agreement cannot be reached but disagreement can't be tolerated. In its simplest form, it is evident in incomplete sentences and in verbal habits such as ending statements with 'you know' on a rising inflection when the other person is not invited to reply, 'No, I don't know'. Other verbal ploys to reduce or handle disagreement are speaking for others and mind reading – anticipating what the other might say. Generally these disqualifications should be avoided in social work interactions.

THE CONTEXT OF CLASS, GENDER AND CULTURE

We have already noted the importance of developing skills in working across difference and that the three dimensions of class, gender and culture interact in discussion, in non-verbal behaviour and in the meaning we assign to messages to create different contexts in which communication occurs. An understanding of language tends to reflect an understanding of culture. In Australia, for example, Aboriginal English has emerged as a distinct dialect 'which reflects, maintains and continually creates Aboriginal culture and identity' (Eades, 1992: 25). There are differences of pronunciation, grammar, vocabulary, meaning, use and style. As Eades suggests, the starting point for developing good communication with people from different cultural and linguistic backgrounds to our own is knowledge of, and a willingness to respect their culture. This provides a basis upon which to understand communication difficulties that may arise. For example, a direct questioning style, common in white British culture, may be perceived as hostile and distressing to someone from another culture. This highlights the importance of establishing that there is sufficient 'common ground' to allow effective communication to occur. The use of interpreters requires special skills and the reader is referred to Cox (1989: 253–63), Pugh (1996: 118–39) and Rack (1982) for consideration of this topic. Similar issues to the ones identified by Eades (1992) could be discussed in relation to the varieties of English spoken in the UK by people of different cultural backgrounds. Research was done, for example, into the use of 'London Jamaican' creole by black (and white) adolescents in London in the early 1980s (Hewitt, 1986) and in the mental health field, Rack (1982) and Littlewood and Lipsedge (1982) have considered the impact of particular forms of language used by people of African-Caribbean and Asian backgrounds. For example, Rack draws attention to the way something that is perceived as mental illness in the western tradition – depression – is framed in terms of social function/dysfunction by an Asian patient and her husband rather than 'inner psychological/emotional states'. He shows the way in which health, in this cultural context, is defined as the ability to carry out your social and family obligations. In the example he gives, the (white English) psychiatrist is trying to establish whether or not the depressed woman is 'feeling better'; he cannot get an answer that makes sense in his terms because the only answer the patient and her husband can give is in terms of her renewed ability to carry out her expected family and social roles. 'If you can do these things you are well, if you are unable to do them you are ill, and no more need be said' (Rack, 1982: 110).

Gender differences in human communication have received considerable attention in the literature. Western cultures have traditionally valued different communication patterns by men and women (Tannen, 1990). These differences reflect and support structural inequalities between the sexes. At a behavioural level, women have been expected to interrupt less and to take the 'one-down' position in interactions. Traditionally women and men have tended to use different language. As communicators, we need to be aware of the effect our gender has on others. Despite the increasing recognition of less rigid gender roles and identities, many of us still tend to typecast people by gender and to attribute a whole range of characteristics purely on that basis. This results in our editing out those parts of the communication we do not expect to hear, or in hearing what hasn't been said at all (e.g. Fook, 1986).

COMMUNICATION SKILLS

Communication skills are often described in the context of specific methods such as counselling (Seden, 2005) or community work (Ife, 2002) and in relation to specific theoretical approaches (Trevithick, 2000) or groups of service users (Trotter, 1999). While many of the communication skills we use in social work practice are used in everyday life, it is particularly important that social workers understand these skills and how they can be used to assist others. Being able to describe to service users, to supervisors, or to co-workers what it is you are doing is an essential ingredient in being able to account for your intervention. The first stage in skill development, therefore, is learning a language to describe our communication behaviour and our communication processes. This goes hand in hand with increasing self-awareness and gaining a clearer idea of your sense of purpose as a social worker. In Table 3.1 we classify communication skills in relation to their behaviours and intentions.

NON-VERBAL COMMUNICATION

It is quite possible to convey a whole story without the use of words. The silent movies did not rely on the few subtitles to get their story across. Non-verbal communication, sent and received, includes observations about what people are wearing, how they are sitting, what they are doing with their hands, the expressions on faces, eye contact and the physical

Table 3.1 Communication skills

Skill classification	Behaviour	Intention
Non-verbal behaviours	Body language Organization of the setting Eye contact Silence Touch Physical appearance	To encourage the other person to express themselves with minimal direction from you. The form these behaviours take and their interpretation have gender and cultural overtones. We have to make our behaviour fit in with the other person. Eye contact especially is governed by cultural norms. There is also a fine line between comfortable eye contact and staring someone out! Usually one's eyes roam over the service user's face rather than being fixed on their eyes. Beware the social work head nod.
Minimal verbal	Encouraging noises Repetition of a single word or phrase	To encourage the other person to tell their story with minimal interference, though it is possible to be quite directive using these behaviours.
Questions – closed	The question contains the categories for the answers. They can be answered by 'yes', 'no' or a number, though the respondent may build on this.	Establish the relevance of the topic for discussion. Obtain information in a form required by others as distinct from the other person relating their story. The interviewer does the work of thinking up the categories.
Questions – open	Questions which commonly start with What? Why? How?	Invite the other person to contribute their ideas on an identified topic. The interviewer directs the other person's attention to particular areas but does not provide the categories from which to select an answer. To be effective, all questions have to build on each other in an orderly manner and need to be interspersed with other behaviour if the interview is not to resemble an inquisition.
Reflection	Paraphrasing what the other person has said, putting words around how they seem to be feeling and what they are doing and thinking.	Enables the interviewer to check that they are on the right path, or encourages the other person to think further ahead about what they think, do or feel about a particular situation.
Interpretation	Offering an explanation of why things appear the way they do – these are usually presented in the form of a question.	Interpretation should only be offered when the interviewer is sure of having a reasonable understanding of the situation. It should be offered in such a way that the other person would feel comfortable in querying it. It follows that it should also be framed in language that is familiar to the other person. Interpretation may have an educative intention – it is offered as a framework to be applied to the particular situation.

Table 3.1 *(Continued)*

Skill classification	Behaviour	Intention
Confrontation	Letting the other person know you have information that challenges the way they are presenting themselves. It takes the form of a statement or a question.	Confrontations are necessary when the content is becoming detached from reality as others see it. Confrontation often takes place within the process of conflict.

distance separating them. Nunnally and Moy note: 'Nonverbal communication can serve to repeat argument, contradict, accent, substitute or regulate verbal messages' (1989: 82). As practitioners, we should strive to keep our verbal and non-verbal behaviours congruent and, at the same time, to observe any inconsistencies between what people are verbally saying and what their non-verbal communication suggests they really mean.

One major form of non-verbal behaviour is what is popularly referred to as 'body language'. Our gestures may well convey more than we know about how we are feeling. The interpretation of body language has a strong cultural component – for example, some, but not all Asian and African people would regard maintaining eye contact as rude, intrusive and showing a lack of respect. For white British people however, lack of eye contact may indicate evasiveness, depression or a desire to terminate the contact. Cultural differences are also discussed by Robinson (1995: 38–44) who analyses patterns of eye contact/gaze, touching and personal space; she highlights the importance of attending to these differences for if they are ignored 'then the potential for misinterpretation will remain' (p. 44).

Much of our non-verbal communication regulates the taking of turns in who is speaking and who is listening. Behaviour such as breaking eye contact, shifting about on the chair or changes in facial expression may mean you begin or stop talking. A further method of regulating the flow of communication is the use of sounds such as 'mmm' (nodding the head to indicate you understand what is being said) or the use of silence. However, silence is often perceived differently. You may think a silence is supportive, giving the other person space to think but they might find it hostile (Brill, 1995: 77). Knowing how to use silence is often an issue for beginning workers. Our own anxiety to appear competent or our desire to rush along must be balanced against our assessment of how useful silence might be.

We all draw conclusions about people from the way they look: are they short or tall, fat or thin, are they bald, do they smoke, and how do they dress? Sometimes it is difficult to know how to dress for an occasion when we do not know enough about the context we will be in. At different times in our history, dress has indicated in a detailed way both the social occasion and the social class of the wearer. Occasion and class have become less predictable from clothing, but we may think, 'What should I wear today?' in the context of who we will be meeting as well as what we will be doing. We notice when clothes make people look good and when they seem out of place because they are unsuitable. As workers we are required not to judge a book by its cover, but at the same time to present an appropriate enough cover so people feel confident that we can deliver what they need.

Touching people is obviously an important part of non-verbal communication in our everyday lives. How does it fit with social work? Of course, to some extent the answer depends on what part of the body is touched, why, and how. Touch can communicate caring, concern; it can be playful; it can also be angry or threatening. In some circumstances it feels right to reach out to someone when they are upset or are displaying other strong emotions. At other times we should wait and give people space (Geldard, 1989). Touch has strong cultural overtones. The age, sex and ethnic origins of people, and indeed agency policy may provide guidelines or rules about what is or is not appropriate.

VERBAL COMMUNICATION

One of the most common forms of verbal communication social workers engage in is the process of asking questions. An analysis of the type of questions used by a worker reveals their assumptions about their purpose and how they understand the tension between the individual and social arrangements. An understanding by the worker of the implication of using different questioning styles enables the worker to make a conscious choice that best facilitates the process and outcome of the interaction. In Tomm's (1988) view, there are four major types of questions: lineal, circular, strategic and reflexive, and each type of question may be differentiated in terms of its intentions and assumptions.

Lineal questions have the intention of orienting the worker to the situation of the other and assume phenomena are related in a linear way. They are investigative and start with words such as 'Who?', 'When?', or 'Why?' or 'What?'. These would be regarded as open-ended questions in Table 3.1. They may also be closed-ended, so that, 'What difficulties are you having?' or 'Are you sleeping well?' are both examples of lineal questions. When used consistently, these questions imply that the interviewer is trying to locate the cause of the problem in the individual.

Circular questions have the intention of being exploratory and assume that everything is somehow related to everything else. These questions are asked to try to find patterns that link people, ideas, feelings, events, beliefs and so on. They start with words such as 'How?', 'Who?' and 'What?'. They may be open-ended questions such as: 'What happens when you both get angry?', or 'Who is it that generally decides what to do?', or closed-ended questions such as 'Do you all think that?' They generally explore differences and contexts, and are focused on possible connections rather than causes of difficulties.

Strategic questions have the intention of correcting the view of the other in line with the understanding of the worker, and assume that there is a lineal connection between a particular situation and a particular cause. The worker who consistently uses this form of questioning will be quite directive and confronting. Examples show that these questions too can be both open- and closed-ended. 'When are you going to take some responsibility for your own life?', or 'Wouldn't you like to move out from here?'

Reflexive questions intend to influence the other in a more general manner and are based on circular assumptions about the issues faced, so that the worker tries to facilitate the other in coming to appropriate conclusions about appropriate action based on a wider view of the situation. Questions such as 'If we were able to do something about your housing, how would your life be different?' have the effect of perhaps opening up new ways for those involved to view their situation.

Tomm makes the point 'that exactly the same words can mean and do very different things in the course of a single interview' (1988: 10). The intentions listed in Table 3.1 can be expanded by considering them in relation to how we view the world and where we consider the focus for change to lie. The quality of the relationship, the pattern of behaviour overall and the way the other interprets the intentions of the worker all contribute to the end result.

Verbal communication also takes the form of statements that may have one or more of the following intentions:

- offering an interpretation of events (see Table 3.1);
- providing information for the use of others;
- confronting or giving directives on what is to be done or thought about; or
- defining how you expect or hope to be seen by the other.

When confrontation is necessary, it is appropriate to do this in such a way that it is the behaviour rather than the character of the person that is challenged. In western cultures when someone asks for help they often expect to be asked a series of clarifying questions and then told what the resulting information means and what will be of assistance. In some circumstances this process may be appropriate, for example in determining whether someone is eligible for a benefit; but in other situations it can lead to unhelpful processes variously labelled 'rescuing' and 'disempowering'. The points made earlier under 'Use of self' are helpful in identifying our motivations in offering answers rather than working with the other to identify available options.

Having developed some facility with the various sorts of behaviour we use in communication, it is necessary to structure these skills into interviews and discussions.

INTERVIEWS AND DISCUSSIONS

Social workers put their communication skills into practice in different situations, most commonly in interviews and discussions. An interview may be conceptualized as structured discussion designed by one party to elicit specific information from the other(s). Interviews and discussions differ from each other in terms of their structure and process, but they also share many common aspects:

- all involve verbal and non-verbal communication between people during which ideas, attitudes and feelings are exchanged;
- all, apart from telephone interviews or discussions, are normally face-to-face interactions;
- participants reciprocally influence each other;
- all may be formal or informal, planned or on the spur of the moment.

An interview is distinguished from a discussion in that:

1. It is both purposeful and directed to accomplishing certain goals. Communications are limited to achieving a purpose which is generally seen as gaining information, making an assessment and effecting change. These purposes are only distinguished here for ease of description – most interviews include more than one purpose;
2. Its content is limited to material which will facilitate achievement of the purpose – the content is likely to have a unity, a progression and a thematic continuity, that is, it has a beginning, a middle and an end;
3. It involves specialized role relationships and differential allocation of air space – somebody takes responsibility for directing the interaction so it moves forward towards the goal. The role relationship is structured as follows:

   a) It is a non-reciprocal relationship structured primarily to service the interests of the service user;
   b) The interviewer acts in a manner that encourages the interviewee to reveal a great deal about him- or herself, while the interviewer reveals much less;
   c) The actions of the interviewer must be planned, deliberate and consciously selected to further the purpose of the interview. The pattern of behaviour is predetermined by the positions people occupy in the interview, by the formal structure of reciprocal roles and by expectations;
   d) It has a context or setting of a definite time, place and duration and of an agency, which sets limits on the functions of the worker and hence the content of the interview.

INTERVIEWS

The purposes of interviews range from assessing need, resolving conflict, offering therapy, obtaining information to offering people ongoing support. The degree of control over content that the worker exercises depends on the purpose of the interview, the practice theory the interviewer adopts and the relationship between the participants.

Most social work and counselling texts highlight the advantages that ideal interviewing conditions offer. Though it is desirable to have a quiet, comfortable, uninterrupted environment, interviews often take place in noisy environments with interruptions from phone calls, children, other workers, neighbours and the distractions of television or whatever else might be happening in the service user's home or in places like a social services office or a hospital ward.

A creative worker can capitalize on at least some of these distractions by using the medium of the distraction to offer less direct ways of gaining information or putting forward alternative ways of understanding what is happening. For example, if a young father is finding it difficult to cope with a two-year-old child who is not able to meet his demands for obedience and logical thought, the worker may be able to model different ways of behaving with the child who continually demands attention. This then becomes a basis for talking about strategies the father might be comfortable with himself. Similarly, with a television blaring in the room, it is difficult to begin, sustain and terminate an interview.

However, it may be possible to have a discussion around what people think about the programme and then to negotiate to turn it off or move to a different room.

STAGES OF THE INTERVIEW

Beginning: The start of any contact is affected by the work done before the interview by those concerned, as well as the task of getting started in the here and now. Before the beginning of a first interview the potential service user may have asked around to get an idea of what to expect. Alternatively, they may have had no inkling at all that anyone was going to visit them, nor that they had been the subject of discussion by others. Similarly, the worker may have received a detailed referral report or had discussions with others before the first contact, or they may have had no preparation at all and simply start with what the person tells them. For a first contact, there are also inquiries about why, how and what this contact is for and what we can expect from each other.

If this interview is a part of ongoing work, then much will have happened since the previous contact. An important part of beginnings is therefore to catch up with each other, to find out what has happened. Part of the work of beginnings is to establish the focus for the interview and the manner in which the worker and the service user will work together to achieve their shared objective. This planning is undertaken with the realization that agreements can change and be renegotiated if they are not meeting the goals we have. Beginnings, then, are about explicitly setting agendas and structures for the bulk of the interview.

On many occasions this phase of the interview will be relatively short. However, if there is conflict about either the need for contact or the content of the interaction, it may take much longer to arrive at an agreement. Perhaps no agreement can be reached; in this case, contact would be terminated at that point.

Sustaining: Having agreed on a focus and structure for the interview, those involved are able to start work on developing ideas and options to be discussed. As has been stated, the process of working on these agendas is mediated through the relationship that has been established. Hopefully this relationship is open, with a sharing of thoughts and feelings, rather than being a process of one person (not necessarily the worker) pulling the strings to make the other one dance. The establishment of a relationship is not enough in and of itself to solve all problems. It should be supportive of the service user so that they feel valued and that their situation is knowable. The critical focus of the work will depend on the assessment of the issues involved and of the appropriate strategies to achieve resolution of the identified difficulties. The focus for change may be identified as being with the person, with their interaction with others, with organizations or with policies that define how resources are allocated. Clearly the content and process of the interview will reflect this.

Sustaining therefore involves deciding what needs to be achieved and getting on with doing that. Generally interviews, when formally structured, last for an hour or less. This seems to be about the length of time we are able to concentrate on what can be an exhausting task. Ideally, when we have worked through the agenda decided for the interview, we move to finishing up for the day.

Finishing up: It is important to terminate each piece of work formally rather than stopping abruptly and suggesting, 'See you next week'. This involves considering the following questions:

- What has been achieved?
- What ways did we use to go about that?
- Was that a comfortable way of getting through the work?
- What needs to be done next and who will do it?
- When will we meet again (if appropriate)?
- Do any formal reports on this contact need to be recorded?

Sometimes we might feel that we have pulled the threads together in the termination process and then, as the meeting concludes, the service user might indicate what is really worrying or scaring them. These 'doorstep comments' are not uncommon and must be acknowledged. The worker must quickly decide whether to suggest that they discuss the issues raised next time, or perhaps renegotiate to continue the interview then and there.

DISCUSSIONS

A large proportion of social work practice takes place in discussions or conversations with one or more people (for example, local residents) who are concerned with the welfare of the person identified as the service user, or who are working collectively on a particular issue. In group situations, the worker aims to maximize interaction among the participants so as to foster the development of relationships between people, to enable them to exchange ideas and perhaps plan to work together. In one-to-one situations, the worker may mainly want to learn from the other and to exchange ideas on the feasibility of various types of action. Brill (1995) makes the point that what might start as an interview between a practitioner and two or more people may end up as a discussion if the worker is able to open up channels of communication between, and hence interaction among, the various participants. The aim here is to foster the development of relationships between people so that they can exchange ideas rather than seek to channel all information through the worker.

RELATIONSHIPS IN SOCIAL WORK PRACTICE

In any situation the relationship between people is the medium or the vehicle through which events are interpreted, decisions are made and work is done. This is true of social work in all its forms. All relationships involve communicating across difference. As we noted earlier in this chapter we have a range of 'selves' and we guess at the selves of others when we attempt to communicate and establish links in the form of relationships. We can only see a small part of the other and each of us constructs ourselves in interactions in ways that we believe will protect or advantage us. Jordan (1990: 186–7) points out that workers can feel in a weak and vulnerable position, 'manipulated' by service users who in turn see workers as powerful gatekeepers to needed resources. The differences in perception of each of the players make effective work very difficult unless the worker is prepared to explore what the struggle is actually about (Jordan, 1979).

THE NATURE OF EFFECTIVE RELATIONSHIPS

Positive, constructive relationships are essential for a happy and healthy life. People without such relationships tend to be less healthy than those who do have them (George and Davis, 1998). We develop relationships from sharing experiences. Some of these experiences, such as parent–child or employee–employer, are structured by society. Our concern here is with helping relationships in social work and social care practice. As we have seen, these are constructed by the social arrangements of social work and social care. Perlman suggests that helping relationships are a process in which at least two persons interact with feeling: '[The] relationship leaps from one person to the other at the moment when some kind of emotion moves between them' (1957: 65). Whether this interaction creates a sense of union or of antagonism, the two people are for the time connected to each other. The relationship starts at first contact and continues to develop in a reciprocal and cumulative manner throughout the time of contact. What goes before is instrumental in defining what will follow.

Good helping relationships result from a conscious effort on the part of the worker. It is necessary for the worker to make conscious use of what is naturally him- or herself – to use your whole self and not just your analytical or technical skills – to achieve a purposive relationship with someone else. Such relationships involve lending part of your self to the other person so that they can make sense of their lives, resolve problems they face, or maintain themselves in the face of an ongoing uncomfortable reality. We can become more skilled in our ability to relate to others through a process of reflecting on what has happened, learning and practising specific skills, and through having a body of knowledge and values related to our purpose.

Not all relationships in social work practice are focused on helping. Much of a worker's involvement with others may be with people who are not service users, but rather targets for change in relation to the service user or service user group.

SOCIAL WORK VALUES IN RELATIONSHIPS

In our practice framework, we argue that the purpose of social work is to promote equitable social relationships and support people in taking more control over their lives where this does not unduly affect the rights of others. This purpose reflects social work values which, in turn, can be seen to shape the important elements of social work relationships. Thompson (2005: 109) suggests that values are things we see as worth safeguarding and as an important influence on how we behave and how we understand issues. Social work values are usually framed as ethics – statements about desirable practice – framed in formal documents, such as a *code of practice* (for example, as produced by the National Care Councils) or a *code of ethics* (as produced by the British Association of Social Workers). In Chapter 8 we will return to a more detailed examination of the ethical and moral base of social work and the tensions experienced in putting these principles into practice. Our focus now, though, is on how the values of social work are reflected in the relationships formed between workers and service users. Important to consider are those values that focus on the way we should relate to others because of their inherent worth as individuals and those that focus on the individual in the context of cultural and structural factors (Thompson, 2005: 121). Thompson argues that these two approaches can build on each other to guide us in forming and maintaining effective helping relationships. Social work values guide and construct the core elements of social work relationships.

ELEMENTS OF SOCIAL WORK RELATIONSHIPS

In forming and maintaining relationships in practice, our behaviour (the purposeful use of self) should be consciously directed by a number of factors. Those commonly noted in the literature are:

- concern for others;
- acceptance and expectation;
- commitment, obligation and congruence;
- empathy;
- authority and power;
- confidentiality;
- self-determination;
- partnership;
- deindividualization;
- citizenship;
- empowerment;
- transactions.

These are ways of conceptualizing the manner in which we make conscious use of ourselves in relationships and which act as imperatives to behaviour. But we also need an understanding of the give and take of the relationship, the reactions and patterns of behaviour which Jordan (1970) called 'client–worker transactions'. A consideration of some of the dynamics of these transactions concludes this section.

CONCERN FOR OTHERS

Concern for others involves caring about what happens to the service user or service user group and being able to communicate this feeling. Compton and Galaway (1989) suggest that it is an unconditional affirmation of the service user's life and needs – a desire for them to be all they can be and to do all they want to do, for their own sakes. It is necessary to guard against becoming involved to the point where we find ourselves wanting or needing people to succeed for our own sakes. Concern for others involves responding with our skills, knowledge and time – within, of course, certain limits of purpose, available time and place – as the service user needs, rather than as our need to help demands. It is useful to reflect regularly on whose needs and problems we are addressing.

This element of the relationship also indicates that, in gathering information about the situation, we should respect the privacy and rights of the service user and only try to find out as much as is needed to be helpful, rather than demonstrating how skilful we are at ferreting out information.

Concern and respect for others is also demonstrated through structural considerations – making and keeping appointments, trying to make the interview space attractive, keeping discussion time undisturbed and trying to dress in a way in which the service user's culture suggests a helping person should dress.

Active listening is an important skill used to show you do care and are concerned. You may not agree with what is said, but you should value the sharing that is going on. Even where feelings are high, as in a conflict situation, we must still try to communicate the value of the other's contribution and show that we are seeking to understand – generally by asking relevant questions or making relevant comments.

ACCEPTANCE AND EXPECTATION

Acceptance and expectation encompass actively seeking to understand with the expectation that people have the capacity to change. Basic to any helping relationship is the acceptance of the person's importance and value, as distinct from the importance or value of the roles they may play in society. Brill notes that: 'Indifference or lack of concern can completely inhibit the development of any meaningful exchange and can be more destructive than actual dislike' (1995: 96). Acceptance frees the other person to express themselves without fear that the relationship will be altered or terminated. It is the climate within which growth is possible.

Achieving this acceptance requires the understanding of the reality and values of another. In some cultures, for example, the needs of individuals may often be seen as secondary to the needs of the family group. We need to understand and respect that as far as possible and work to develop appropriate ways of work in this context. We need to have a reasonable acquaintance with ourselves and know how to recognize acceptance (or lack of it) in ourselves. From this base we can recognize the individual, differentiated from all others – including ourselves. We understand the individual in the context of general knowledge and in the light of the knowledge that no two people are the same, physically, mentally, emotionally or socially.

A potential problem in coming to terms with the concept of acceptance is that it is possible to confuse liking (in an acceptance sense) with approving the behaviour of that person. So, if we say, 'I can't accept anyone who abuses children', we have moved to judging behaviour and have forgotten about these people's right to existence, their right to be valued and to be understood. It is certainly easier to be accepting of some people than of others. The ease or otherwise we feel generally comes from ourselves and an interpretation of the other, not from the other *per se*.

Acceptance is closely linked to the expectation or trust that people can change in a self-determined, self-directed way. It is a vital part of the total growth process in life, no matter what the stage, to have people believe in us and in our abilities. We try to communicate acceptance by trying to understand the person in the context of their situation. We reflect on what is said and ask questions that relate to what the other person is saying, as distinct from demonstrating the ability to presume what life is like for this person. It involves a feeling of being with the person, as distinct from feeling as if you are shoving them along or handling them with pincers. It is important to accept, respect and believe in ourselves to be able to offer this to others.

COMMITMENT, OBLIGATION AND CONGRUENCE

These factors suggest that our involvement with others is, as far as possible, unqualified by our personal needs and that we bring to the relationship a consistent and honest 'realness'. This requires us to set out the terms of our commitment and obligations to those we work with as explicitly as possible, so that we can be responsible and accountable for what we say and do with the service user or service user group, to the system that employs us, and to ourselves.

The maintenance of integrity is important to this process. This involves honest knowledge of ourselves and clear knowledge of agency procedures, policies and our professional role. We demonstrate congruence when we don't feel we have parts of ourselves that we have to protect, when we can be honest with the service user and when we can appear as a whole to others – head, heart and hands in open communication with each other.

EMPATHY

Empathy is a capacity to enter the same perceptual frame as the other, without losing ourselves in the process. It requires us to feel the emotions experienced as the other feels them, although this is always only an approximation of what it is like for the other person. At the same time we must remain separate enough from it so that we can use this knowledge.

It involves the imaginative consideration of others and a recognition and relinquishment of the stereotypes we carry so that we may relate to this person as an individual rather than this person as a representative of a class of persons. Empathic behaviour may be hampered by a limitation in our ability to communicate verbally or non-verbally. To use ourselves effectively, we must also accept that we cannot fully know another, even if the other is willing to fully share him or herself with a stranger.

The essence of relationships is emotional rather than intellectual. It is the interchange of attitudes and feelings that builds relationships. To be able to understand what it is like to be in someone else's shoes, the worker has to be honest with him or herself and with the other person. Honesty is associated with realism and responsibility and is difficult to attain.

AUTHORITY AND POWER

A helping relationship is always an authoritative one to some degree. This authority has two sources. The first is institutional and derives from the worker's position in the agency. This authority is obvious if the agency is sanctioned to make decisions about people's liberty or their access to basic resources, such as money and so on. But all agencies carry the power to help as well as to limit the use service users make of the resources society has put at their command. The second source is psychological, and derives from the authority of knowledge. In this context the worker has the power to influence or persuade the service user because the worker is accepted as having relevant expertise. Quite often service users know what is wrong but need help in knowing how to handle their difficulties. If the worker is perceived as having authority in an institutional and expert sense, the service user is relieved to have found someone they believe can help. The exercise of authority in this context is what people expect and value in their worker.

The power the worker has comes from the authority they are perceived to have and critically exercise. At times workers are very uncomfortable when they see themselves cast in this powerful position. They worry, quite understandably, about their capacity to meet the expectations they feel other people have of them. One possible antidote to this position is to realize that the exercise of authority does not mean we become responsible for other people's lives but it does mean we must be accountable to service users and to our employers for what we do. What we do is enable other people to make decisions about their lives. The expertise we have provides the service user with the opportunity to review, assess and plan for what it is they want; it does not give us the power to know what it is other people should do.

CONFIDENTIALITY

Confidentiality is a simple concept that becomes extremely complex in its execution. Confidentiality simply means that we do not pass on information other people have told us about themselves unless we have approval to do so from the person concerned. The significance of confidentiality is largely culturally determined and, as Shardlow points out, 'What is acceptable with one person may not be acceptable with another who has a totally different personal biography' (1995: 65; see also Rooney, 1980, cited by Dominelli, 1997).

Issues immediately arise when you work cooperatively with others – the limits of confidentiality may be a whole team or a work group rather than an individual (see Chapter 6). How can agency records respect this principle? When you are advocating on someone's behalf and it seems advantageous to introduce information you haven't 'cleared' with the service user, do you do so? How faithful are we in reporting back later just how much information we did pass on, or do we only mention the outcome? However, the difficulties of respecting the service user's right to confidentiality do not provide a *carte blanche* to dispense with this right. It is important to develop the habit of talking to the service user about what information others need to know, how it is to be presented and whether there is some material that is not to be mentioned. In many contexts in social work, we seek to minimize the power differential between ourselves and the service user by sharing our knowledge, our way of doing things. The process of 'clearing' information in this way demonstrates to the service user how to order information, to see connections within the whole story and to identify the points where change is possible.

SELF-DETERMINATION

Interpreted liberally, the word 'self-determination' refers to that part of someone's behaviour that emanates from his or her own wishes, choices and decisions. Most human beings have a capacity for self-determination. We are capable of making our own choices and decisions, no matter how silly these choices may appear to others.

There has been much debate about whether self-determination is a basic value to be held on to at all costs, or whether it is an operationally useful principle but not an imperative (Freedberg, 1989). Some of the confusion relates to whether self-determination is seen as reflecting the person's basic right to manage his or her own life and to make decisions about it, or whether it is seen as extending the range of choices available both in how the person regards him- or herself and in his or her environment. That is, do you regard it as a basic right or an ideal to strive for in practice? The fact that it is undeniably difficult to implement is no excuse for not trying to accord people the right to make decisions about themselves (McCouat, 1988). Justice, freedom and equality are equally difficult values to implement.

It is important for the worker and the service user to look for as full a range of alternative choices as possible, since without alternatives there is no opportunity to make decisions, and thus no opportunity to be self-determining. It is sometimes not enough for people to have alternatives; they need help to come to a decision about what choice to make. The social worker is not asked to choose for the service user, but to help the service user choose for him- or herself. The worker may often be asked for their suggestions and these should be put forward as possible options – part of the presentation of choices available.

Where there is a conflict between the value or right of self-determination and knowledge, and where what might be chosen is harmful to others, the worker will probably give greater weight to what they know and less to the value of self-determination in making a decision. An example would be the removal of someone to a psychiatric hospital against their will because you know that the likelihood of their recovery without treatment is very low and their deteriorating mental health is likely to put themselves or others at significant risk. When such knowledge is lacking, the value of self-determination takes precedence in determining what the worker does. If an elderly person wishes to remain alone at home when he or she is bedridden or very frail, the worker will support this choice and try to get together a group of services appropriate to his or her needs (Jordan, 1990). The worker cannot know what is best for the person, even though they might worry about the loneliness and danger in the situation. Often the self-determination we extend to others is limited by our desire to avoid giving ourselves problems. It may be easier to manage an old person in a residential setting than at home, but it may not, by any stretch of the imagination, be the best 'choice' from this person's point of view. In our relationships with others, we should be consistently asking ourselves who owns the problem and who is being asked to resolve the problem.

PARTNERSHIPS

It is a well-established principle in social work that we should work with, rather than for others and this is what partnerships are about. In some contexts the partnership is with an individual, and in others it is with a group. This collaborative, rather than top-down approach is favoured because of the respect it shows to the expertise of individuals as they live sometimes difficult lives, and because the outcome is likely to be more sustainable and successful if individuals or families are involved in setting a direction for work. Partnerships involve being explicit about what you can offer in a situation and listening to and respecting the contributions of others. Valuing working with others is also a feature of successful team, inter-agency and community work as outlined in Chapters 5 and 6.

DEINDIVIDUALIZATION

Thompson offers this concept to encourage us to see service users in their wider context, particularly their membership of disadvantaged groups, and to recognize that 'we are not just unique individuals' (2005: 121). This value is strongly linked to the feminist injunction to see the political in the personal, or to refrain from blaming the victim. By helping people to understand the impact of social structures on their situation you as the worker and they may be able to identify culturally appropriate ways of responding.

CITIZENSHIP

As we noted in Chapter 2 the concept of citizenship focuses on our rights and capacity to be fully involved in the life of our community or society. Thompson notes that social work practice 'plays a pivotal role promoting or undermining the citizenship status of particular individuals, families or groups who are otherwise prone to social exclusion' (2005: 124). This value emphasizes the social rights of the individual to make claims against the state for basic welfare needs, to be included in society and to be treated in a just and equitable manner. Crimmins and Whalen address citizenship and youth work. They suggest that a commitment to citizenship in this area of practice will be reflected in a 'set of values which recognise young people as active participants rather than passive service users' (1999: 168). The onus is on the worker to find ways to enable young people to be more engaged in their communities and to contribute to the development of appropriate resources for this group.

EMPOWERMENT

'Empowerment is not only a psychological process but also a social and political one' (Thompson, 2005: 125). Thompson suggests that the focus of empowerment is on educating people so that they might tackle the disadvantages they face and hence gain greater control in their lives. An understanding of empowerment requires an understanding of power, a complex and multilayered phenomenon, which is discussed briefly in Chapter 5. The values associated with this concept include a commitment to continually exploring the social arrangements that advantage or disadvantage people in our communities and seeking to help people remove barriers to achieving their goals – it involves helping people to help themselves. In defining the purpose of social work as encouraging people to take more control over their own lives and to promote equitable relationships, our practice framework emphasizes the importance of empowerment, although recognizing that it should not be used to oppress others (and thus not facilitate equitable relationships).

TRANSACTIONS

Transactions refer to the manner in which the worker and the service user affect each other, acknowledging interdependency in helping relationships. Jordan (1979) notes that often the worker can arrive at an understanding of what it is someone needs by good listening. Sometimes this is not enough. The worker may feel manoeuvred into doing what the service user wants without a carefully thought-through assessment of whether this action will really help. He goes on to describe a process where some service users 'seemed to ask for help or use the help offered them in an essentially defensive way, which precluded any real change in them or improvement in their circumstances' (p. 41). They did this by emotionally separating off those parts of themselves that made them anxious; at the same time these parts struck a chord in the social worker's own feelings. Jordan argues that 'this process of influence can only work through the social worker's own feelings being reinforced and exaggerated by the clients' (p. 42). These feelings have their origins in the earlier lives of workers, as well as in their feelings about service users who threaten them and undermine their confidence in themselves as social workers. It follows that the potential for such transactions lies in all of us as workers.

It is often stated that 'feelings are facts'. How we feel about a service user throughout the course of an interaction is just as much information to be thought through as the report the service user has given us. It is especially important to think about our reactions when they do not seem to be obviously linked to the content of the interview. As Jordan suggests, the worker's response to the service user in this situation represents an important clue to what the central issue might be for the service user. The worker's own feelings 'often show (the worker) the part of his problem that the client is least able to communicate verbally, yet most needs to share' (1979: 42). How do we make use of such transactions with the service user when we are aware a discrepancy exists? Generally speaking we let the service user know, in a constructive way, what our feelings are. This may produce anger and disbelief as well as increasing the potential for growth if the need for the defensive manoeuvre can be removed.

CHAPTER SUMMARY

We have considered why it is important to have some understanding of ourselves in terms of what motivates us as social workers. This understanding of ourselves is a necessary starting point in understanding the process of social work and what service users value in the process. Community members or service users value good communication skills and the capacity to relate to the whole person as well as to the problem they bring to the social worker.

The broad approach to relationships in social work practice is built on good communication skills, as outlined in this chapter, combined with an understanding of the values and purpose of social work in different contexts. Thus communication skills comprise one of the essential building blocks of social work practice which we must acquire in order to make use of ourselves in relation to others. We turn now to consider assessment of needs and resources as the next step in practice.

FURTHER READING

Brill, N. and Levine, J. (2005) *Working with People: The Helping Process*, 8th edn. Boston, MA: Allyn and Bacon.
This classic introductory text from the United States encourages students to take a reflective approach to practice, emphasizes the need for self-awareness and skilful use of self, and examines the development of practice skills.

Thompson, N. (2005) *Understanding Social Work: Preparing for Practice*, 2nd edn. Houndmills: Palgrave.

Thompson's introductory text provides a realistic account of social work today and encourages readers in the development of their knowledge, value and skill base. He engages honestly with the challenges facing those who are entering the profession.

Jordan, B. (1979) *Helping in Social Work*. London: Routledge and Kegan Paul.

Much of Bill Jordan's honest and personal account of social work in 1979 rings true today. While constrained by organizational and policy factors, social work relationships should be informed by social work values, such as respect and authenticity, so that workers and service users are supported in the demanding experience of helping.

USEFUL WEBSITES

Centre for Evidence Based Social Services: www.cebss.org.
Centre for Human Service Technology: www.chst.soton.ac.uk.
Information for Practice: www.nyu.edu/socialwork/ip.
Research in Practice: www.rip.org.uk.
Social Care Institute for Excellence: www.scie.org.uk.
Society for Social Work Research: www.sswr.org.

REFLECTIVE QUESTIONS

1. Identify a range of ways in which you can characterize your communication with others. What would you characterize as 'good' communication as a worker? What cultural assumptions are you making in your answer?

2. What do you see as the main challenges for you in communicating across difference? Imagine you are someone with a very different life to your own. How would you answer this question now?

3. Think of an interaction you have recently had, any interaction will do. Thinking back over what happened, how would you say the process of interacting affected the outcome?

4 ASSESSMENT

In this chapter we examine:

- What assessment is and how it relates to intervention;
- A systematic approach to assessment located within our practice framework;
- The process and stages of a systematic assessment;
- An example of an assessment with children and families;
- Issues for social workers in conducting assessments;
- Community profiles and network analysis as assessment activities.

Social workers engage with individuals, groups and communities who experience difficulties in their lives and tensions with their social arrangements. In our practice framework we argue that the focus of social work practice should be understanding these tensions, while its purpose should be assisting people to resolve the tensions by helping them to take more control of their lives and by promoting equitable relationships. Thus far we have examined the social welfare context of social work practice and have highlighted the importance of social workers' use of self in developing relationships with service users and in putting the social work purpose into practice. In this chapter we consider the assessment aspect of our practice framework: the 'understandings' that workers develop about the situations in which they seek to intervene.

The discussion in this chapter is framed in quite general terms and looks at some underlying ideas or principles in relation to assessment. However, these will need to be 'mapped onto' the more specific frameworks that govern practice in different areas of social work practice – for example, the Framework for the Assessment of Children in Need and their Families (DoH, 2000d) and the Single Assessment Process (SAP) for older people, introduced in the National Service Framework for Older People (DoH, 2001b, 2002b). We illustrate the principles of assessment through examples drawn partly from social work students' own practice learning experiences. In Figure 4.1 we include the assessment dimension in our practice framework.

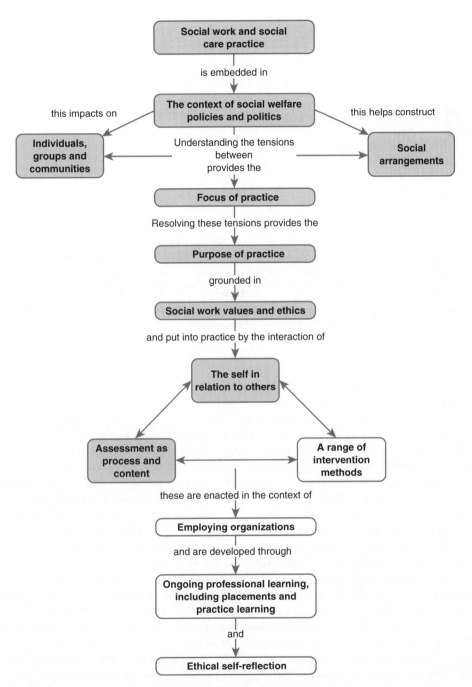

Figure 4.1 Assessment in the practice framework

THE VALUE OF A SYSTEMATIC APPROACH TO ASSESSMENT

Our purpose in seeking to understand a particular situation influences the way we understand that situation and our understanding in turn influences the outcomes established with service users or communities and the actions taken to achieve those outcomes. In Chapter 1 we discussed the importance of an explicit sense of the purpose of practice, to provide direction for assessment, application of theory and knowledge and choice of interventions that maximize benefits to those we work with. As 'helpers', 'facilitators' or 'agents of the state', we are accountable to service users, our profession, our employers and ourselves for the results of our interventions in people's lives. Being accountable means being able to articulate the details of our assessments, the decision-making processes that guide our assessment and the rationale for our choices of intervention.

In developing our practice framework in relation to assessment, we argue for a systematic approach to assessment processes and content. This can assist in three ways. First, our practice framework focuses our attention in assessment activities on the interaction between people (individuals, groups and communities) and their social arrangements. Second, it provides a systematic way of ordering, of making sense of the specific situation in terms of the tension between people and social arrangements, and the manner in which they are empowered or disempowered by these interactions. This means that, as practitioners, we are engaged in a process of seeking to understand situations by locating people in their contexts. Third, our practice framework, as applied to assessment, facilitates the systematic application of professional knowledge to deepen understanding and test developing explanations related to our understanding.

The knowledge and ideas of a profession – its discourses – are important because they provide a routinized way of sorting and assigning meaning to complex situations so that considered intervention can be undertaken. Professional discourses also form part of the social arrangements with which people (practitioners included) interact. Professional discourses and knowledge can influence the construction of problems and the way these can be disempowering or empowering for service users. For example, professional discourses on ageing reflect both stereotyped societal views of older age as a time of loss of capacity, senility and passiveness (Palmore, 1999), as well as more positive views of ageing (Beckingham and Watt, 1995: 483). Practitioners are often influenced (both consciously and unconsciously) by ageist stereotypes and consequently may reproduce these stereotypes in their interactions with older people (albeit subtly and with best intentions). In an elder abuse situation it is not uncommon for health professionals to use a child protection theoretical model to construct understanding and action. The older person, although mentally competent, is viewed in a paternalistic and ageist way as a vulnerable child for whom decisions must be made for their 'own good'. However, many older people argue for an adult protection model where they retain control over choices and decisions regarding strategies to ameliorate abuse and the right to make 'poor' decisions even though fully informed of various possible consequences of such decisions (Harbison and Morrow, 1998).

The knowledge of any profession needs to be applied with a critical appraisal of the way it shapes an understanding of a person's situation, and how it empowers or disempowers. It also needs to be understood as socially constructed rather than as an absolute statement of what is. Thus it is essential to engage in critical reflection in all aspects of practice. In assessment, critical reflection involves:

- the worker making explicit the assumptions and propositions that emerge;
- applying knowledge and theories to inform understanding and test propositions;
- generating alternative explanations;
- weighing different information; and
- making explicit the decision making regarding the conclusions reached and the outcomes agreed upon (Gibbs and Gambrill, 1999: 4).

This process guards against behavioural information bias (Gambrill, 2000: 45) where practitioners search for and shape information to support a favoured position, approach or theory, and ignore disconfirming information (see also Milner and O'Byrne, 1998: 27–8).

The systematic application of professional knowledge – which encompasses theoretical, personal, empirical and procedural knowledge and practice wisdom (Drury Hudson, 1997: 38) – in a critically reflective manner, increases the likelihood that our assessments will accurately reflect the nature of problematic situations and that our interventions will be effective (Gambrill, 2000: 46). While social workers often need to take action before all the data is in and different explanations and choices are comprehensively tested, it is unacceptable to adopt an ad hoc approach to assessment or rely uncritically on 'gut' feelings. We intervene in people's lives – sometimes against their will – so it is essential in formulating your understanding and interventions to understand what you are doing and to know why you are doing it.

THE NEED FOR SPECIALIZED KNOWLEDGE

In developing our practice framework in relation to assessment we select particular areas of the world for attention. Our framework makes certain assumptions (detailed in Chapter 1) about the nature of our understanding of the world and the purpose of practice. It does not provide the specialized knowledge necessary to understand the situation, but rather suggests where you might start to inquire. Every area of practice needs specialized knowledge relevant to that area and to the particular practice context. Consider the following examples:

You work in a local authority Children and Families Team and are required to investigate an allegation that a child is neglected by her parents – that they show her very little attention. When you visit the home you ascertain that the child is 13-months old, can sit, rarely crawls and can't walk. Would you ask yourself: 'Is this child a late walker? Why?'. What about if the child were 16 months and exhibiting the same behaviour?

You are a worker at an advice centre for young people. From talking to a number of the service users, you become aware that some of the 14-year olds are sexually active and not practising safe sex. Would this suggest anything to you?

You are a community worker trying to establish a group for older unemployed people on a local housing estate. The husband of one of the women in the group dies suddenly. From the times you had contact

(Continued)

(Continued)

with them as a couple and from what you have heard from others in the group, they were very happy. Much to everyone's surprise, she now seems very angry with her husband. The others in the group think she shouldn't destroy the good memories from the relationship. Is there any reason why she should be angry? Should the group try to foster and reinforce positive images?

Each of the above situations requires specialized knowledge to understand the meaning and the possible consequences of the behaviour for the individuals involved. Those issues may be dealt with in a manner which enhances the person's ability to control life or in one which minimizes that ability.

In this book we can only provide the guideposts to direct the assessment; the acquisition of the specialized knowledge is a lifelong process. It is reworked in each new context in which you practise social work and is broadened and developed through the process of continuing professional education as new knowledge and technologies come to hand.

ASSESSMENT AND INTERVENTION AS SEPARATE PHASES OF PRACTICE

Like two sides of a coin, assessment and intervention are interrelated parts of social work practice. For example, in coming to understand the situation of another, the interactions that take place, such as the type of questions we ask and our ability to respond sensitively to the perspectives and feelings of others, both deepen our understanding and have an impact on people. People may, for example, feel better understood, relieved or more anxious as a result of the process. We need to take account of the impact of our assessment in order to evaluate and re-evaluate our understanding and consequent actions. For these reasons we conceptualize practice as an iterative process rather than a linear one.

Often social workers are engaged solely to conduct an assessment and not to provide the consequent intervention. This is particularly the case in care management where the social worker's role (given the purchaser/provider split) is mainly limited to assessing people's care needs, for example using the Single Assessment Process (DoH, 2002b), and setting up care plans. However, the experience of the assessment and the subsequent reviews may feel like an intervention, both to the service user and the social worker, because of the positive benefits the assessment may offer: to talk through problems with a trained professional and consider options for the future.

While the interconnectedness of assessment and intervention must be kept in mind, we discuss the process of assessment separately from intervention. We believe that this approach helps practitioners to reflect on the specifics of practice and to develop an active, disciplined approach to understanding the circumstances of their interactions.

AN APPROACH TO ASSESSMENT

Our practice framework guides the development of our approach to assessment. This consists of a conceptualization of assessment, stages in undertaking an assessment and the processes and content of assessment. What then is assessment? We define it in the following way:

> Assessment is the process of coming to understand the nature of interactions between people and social arrangements in order to understand the areas and sources of tension between people and social arrangements. Assessment is undertaken to facilitate purposeful intervention, that is, to aid in the development of strategies and tasks which assist people to develop power and control over their own lives and to form equitable relationships.

Formulating an assessment involves attention to both process and content. In Figure 4.2 we set out the stages of assessment and the processes of relationship building and analytical thinking that support these stages. Within each stage there are questions designed to assist the worker to develop an assessment which reflects the purpose of social work practice and the related definition of assessment put forward in this text. We now turn to discuss this approach in more detail beginning with processes in assessment.

PROCESSES IN ASSESSMENT

Assessment involves a process of coming to understand the other. Necessarily it also involves a process of coming to understand yourself in relation to the other. Assessment can never be just a one-way process: it is never simply the worker influencing the other. The other person is seeking to make sense of you and the interaction. The people you work with have open and hidden agendas for the interaction and hence will provide or withhold information to influence the assessment you make. The extent to which practitioners are able to formulate an accurate understanding of the problematic situations of other people will in part depend on the quality of the relationships in which the understanding develops and their analytical skills. Each stage in the formulation of an assessment is supported by relationship building and analytical processes.

Effective assessment takes place in the context of effective relationships and therefore involves a relationship-building process. In developing this process the worker utilizes those skills and interactions outlined in Chapter 3 that support or facilitate people developing trust in the worker and being able to share the often sensitive and traumatic aspects of their lives that have led to their contact with the worker. It also involves striving for mutuality in the worker–service user relationship, where the worker consistently shares their developing understanding of the other person's situation and explores outcomes and solutions that are both effective and as acceptable as possible to the service user. Assessment therefore involves coming to understand yourself in relation to the 'other' rather than yourself as simply influencing the other. Social workers do not have the sole preserve on understanding and intervention. Individuals, groups or communities have lived and sought to order their own lives and resolve their difficulties usually without the assistance of professional helpers. We must therefore evidence respect for the expert knowledge and experience associated with this understanding of their own lives.

In addition, assessment (and any subsequent intervention) is likely to be taking place in an inter-professional context, so understanding also involves acknowledging and working with the different perspectives of other professionals involved with the family. For example, a key part of accurate assessment involves bringing often disparate pieces of information together and establishing a full and holistic understanding of an individual or family's situation; different professionals may each have a different part of the jigsaw and the whole picture may

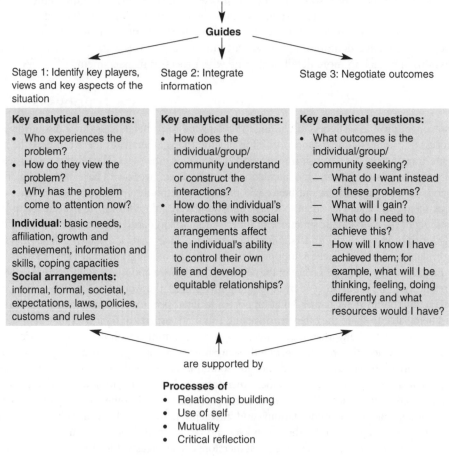

The purpose of social work and social care practice
To promote the development of equitable relationships and the development of individuals' power and control over their own lives, and hence to improve the interaction between individuals and social arrangements.

Assessment
Assessment is the process of coming to understand the nature of interactions between people and social arrangements in order to understand the areas and sources of tension or lack of fit between people and social arrangements and to facilitate purposeful intervention, that is, strategies that assist people to develop power and control over their own lives and equitable relationships.

Guides

Stage 1: Identify key players, views and key aspects of the situation

Stage 2: Integrate information

Stage 3: Negotiate outcomes

Key analytical questions:

- Who experiences the problem?
- How do they view the problem?
- Why has the problem come to attention now?

Individual: basic needs, affiliation, growth and achievement, information and skills, coping capacities
Social arrangements: informal, formal, societal, expectations, laws, policies, customs and rules

Key analytical questions:

- How does the individual/group/ community understand or construct the interactions?
- How do the individual's interactions with social arrangements affect the individual's ability to control their own life and develop equitable relationships?

Key analytical questions:

- What outcomes is the individual/group/ community seeking?
  — What do I want instead of these problems?
  — What will I gain?
  — What do I need to achieve this?
  — How will I know I have achieved them; for example, what will I be thinking, feeling, doing differently and what resources would I have?

are supported by

Processes of
- Relationship building
- Use of self
- Mutuality
- Critical reflection

Figure 4.2   A systematic approach to assessment

only become clear when all the pieces are assembled. Inter-agency working has not always proved either easy or effective, as a succession of child death inquiries has highlighted; however, it is an essential part of good practice and requires careful consideration. With the development of Children's Trusts, social workers are more likely to find themselves working in integrated multi-professional teams, but whatever the context, there will be a clear need to understand the dynamics of inter-agency, inter-professional and multi-professional working.[1]

Analytical processes in assessment relate to the critical reflective process elaborated earlier: formulating propositions, developing explanations, questioning assumptions, considering alternative points of view and applying evidence to judge the strength and soundness of the explanations being developed (Gibbs and Gambrill, 1999; Gibbs, 2001).

The content of assessment refers to the areas of people's lives which are appropriate to explore to gain a comprehensive understanding of their situation. There are a number of different ways of conceptualizing the content of assessment, often with a particular service user group in mind. Frameworks may be generic, for example, Milner and O'Byrne's (1998) framework which incorporates six different 'maps' to guide workers towards 'helpful analyses'. They may also be specific to particular situations, for example a framework for assessing older people and their families (Hughes, 1993), the three 'domains' identified within the *Framework for the Assessment for Children in Need and Their Families* (DoH, 2000d) or a framework for assessing risk in child protection work (Munro, 2002). In applying our practice framework to assessment, we incorporate a schema developed by Monkman (1991) which elaborates individual and environmental factors (social arrangements) that interact in problematic situations. Monkman's schema is informed by ecological and systems theories in social work, including the work of Germain and Gitterman (1980), and we acknowledge the subsequent influence of these approaches in our own framing of assessment.

We now turn to examine more thoroughly the stages, processes and content aspects in formulating an assessment as outlined in Figure 4.2.

STAGES IN FORMING AN ASSESSMENT

The following stages are recursive and overlap in practice. However, in most situations one of these stages is likely to be more dominant.

1. Identify the key players, their views of the problem and the key aspects of the situation;
2. Integrate information, particularly the nature of the transactions with social arrangements that play a significant role in creating and maintaining the tension or difficulties;
3. Negotiate and establish outcomes with service users or groups and develop a plan of intervention.

STAGE 1: IDENTIFY THE KEY PLAYERS, THEIR VIEWS OF THE PROBLEM AND THE KEY ASPECTS OF THE SITUATION

The primary concern in this part of the process is to locate people in their contexts so as to formulate an understanding of the interactions between people and social arrangements. The mutual task is one of locating the transactions between people and their social context and identifying visible sources of pressure and support. It is clear that this is directed by social work purpose and requires, in addition, specific knowledge of the areas in focus.

In this stage the worker should consider the following questions and content area: *Who experiences the situation (person-in-social arrangements) as problematic and how do they perceive the problem(s)?* Is this situation 'self-referred', or is contact with a social worker made at the instigation of another? Some individuals or groups seek assistance with specific difficulties in their lives which they experience as problematic. In other situations, people 'seek' assistance because others consider that they have a problem. Alternatively, the state sanctions intervention in certain areas of social life to maintain adequate 'standards' or 'modes' of living, delegating responsibility to investigate and remedy certain breaches of modes and standards of living. For example, neighbours might make a referral if they think that a child is being mistreated by his or her parents, or policy makers can identify a 'problem community'.

The answer to this question of who experiences the problematic situation has an impact on how the problem is defined and perceived and also influences motivations and expectations in relation to social work practice. It is clear that the understanding of a situation may and will vary between different people or organizations (such as self, family members, peers, other communities, school, employer, social services, voluntary agency, local politicians, shopkeepers and so on). For example, the police, social workers and youth workers frequently formulate different perspectives of the same situation where adolescent misbehaviour is involved. Local home owners may have a different perspective on a suitable location for a hostel for people with chronic mental health problems than workers in the field. Each of these 'understandings' is important. However, some players will exercise a greater force of definition. The courts, for example, can impose their definition, while those with least power have greatest difficulty in having their definition heard or accepted. Sometimes our task as practitioners is to ensure that the definitions and understandings of service users are heard. Indeed, the very process of problem definition may create the problems or difficulties experienced.

Why now? Social workers become involved in situations when a problem has been identified – either self-identified or identified by others (for example, a council, community group or neighbourhood). Rather than seeing an event as discrete or isolated, it is necessary to look for its meaning in the individual's/group's life stream. We ask:

- Why did this person (group) seek help now and not before? or
- Why did others seek intervention now and not before?
- Why is it seen as a problem/issue now?

What aspects of the individual, group or community and what aspects of the social arrangements are relevant to the problematic situation as resources or restraints? People are partly formed by and from interactions with social arrangements. Hence we need to understand both individual and social arrangements that are operating in any situation and the nature of the interactions between them, to deepen our understanding of the situation. Monkman (1991: 254) locates social work intervention in the 'reciprocal transactions between the person and the environment' and identifies five factors in relation to the individual and five in relation to social arrangements which need to be considered. These are outlined in Table 4.1. Within our conception of social arrangements, it is important to reiterate that the worker needs to include the influence of professional and lay discourses, as well as the organizational context on the problematic situation. These factors would fit under Monkman's last category of laws, policies, customs and rules.

In this stage, the analytical process is directed towards application of knowledge, theories and information to assist understanding and critical reflection on the application of

Table 4.1 Factors for assessment in individual and social arrangements

Individual factors	Social arrangements
Basic needs: behaviours which enable the person to obtain and use resources to continue life (such as food, shelter and degree of mobility).	**Informal resources:** family, friends, neighbours, co-workers and others who can provide support, affection, advice, services.
Affiliation: behaviours which enable a person to establish close connections with others (capacity to form personal relationships, use organizations).	**Formal resources:** membership of organizations or formal associations that promote the interests of members, provide services, including employment opportunities.
Growth and achievement: behaviours which enable a person to perform for and to contribute to him/herself and others (includes cognitive, physical, economic and emotional capacities).	**Societal resources:** structured services and service institutions such as hospitals, social security offices, courts, police services.
Information and skills: behaviours which enable a person to increase knowledge of specific events or situations.	**Expectations:** patterned performances and normative obligations that are grounded in established societal structures. Expectations involve roles and tasks. It is important to note that achieving outcomes in this category does not equate with assisting individuals to adapt to normative expectations; it may mean adjusting expectations to suit individuals.
Coping patterns: refers to consistent, habitual behaviours (may be cognitive, behavioural or affective) developed over time and applied to a situation.	**Laws, policies, customs and rules:** refers to binding guidelines for conduct created by a controlling authority. Customs may refer to those held by informal resources (e.g. family) and formal resources. We include the influence of professional and lay discourses and the organizational context in this category.

Source: Adapted from Monkman (1991).

knowledge. The practitioner is asking what knowledge am I using here, what further knowledge do I need, how is my use of knowledge influencing the way I understand the key aspects of the situation?

STAGE 2: INTEGRATE INFORMATION, PARTICULARLY THE NATURE OF THE TRANSACTIONS WITH SOCIAL ARRANGEMENTS THAT PLAY A SIGNIFICANT ROLE IN CREATING AND MAINTAINING THE TENSION OR DIFFICULTIES

In this next stage the focus is on the constructions or meaning that the key players place on their experiences of self in relation to their social arrangements. The stage also involves developing a deeper understanding of the various ways in which each factor, singly and as a whole, influences the ability of the individual to exercise power and control in their life and to resolve difficulties or tensions in their interactions with the environment. Therefore it is important to consider the manner in which social processes and social characteristics such as age, class, gender, ethnicity and so on are experienced by people in a way which either enhances or restricts their ability to control their own life.

Clearly it is not possible to use one variable such as age or class to totally explain a particular situation – for example, poverty and unemployment do not always lead to criminal behaviour. But a combination of factors such as poverty, unemployment, lack of legitimate opportunities and the experience of discrimination, taken together, can give rise to criminal behaviour. This suggests that the assessment process seeks to broaden the immediate understanding of the situation and direct the attention of the participants to the complexity of the issues.

- How do people's interactions with social arrangements (including the associated discourses) affect the individual's ability to control their own life and develop equitable relationships?
- To what extent does the formulation of the situation by those involved disempower the individual and maintain their problems?
- In what areas of their life does the individual exercise some power and control?
- What resources (personal and environmental) are available to develop control?
- What role does the agency play in constructing/solving the problem?

In this stage the analytical process is directed towards making causal links between various factors, developing propositions, testing propositions with service users, and synthesizing information to account for complexity. The worker critically evaluates the formulation that is developing, considers alternative explanations and makes explicit the theory and knowledge being used to inform and test understanding.

STAGE 3: NEGOTIATE AND ESTABLISH OUTCOMES WITH SERVICE USERS OR GROUPS AND DEVELOP A PLAN OF INTERVENTION

In this stage the worker uses the assessment to work with service users towards specifying what changes or outcomes the service user wants in the individual and environmental aspects of their problematic situation. Service user outcomes can be defined as identifiable events or changes as a result of intervention. It is important to note that although such changes are intended, there may also be unintended consequences of interventions which need to be considered in implementing, monitoring and evaluating of interventions. We can gain an early overall impression of a service user's desired outcomes while formulating an assessment by making sure that we balance a problem focus with an outcome focus. Once a comprehensive understanding has been reached we need to be more specific about outcomes by encouraging service users to ask:

- What do I want instead of these problems?
- What will I gain?
- What do I need to achieve this?
- How will I know I have achieved them – for example, what would I be thinking, feeling, doing differently and what resources would I have?

Although outcomes are service user centred, they are necessarily limited by societal resource constraints, practitioner constraints and of course ethical constraints (you cannot agree to work with service users towards an outcome that would be harmful to themselves or others). Importantly, there are also organizational constraints in that the social worker will be bound to carrying out the agency's purpose, in line with its community and statutory role. In this sense then, outcomes are always agreed outcomes, with agreement being the end product of a negotiation between service user and practitioner, in the context of organizational constraints and opportunities.

As far as possible, outcomes should be worded in quantifiable terms. For example, an outcome for someone to receive services under the NHS and Community Care Act 1990 could be worded, 'Mrs P will get more help at home'. However, this wording of the outcome would be difficult to evaluate. It would be more specific and quantifiable to say 'Within two weeks, Mrs P will have in place delivered meals at least two days per week and assistance with dressing twice a day for at least five days per week'. The second statement provides more direction for the choice of interventions and the tasks needed to achieve the outcome and ultimately evaluation regarding whether or not the outcome was achieved and the interventions were successful.

We have so far discussed the process and content of assessment, in line with our practice framework. The approach to assessment which we have detailed will, of course, need to be considered alongside the formal frameworks we have referred to earlier, particularly those governing assessments in community care and work with children and families. Most written assessments have had the process stripped from them – they appear as a formulation or statement of what is, without much sense of how the worker arrived there. A clear statement of the conclusions reached through the assessment helps in clarifying our ideas, negotiating with other professionals, seeking to influence decision makers and so on. However, it is also necessary to attend to the process issues involved in carrying out the assessment. The following account is partly based on real circumstances and presents the perspective of a social worker who discusses an assessment carried out in a local authority Children and Families Team in a London borough.

Practice example: assessment with children and families

Introduction

In this example, I discuss a piece of work undertaken in a local authority 'assessment and early intervention' team in response to a referral to the Duty (or intake) system.

Family composition

Cerian (aged 32, white, Welsh), her partner Michael (aged 31, white, Scottish) and their children Alys (aged five, white, Welsh, from Cerian's previous relationship) and Rhiann (aged two). Cerian's first language is Welsh. She speaks to the children in Welsh but uses English with Michael and in all communication outside the home.

The case was identified for allocation after Cerian's Health Visitor had contacted Duty on several occasions to express concern about Cerian's mental health and ability to manage the children. Also, a referral had been received from the headteacher after Cerian had twice arrived late to collect Alys. After an initial assessment it was agreed that a core assessment[2] should be undertaken; services were provided under s17, Children Act 1989.

(Continued)

(Continued)

My account draws on material in the SSD family file, a series of home visits to Cerian and the children (Michael was also present on three occasions), as well as (with Cerian's agreement) meetings and/or telephone conversations with her Community Psychiatric Nurse (CPN), the family's Health Visitor and Alys's teacher.

Background

Cerian and Alys moved to London from Caernarfon about three years ago, shortly after Cerian split up with Alys's father. He has not been in contact with the family since his relationship with Cerian broke down rather acrimoniously. She thinks he also moved away. Michael and Cerian met soon after her arrival in London and their first child, Rhiann, was born two years ago. Cerian is currently pregnant again, and the baby is due in two months. Michael spends most of his time with Cerian and the children but his relationship with Cerian is volatile and he returns to his own flat periodically.

Cerian has been diagnosed with schizophrenia, which is generally controlled by medication. She is known to the local Community Mental Health Team (CMHT) and has an allocated CPN. Cerian normally copes well, getting Alys to school daily and providing good care for both children. However, if she stops taking her medication, her health deteriorates. In the past this has left her unable to look after herself or the children adequately and has resulted in her being 'sectioned' (i.e. detained under the provisions of the Mental Health Act 1983) twice before, the last time during her pregnancy with Rhiann. Social Services became involved on each of these occasions, to make arrangements for Alys to be accommodated (s20, Children Act 1989) but Cerian declined further involvement once she was well enough to resume Alys's care, preferring just to keep in regular contact with her Health Visitor.

On reading through the initial assessment and the case file, I learned that Cerian was again becoming unwell; she had stopped taking her medication as she feared it would harm her baby and could not be persuaded to resume treatment. As part of my core assessment in the short term, I needed to:

a)   Assess the level of care that Cerian and Michael were each able to offer the children, to ensure that the children's different care needs were being met and to see if any additional support was needed;
b)   Carry out a risk assessment of the impact of Cerian's mental health difficulties on each of the children;
c)   Clarify arrangements for the care of Alys and Rhiann when Cerian went to hospital to have the baby. It also seemed possible that if Cerian's mental health deteriorated further she could require in-patient treatment again, which would also have direct implications for the children.

Stage 1: Identify the key players, their views of the problem and the key aspects of the situation

Who experiences the problem and how do they perceive the problem?

This referral has come from external sources rather than directly from Cerian. The problem is framed in terms of Cerian's ability to care for herself and the children as her mental health appears to be deteriorating. Cerian is aware of the concerns and understands that her mental health is affected if she stops taking her regular medication. However, she does not want to take it while she is pregnant.

Her concerns relate to arrangements for Alys and Rhiann when she goes into hospital to have her baby.

(Continued)

Why has the problematic situation arisen now?

Two outside agencies/individuals have raised concerns about Cerian's current situation. She is becoming increasingly unwell and this is impacting on her ability to look after herself and the two children. Her relationship with Michael is unstable, and it appears likely that they will split up. This is an additional source of stress for Cerian.

What aspects of the individual in interaction with their environment are impacting on this situation?

Basic needs

Cerian was born in Caernarfon and lived there until she moved to London three years ago with Alys. She met Michael soon after and they have one child, Rhiann. Cerian is currently pregnant again. She is physically in good health but suffers from schizophrenia which has to be controlled by medication. However, she is unwilling to take medication when she is pregnant, with the result that she has had serious relapses with each pregnancy.

Cerian worked as an illustrator in Wales but has not had paid employment since being in England so receives Income Support. She says that she really enjoyed her work and that it fitted in well with her childcare responsibilities. However, she lost most of her contacts when she moved from Wales and has not been able to find appropriate work in London. She lives, with the children, in a large, sparsely furnished, two-bedroom council flat.

Michael works part-time as a gardener. From time to time – particularly when he and Cerian are not getting on – he goes back to his flat in West London. On these occasions, Cerian is left without any other support or help with the children.

Alys attends the local primary school.

Affiliation

Cerian has some contact with her mother and sisters but, given their distance from her, they cannot provide any practical help, day to day. Her mother has invited the family to visit in the holidays and has said she would be happy to have the children to stay when they are a bit older. Michael provides some 'hands-on' care with the children but this is not always seen as supportive by Cerian.

Alys attends the local primary school and has settled in well. She speaks both Welsh and English and has started to make friends. Her health is good and she is a lively and outgoing little girl who enjoys stories and drawing.

Rhiann is looked after at home by Cerian, with some input from Michael. During the initial assessment, a nursery place was offered but Cerian refused it on the grounds that it was too far away and the travel arrangements too awkward. Later discussion with her Health Visitor suggests that she had seen it as a criticism that she could not care for Rhiann adequately.

(Continued)

(Continued)

Growth and achievement

Cerian misses the friends she had in Wales and has so far found it difficult to establish new friendships. She likes films and visiting galleries but does not manage to get out much. Michael has more friends but tends to see them on his own on the grounds that they do not have anyone to babysit for the children.

Alys enjoys school and gets involved in class activities. She has started swimming lessons at school and is proud of being able to swim a whole width with her armbands on! Rhiann seems quiet when she is at home with Cerian but becomes quite a lot more boisterous when Alys is around. She enjoys having stories read to her and also likes being pushed on the swings at the local park.

Information and skills

Cerian has been given information about various local resources for herself and the children but has so far not wanted (or been able) to access more formal resources outside the home. She takes Rhiann to the park some days and has found out about a local toy library but has not yet been along.

Coping patterns

Cerian has been managing the children's care with little additional support, but this is becoming less sustainable as her mental health deteriorates, leaving her more dependent on Michael's input. Before this current episode, she was coping well and had been quite optimistic about arrangements once the new baby arrives. However, her present mood is more unpredictable and she finds it hard to deal with anything unexpected – for example, when school closed early because of bad weather. In addition, she has become more resistant to offers of support and home visits that she normally welcomes (e.g. from the Health Visitor), becoming agitated and increasingly wary of the different professionals involved with the family.

Social arrangements

Informal resources: Cerian's mother and two sisters all live in Caernarfon; she tends not to initiate contact with her family but has some contact with one of her sisters who phones regularly and visits approximately twice a year. Michael keeps in touch with his parents and siblings, mainly by phone. His parents live in the same town that he was brought up in, but his siblings have all moved away.

Currently, Cerian is quite isolated and lacks informal contacts. She says that she has never been particularly outgoing and so can find it hard to make new friends. She did meet up with the mother of one of Alys's friends a couple of times but has not felt well enough to pursue this recently. She has taken Rhiann to a toddler group which she enjoyed, but again, attendance at the group depends on how Cerian is feeling from week to week.

Formal and societal resources: Cerian has regular contact, and generally a good relationship, with her Health Visitor who she sees at least weekly. Her relationship with the CMHT is less good as she associates them with her periods of compulsory hospitalization and separation from the children. The CPN visits approximately fortnightly, but Cerian does not always answer the door when she calls. Cerian describes

(Continued)

their relationship as 'fairly formal and a bit awkward' and does not find it easy to talk to the CPN who she feels is judging her. Cerian has had some contact with Alys's class teacher and with the headteacher, both of whom she likes. She can see that Alys is well settled and enjoying school and commented that Alys is always talking about 'her' teacher. This relationship is clearly one that Alys enjoys, and which provides continuity and consistency at times when Cerian's behaviour is more erratic.

Expectations

Cerian sees herself as the main carer for the children and enjoys this but misses having a professional work role (and identity). She sets very high standards for herself and is sensitive to any implied criticism of her care of the children (as seen in her response to the offer of a day-nursery place). She appears to have a lot invested in being seen as 'a good mum' – and in her view a good mother does not take any drugs when pregnant (including prescribed medication).

In terms of role expectations, both Cerian and Michael seem to expect the girls to be fairly quiet at home and discourage what they see as too much 'silliness', particularly from Alys.

Policies, laws, customs

This assessment was carried out in the context of s17 of the Children Act 1989 and according to the *Framework for the Assessment of Children in Need and Their Families* (DoH, 2000d). (The example is mapped according to the dimensions of the DoH Framework later in this chapter.)

Stage 2: Integrate information, particularly the nature of the transactions with social arrangements that play a significant role in creating and maintaining the tension or difficulties

- What is the nature of the interactions between the person and their environment?
- How do the individuals, group or community understand or construct the interactions?
- How do these interactions affect the individual's ability to control their own life and develop equitable arrangements?
- What avenues are available to develop control?

From both my own observations and information from the Health Visitor, it appears that both children are generally developing well and seem securely attached to both parents. However, there are some concerns about the longer-term effect of Cerian's mental health difficulties on them. Cerian herself is extremely isolated; her main source of support up to now has been Michael, but their relationship is more a source of stress for her at present. However, he does provide some help with the children, although he has never looked after them on his own for more than a couple of hours. Cerian is concerned about arrangements for the children when she goes into hospital to have the baby. Although Michael has said that he is willing to look after the girls, he does

(Continued)

(Continued)

not appear to have discussed this in detail. When Cerian was hospitalized previously (before Rhiann was born), he was initially keen to look after Alys but then at the last minute decided he could not, which meant that she was accommodated each time. I would therefore need to discuss carefully with him whether he felt able to take on the care of the children – and Cerian would need to agree any arrangements that were made.

There are, additionally, concerns about the care of the children if Cerian should need hospital treatment to address her mental health problems. At the moment, she is unwilling to accept that this may happen and is therefore not prepared to discuss possible care arrangements.

A range of factors seems to be influencing the individuals' relationship with social arrangements: Cerian experiences multiple disadvantages as a poorly supported lone parent, and at the moment she runs the risk of becoming quite socially excluded. She is economically disadvantaged (unemployed and receiving benefits) and the caring work she does as a mother is generally not valued. She is also dealing with the stigma associated with mental illness and fears that the children will be taken away from her if she acknowledges any difficulty in coping. So she fends off Michael's offers of help and won't accept other resources (like a nursery place for Rhiann) as this just confirms her anxiety that she is not a 'good mother'.

Michael says he wants to be an involved parent but this seems to be in conflict with ideas he grew up with, namely that childcare is really women's work. He has not had much experience of looking after the children on his own but at the same time, he seems to feel that he should be able to manage 'as it can't really be that hard to look after a couple of little kids' and is therefore unwilling to ask for help.

Alys appears to be managing well at the moment. She does not like it when Cerian behaves erratically but seems able to accept and make use of other relationships – with Michael and also with her class teacher – to provide stability for herself. In that sense she appears quite resilient (Daniel et al., 1999). It is therefore important to ensure that these links are supported, particularly while Cerian is unwell. The situation is harder for Rhiann who, because of her age, is much less able to establish other supportive and sustaining relationships. She does appear to be well attached to Cerian but has been quite unsettled by her mother's sometimes inconsistent responses in recent weeks.

Children, young children especially, are one of the least powerful groups in society and it is often the case that adults decide for them and speak on their behalf. The Children Act 1989 expects social workers to ascertain the child's wishes and feelings, as far as this is possible. So in this case, it feels important to try and get the best understanding possible of how each child sees the situation. Obviously, this is harder to achieve with Rhiann who is not yet able to say very much but it is clear that she, like any small child, has ways of expressing herself! Also, careful use of observation will help in understanding something of her world.

Stage 3: Negotiate and establish outcomes with clients and develop a plan of intervention

(See Background section for the aims of the assessment)

I encouraged Cerian and Michael to identify what they wanted for themselves as individuals and also (possibly) as a couple, and for the children. In addition, the children's wishes and feelings were ascertained, as far as possible.

At this stage, although not all matters were resolved, a number of main outcomes were agreed and confirmed in a written agreement:

(Continued)

- Cerian and Michael will have firm arrangements in place to cover the period when Cerian is in hospital having the baby. This may involve the use of a foster placement if all agree that is in the best interests of the children. If so, efforts will be made to introduce Alys and Rhiann to the carer before the placement begins;
- Cerian will continue to have regular contact with her Health Visitor and social worker and will also attend the CPN's out-patient clinic. Cerian has agreed that I will continue to liaise with both the Health Visitor and CPN to ensure that her health needs and the children's care needs are being met;
- In the longer term, I will discuss with Cerian ways to address her social isolation. This may include attendance at the Southborough SureStart parents' group and fortnightly craft sessions. In addition, Michael will be encouraged to take on some regular childcare to allow Cerian time to pursue her own interests.

The importance of process

Although overall the assessment went smoothly, the process raised a number of issues for me. I had not worked with someone with a diagnosis of schizophrenia and did not know much about the condition but was aware of the negative stereotypes associated with mental illness (schizophrenia in particular). I found it very helpful to be able to work closely with the Health Visitor and CPN and to discuss my assessment with them. Also, Cerian was quite open about her previous acute episodes which helped to break down any taboos about discussing her illness.

At the same time though, her apparent lack of insight into her immediate situation was worrying and I had to spend a lot of time discussing with her my concerns about her current ability to cope with the children. Again, this felt quite fraught as Cerian, not surprisingly, has a lot invested in her view of herself as a good mum and found my questions about her childcare pretty threatening. I think I was able to reassure her that my aim was not to break up the family but rather, to try and help her find ways to manage when she was under stress. There are considerable strengths within the family, and the object was to try and build on these. One of the biggest challenges was to get Cerian to see that accepting help was not a sign that she was failing.

Working with small children was also a challenge but one that I found I enjoyed! I made sure I spent some time with each of the children and tried to get to know them properly. I have learned from this that there are many ways for young children to communicate their feelings and that good observation skills are critical.

It is possible to see how the information presented here also addresses the areas or domains identified in the *Framework for the Assessment of Children in Need and Their Families* (DoH, 2000d): the child's developmental needs; parenting capacity; and family and environmental factors. The social worker should be able to work according to this framework and provide evidence relating to each of the key domains. The example below works through one of the domains in detail and then includes elements of the other two to show how they interrelate.

Children's developmental needs

Health: Alys and Rhiann's health needs are being met and there are no concerns from the GP or Health Visitor. The children's immunizations are up to date and they have had no major illnesses.

Education: Alys attends school regularly and although occasionally late, she is doing OK. The Health Visitor suggested that Rhiann would benefit from attending nursery and a place was offered but Cerian turned it down. At the time, she said that it was because the nursery was too far away, but later discussion with her Health Visitor suggests that she had seen it as a criticism that she could not care for Rhiann adequately.

Emotional and behavioural development: Both the children were at home during my initial home visits and I was able to observe them playing by themselves but also interacting with their mother. Alys appeared happy and generally well behaved. On my earlier visits, I noted that when Alys first came in from school, she was quite irritable but Cerian appeared used to this and dealt with it calmly, providing her with a snack and some 'quiet time' looking at a book together. Rhiann is quite quiet when she is on her own with Cerian but gets more boisterous when Alys comes home. She is always interested in what Alys is doing – and can be quite disruptive when she wants to join in!

Identity: The children's identity and cultural needs are being well met within the family. Cerian talks to the children mainly in Welsh and they have some contact with her relatives in Caernarfon. Michael does not understand Welsh and talks to the children in English. Although his relationship with Cerian is strained, he has indicated that he intends to continue to be involved with the children's upbringing. While it is not his religion, he is happy to support Cerian in educating the children about her Catholic faith.

Family and social relationships: Alys seems to have a good relationship with both her parents though I noticed that she appeared more anxious with Cerian on my most recent visits. As Cerian's behaviour has become more erratic, Alys has become quieter and seems to spend more time playing by herself or watching TV. She has settled well at school and talks happily about her class teacher whom she likes a lot. She has started to make friends and has been invited to friends' houses on occasions after school. Rhiann does not have much contact with people beyond the immediate family. As noted earlier, a nursery place was available but Cerian turned it down. Like Alys, she appears rather more subdued with Cerian than with Michael, which I feel may reflect her anxieties about Cerian's more unpredictable behaviour at the moment.

Social presentation: Until recently, both children have been clean and appropriately dressed. As Cerian has become more unwell though, there have been occasions when Alys has appeared at school in clothes that were either dirty or not warm enough. The Health Visitor also commented that Rhiann looked 'grubby' last time she visited.

Self-care skills: Both children are developing age-appropriate self-care skills.

Parenting capacity

Basic care: Levels of care for the children have been satisfactory, though there is some concern at the moment about Cerian's ability to look after them without support. Michael usually does the main shopping but Cerian does the cooking and the bulk of the housework. At the moment, Michael is trying to do more to keep the flat clean and tidy as Cerian is not finding it easy to cope with everyday domestic tasks. When he is away, the flat quickly becomes quite messy. Although up until now Cerian has managed to prepare food regularly for the children, her own eating habits have become quite chaotic and she does not appear to be eating regularly.

(Continued)

Family and environmental factors

Family history and functioning: Cerian was born and brought up in Caernarfon in Wales. Her parents divorced when she was 11 and she lived with her mother and two sisters, seeing her father only during school holidays. She says that she had quite an isolated childhood and as an adolescent had a poor relationship with her mother. She left home when she was 17 and went to live with her then boyfriend. This was not a happy time for her as he was violent towards her and they split up within months. Cerian returned home after this and was able to establish a better relationship with her mother. Her mother and sisters still live in Caernarfon; she has some contact with one of her sisters who phones regularly and visits approximately twice a year but otherwise does not communicate much with her family.

Michael similarly has limited contact with his parents and siblings but sees them occasionally at major family events.

OUR OWN ISSUES AND ASSESSMENT PROCESSES

We can see from this account that unless you understand what you bring to the assessment, your practice will be impaired. Jordan (1979) identifies areas where our own issues (and best intentions) may interfere with the assessment (and intervention) process. While formulated in terms of interpersonal work, Jordan's barriers could equally be identified in our interactions with colleagues, groups or communities. He refers to these barriers as partial empathy and naïve helpfulness.

PARTIAL EMPATHY

Jordan (1979) argues that an essential element of the helping process is the ability to listen to a number of conflicting messages at one time, although this form of listening can cause discomfort for the listener. The process of listening to and feeling with the other is referred to as 'empathy'. Jordan cautions that if the worker is not tuned in to the totality of the conflicting feelings, his or her empathy will be one-sided, partial and ultimately unhelpful.

We often choose to confide in someone who will be 'understanding', in the sense that he or she will accept our characteristic weaknesses or failings, will recognize some validity in our unorthodoxies and some virtue in our vices. It is easier to 'confess' to someone who is likely to follow the steps that have led us into whatever moral swamp we have entered, to see our reasons for starting and continuing down that path. But we have also often had the experience of feeling first rather frustrated and then guilty, annoyed or betrayed, when that acceptance prevents our confidant from hearing the other part of our story. We often do not simply want to be understood – to be told, in effect, that he or she too has been there, or could easily have got there but for a stroke of luck. We may even want to find a way back. We want the listener also to hear why our situation is bad or wrong or uncomfortable for us, or for others. We do not want the listener to excuse us, protect us or apologize for us. We want him or her to help us find the strength to resolve our own conflict, in our own way.

Partial empathy is often exhilarating and exciting for the helper and gives short-term relief to the other person. There is a delight and joy in the recognition and the sharing which comes from total identification with another, but it tends to be short-lived. The true empathy which stems from sharing the pain and confusion of another person's emotional and moral conflicts is usually less dramatic, but in the long run almost always more effective. It demands much more self-discipline (Jordan, 1979: 21).

In Jordan's terms, partial empathy acts to prevent the other person from telling the helper the worst. The worst, of course, is what we do not wish to face – if it were easy we would probably not need help:

> The art of helping by sharing lies in knowing when the other person has not yet reached the worst and letting him or her get there. This is largely a matter of self-knowledge and self-discipline. The helper feels very tempted to block the other person off from reaching the worst, because it is painful enough to share everything else that leads up to it. Very often it is the helper who cannot bear to hear the worst, rather than the other person who cannot bear to tell it. Again, we can probably all bring to mind times when we have tried to confide a dark secret and our intended confidant has subtly refused to hear it.
>
> There are many ways in which the helper can cut the other person short before he or she reaches the worst. One of these is by insisting that the helper understands, that there is no need to say any more. Another is by elaborating and complicating a particular point so that he or she gets stuck at it. Another is to interject some clever interpretation or tricky question which confuses the other person by suggesting that he or she sees all sorts of deeper implications in what has been said. Another is simply to bring the conversation to an end. All these are ways of switching off from listening and sharing beyond a certain point and all are essentially self-defensive for the helper. Partial empathy is often a manifestation of such a defence – the helper gets stuck in one aspect of the other's feelings because he cannot bear to hear the others. (Jordan, 1979: 22–3, reproduced with permission)

NAÏVE HELPFULNESS

The other area that Jordan draws our attention to is what he refers to as 'naïve helpfulness'. Jordan links the emotions and issues which the individual brings to the helping process:

> My own motivation contained a strong but unrecognised desire to protect vulnerable people from the pain of separation or rejection. This same impulse was so strong that I tended to split it off from my own ideas and 'principles' and to shield it from the consequences of my actions. I was not prepared to learn that I was not helping their clients whom I tried to place under this kind of protection. (1979: 32)

In considering the issues related to self in process, it is necessary for you to address questions such as the following:

1. How does my need to help influence what is transacted?
2. How does my need to appear knowledgeable interfere with my ability to hear?
3. How does my need to look competent affect this process?

4. How do I stay with the chaos of the group and not impose solutions?
5. What personal issues does this touch for me?

Finally, in relation to process, it is essential that you approach any assessment with a respectful attitude and make the assessment process as inclusive as possible.

COMMUNITY PROFILE

A community profile is one form of assessment that is useful in understanding the context in which you are working and in helping to identify significant issues, resources and ideas for future work. Developing a profile of the community you work in can be extremely valuable for a wide range of social work roles, including the local authority-based social worker. For community workers engaged in urban and rural regeneration strategies, developing such a profile would assist greatly in understanding the needs of the community and identifying where partnerships need to be established. In the process of gathering information you will come into contact with a range of people, some of whom are likely to be involved in action, and who you will influence as a result of your inquiries (Twelvetrees, 2001: 18). In this way what is essentially a piece of assessment also involves a piece of intervention. Profiles are often used by community workers to help understand how their actions both affect others and are affected by the environment. Most local libraries hold profiles of geographic areas that you can access to see how they were researched and put together.

Community profiles can be very lengthy documents, the result of extensive research of Office for National Statistics (ONS) data, interviews and surveys. The 2001 census data is available electronically so that you can now manipulate some of the data to answer specific questions – for example, how many people of a specified age, in a designated area are living in their own homes? This is often essential for profiles that are used by social workers and other staff in voluntary agencies in funding applications for the development of services. Local authority-based social workers may also draw on community profiles to put forward a case to the local authority for a different use of resources according to community need. On a day-to-day basis workers often build up a picture of the community in which they work from their contacts with people, and by considering available information from the ONS, local histories at the library, the police, local councils, employers and so on. They also listen to people, walk around, use their eyes, ask questions and try to be aware of the limitations of their observations, as well as their uses, and what impact their being in the community asking questions has on how people respond.

As in all forms of assessment, the way we view the world limits and highlights aspects of our community. It is, as noted earlier, impossible to not assess. The challenge is to be aware of the assessment we start with and to be prepared to consider alternative ways of constructing the reality of a community if our assessment is to lead to effective action.

PURPOSE OF THE PROFILE

Purpose is clearly linked to the context we are in. As workers, or students on placement, this context is usually our agency base which focuses the issues we are concerned about and gives us legitimacy in the eyes of those we approach for information. Asking people to think about their community's resources and issues can raise expectations that you will be attempting to resolve concerns. Being clear about your purpose for yourself and with others is important in this context as well as in justifying the use of agency time. Possible purposes for completing a community profile could be:

- to assist a local authority to get a picture of a particular community and its resources and needs;
- to help a community decide how to tackle an issue;
- to provide the basis for developing or evaluating a Local Neighbourhood Renewal Strategy (Cemlyn et al., 2005);
- to enable a voluntary organization to map a community and its needs as a basis for a funding submission;
- to understand the impact of your actions in a community.

In the remainder of this section the general areas a profile should cover are listed. Some examples from profiles done by students in the second year of a social work degree illustrate the points made. The process section features the sort of material you could include and private considerations of the impact doing the profile has had on your understanding of yourself.

DESCRIPTION OF THE PROFILE PROCESS

This section should include a description of how material was gathered. For example, if a survey was undertaken, it would be described here with conclusions drawn about the reliability and validity of the information obtained. It is also important to think about the impact doing the profile has had on yourself and on the community, and how your own assumptions have influenced the whole process. The following is an example of this form of reflection, which would not normally be included in the finished product, but could help in your formulation of the profile.

Looking back, my best encounters were the more informal ones. Here I didn't suffer the aura or role differentiation of 'expert' or 'data collector' but was on more relaxed, mutual terms. In this context I became much more aware of the milieu of transactions in the community and of the circular nature of linkages. Open-ended questions such as 'How do you feel Neighbourhood Watch has impacted on the community?' were not only easier to ask but enabled more exploration. More reflexive questions and propositions were used and expanded the scope of these encounters, for example 'What improvements would you like to see in the neighbourhood?' My assessment involved the residents in dialogue that was shared with them (as opposed to keeping it to myself and me doing all the assessment as the 'expert').

More than this, I became a part of the transactions of the community. In this respect, I found myself being impacted on by those I spoke to. My own relationships with some I talked to have improved and have improved the neighbourly feel with them (O'Connor et al., 1991: 108).

Having grown up here, I can clearly locate myself within the ecology of this community. My own values, the values of my family and the values of the community (and of course, of the society at large) have all

(Continued)

shaped each other to varying degrees. I can locate the community's working-class, patriarchal and traditional values in myself. A sense of commonality and even the working-class 'us-against-them' was with me while building this profile. I can see how I have inherited the space behaviours of the residents and that this has affected how I approached this task (Fitzgerald, 1992).

A more formal description of process that would be included in the formal document can be equated with a research method. Having identified the purpose, you select an appropriate method, paying attention in your description to its advantages and limitations. Henderson and Thomas (2001) provide a very useful outline of approaches to data collection, including the use of existing data and generating data using questionnaires and focused interviews.

DESCRIPTION OF THE COMMUNITY

HISTORY OF THE COMMUNITY

Most profiles give a brief outline of changes over time in the area since history almost always offers an important dimension in understanding the current situation. We would encourage you to pay attention to history from the point of view of the different (cultural/religious/ethnic) groups within the area, as appropriate. How much of this you include in the profile will depend on your purpose.

DESCRIPTION OF THE CONTEMPORARY COMMUNITY

The aspects you choose to describe will be influenced by your purpose and whether you gather your own data or only use secondary sources, such as information contained in the General Household Survey or the latest national Census data. The usual areas include:

- boundaries of the area, as defined by different community and government agencies. This description would pay attention to the degree of fit between formal and informal boundaries as well as physical boundaries such as hills, railway lines, water or busy roads;
- physical descriptions of the area in terms of topography, land use, type of housing;
- population descriptions in terms of age grouping, gender, ethnicity, household types, income, occupation, education, home ownership, mobility and links between these. It is helpful to draw comparisons between local data and broader data to highlight areas of difference if you are arguing for new services or resources or wish to highlight what makes this community different;
- services, locally available resources and the degree to which the area is a centre for other communities or must use services in other areas;
- political representatives and their involvement in the area.

Such material may be presented descriptively and by using graphs and tables.

ANALYSIS

This section of a profile 'makes sense' of the descriptions presented of the community and the information-gathering process. Again, depending on your purpose, your value stance, your knowledge and the politics of the situation, you construct a set of meanings for your material. The analysis should address how and why you see the community functioning: what it does, what maintains it this way, what sorts of things it is good at/proud of doing, what its hopes are and what, if any, gaps in resources/action exist to meet these expectations. Some of the topics an analysis might explore are networks, social exclusion, distribution of power and leadership. The following is an example of a reflective form of analysis of one issue in an area.

The community of elderly people in C became known to me as I talked to shopkeepers in the area. They were obviously their main customers. The older people themselves confirmed this and also the fact that the commercial centre at C catered for most of their needs within walking distance. Buses were regularly used for trips further afield and it was felt that they were adequate. However, it was brought to my attention that there were a number of people who were unable to get out much and who were very lonely.

To the group of mobile families, this community of elderly people hardly exists. It is known that C is an older area but due to different hours of activity the two rarely cross paths. Both home owners/buyers and permanent renters have a similar use for the area: attractive, quiet surroundings and privacy. Their work and shopping, schools and recreation are generally elsewhere. The difference between these groups – home owners/buyers and permanent renters – is mainly their economic circumstances, the mobile families who are home owners/buyers being well represented by the new expensive homes in the area.

C's history has implications for its welfare. The rejection it has suffered continues. I have been put down, specifically because I live in the area, more than once. There are two reactions to this rejection, one: it makes for a deliberate, well-thought out, independent choice which enhances self-image; or two: it demoralizes people in already poor circumstances who cannot afford to move and feel stuck.

The people vulnerable to this demoralization have other problems to contend with. The elderly people who cannot easily get about mostly lack company. The extent of their problem is debated. The doctor's receptionist may have a vested interest in maintaining that their health is fine, since she represents the person responsible for that health. The unemployed and housebound single mums lack age-appropriate entertainment. The glaring problem that affects physical welfare and self-image is the inequality among residents. People in poor circumstances have to deal with living next door to and attempting to mix with some very well-to-do folk who want their privacy and resist most advances.

It is remarkable then, that although burglary rates are high, vandalism is not a feature of C. The disadvantaged groups have not yet spelt out their anger in this way (Kernke, 1991).

ACTION PLAN

Most profiles should lead to proposals for action that are supported by the body of the profile. An action plan should indicate what people want to achieve, who wants these outcomes and what resources are currently available. It should identify various strategies for achieving these goals, and evaluate their costs in relation to hoped-for benefit. This plan should be shared as widely as possible to ensure that others agree with your conclusions about the community and that they agree with the strategic direction. Significant support from influential parties is essential in the political process of negotiating for needed resources. However, as studies into urban and rural regeneration have demonstrated, action strategies are most successful and are more likely to be sustained over the long term when a 'bottom-up' approach is used and a diversity of community members feel like real participants in the processes (Stewart and Rhoden, 2003).

Any planned change is likely to be met with some resistance, since communities function the way they do to meet someone's needs. The resistance could arise from your agency, other service providers or from the community, who may not, perhaps, have much energy to make things different. Such sources of resistance need to be understood, and your action plan should include ways of working with, rather than ignoring those who are not immediately supportive. Alternatively, they may be significant enough to cause a rethink of goals and methods.

NETWORK ANALYSIS

An important element in understanding communities is understanding the various networks between people within those communities. And while not all social workers may get involved in developing a community profile, most social workers will still need to know about how the individuals and families they work with make sense of and relate to their environment. It is also the case that many social work assessments are conducted with a close eye on the social networks of the individual or family concerned, for example those assessments conducted within the context of the DoH (2000d) *Framework for the Assessment of Children in Need and Their Families* and the DoH (2002b) Single Assessment Process for older people. As we discussed in Chapter 2 the state has withdrawn from the direct provision of care in many areas and increasingly relies on community and informal family and friendship networks to provide these services (Keating et al., 2003).

Our practice framework understands the individual in relation to social arrangements and network analysis provides a way of conceptualizing the kinds of arrangements within which people live. Reigate comments that

> interpreting social behaviour through attention to social networks … offers a tool for understanding the social experiences of clients from their own point of view plus an opportunity to compose a picture of the informal support systems that may or may not be available. (1997: 24)

According to Diamond (2004) the identification that certain communities or neighbourhoods are in need of regeneration can often ignore the invisible capacity evident within networks of support among community members and the social entrepreneurship evident in the informal economy of these communities. Understanding these networks and their capacities provides the basis for developing coalitions across stakeholder groups.

In Chapter 5, we will be discussing network building as a social work intervention to help improve the interactions between people and their social arrangements, but it is important to highlight here the contribution that an understanding of networks can make to assessment. Hill (2002) discusses some of the key features of social networks and explores the significance that the concept has for social work. He uses the example of a network exercise developed for social work students to show how a network approach can contribute to assessment and intervention. He highlights the use that can be made of different tools (e.g. genograms, ecomaps and 'life-space representations') and shows how the diagrams they give rise to can be used both as a 'communication tool and as a record' (p. 246), offering different ways of representing the individual's own view of their network and key social interactions. Keating et al. (2003) provide a useful review of how social networks turn into support networks, which can then provide the basis for care networks. They argue that analysing care networks (rather than care dyads) provides a much better understanding of the support available to older people. Additionally, based on network types identified in the *Bangor Longitudinal Study of Ageing*, Wenger and Tucker (2002) present a support network instrument that can be used by social workers to assess the dimensions of older people's networks. In the next chapter we will develop a more in-depth discussion of social networks and examine how network building can be used as an intervention strategy.

NEGOTIATING AND SHARING THE ASSESSMENT – A RETURN TO PROCESS

If you consider the issues detailed earlier, you will see that people have been located in relation to their social arrangements. You should have developed an understanding of who/ what the individual/community is, what the issues are for them, the sources and causes of tensions, the empowering and disempowering aspects of interactions, what resources and strengths exist, organizational constraints and opportunities and service user-centred outcomes.

The validity of the assessment is strengthened by a process of constant sharing of the assessment during the assessment. This does not just mean that, having formed your assessment, you return to the scene and recite your dissertation. Rather, it means that as you interact, you share the information you are collecting and check out your understandings on an ongoing basis. Without sharing, the process of assessment will be flawed, one-sided and dehumanizing. Assessment involves the sharing of a range of perspectives and therefore models the notion of the need to account for the understanding of others, regardless of how challenging that may be. The validity of the assessment also involves analytical processes related to the application of your general and specialized knowledge and critical reflective reasoning, that challenges assumptions, generates alternative explanations and provides an explicit account of your decision-making processes throughout assessment.

CHAPTER SUMMARY

Assessment involves both content and process and is guided by an explicit sense of social work purpose. Assessment provides the basis for formulating outcomes and developing strategies to facilitate individuals/groups/communities resolving their difficulties or tensions in ways that allow greater control over their lives and promote equitable relationships. The approach to assessment detailed here draws on our practice framework and facilitates a comprehensive analysis of the issues affecting people's interactions with their social arrangements. The quality of the assessment will in large part depend on the worker's human relationship and analytical skills. The more comprehensive and valid our assessment, the more likely we are to negotiate service user-centred outcomes and to choose interventions that are appropriate, acceptable and effective in improving the lives of service users. In the following chapters we discuss intervention strategies, or (put more colloquially) 'What can be done to improve the situation?' In Chapter 5, a number of approaches to intervention are discussed. Organizations are frequently an appropriate target for intervention and hence interventions and organizations are considered in Chapter 6.

FURTHER READING

Henderson, P. and Thomas, D.N. (2001) *Skills in Neighbourhood Work*, 3rd edn. London: Routledge.

Henderson and Thomas provide a practical and easy-to-read guide to community development and, in particular, outline the basis for developing a community profile. The strategies discussed in this book are of use to social workers employed in a wide range of organizations.

Milner, J. and O'Byrne, P. (1998) *Assessment in Social Work*. London: Macmillan.

Milner and O'Byrne examine some of the tensions social workers face in being involved in assessment processes, not least the difficulties in separating assessment from intervention. They see social work theories as providing different types of maps to guide assessment: psychodynamic approaches (map of the ocean), behavioural approaches (ordnance survey map), task-centred approach (handy tourist map), solution-focused approaches (navigator's map) and narrative approaches (forecast map).

USEFUL WEBSITES

The following selection of sites provides links to points of reference for particular areas of practice.

The Cochrane Collaboration which provides up-to-date reviews of all the effects of health care interventions: www.cochrane.org.

National Association of Social Workers (US) links on social work practice: www.social-workers.org/practice.

Neighbourhood Renewal Unit: www.neighbourhood.gov.uk.

Research and Training Center on Family Support and Children's Mental Health (USA): www.rtc.pdx.edu.

REFLECTIVE QUESTIONS

1. Think of and describe a personal problem that you have experienced. What social factors were implicated in the problem? In what way did these factors influence the problem?

2. From your point of view, how well did anyone else understand your problematic situation? What factors contributed to or worked against other people gaining an accurate understanding of the problem? How differently might other people have described your problem?

3. To what extent did you feel powerful and powerless while experiencing the problem? Think about how and why these feelings might have fluctuated throughout the duration of the problem.

4. What did you want instead of your problematic situation and how did you know that you did or did not achieve what it was you wanted?

NOTES

1   As part of the drive to ensure more integrated services for children, young people and families that we discussed in Chapter 2, a Common Assessment Framework (CAF) for childen and young people is being introduced in England (www.everychildmatters. gov.uk/caf/). It is intended that the CAF will be used by all agencies working with children and young people, including those working in health, early years, childcare, schools and other education settings, youth offending services, and Connexions. The CAF will not replace more specialized frameworks (for example, *The Framework for the Assessment of Children in Need and Their Families* or the young offender assessment profile, *Asset*), but may reduce the need for some of these assessments to take place by offering a thorough overview of a child or family's situation. It will provide a common starting point for the different agencies and a more standardized approach to the preliminary stages of the assessment of the needs of children and families. At the time of writing, the CAF is being trialed in a number of areas and a final version of the framework will be implemented across the country between April 2006 and 2008.

2   The piece of work was undertaken before the full implementation of the Common Assessment Framework (CAF) and relates to *The Framework for the Assessment of Children in Need and Their Families* (DoH, 2000d).

5 INTERVENTION

In this chapter we examine:

- Building relationships and the purposeful use of self;
- Problem solving;
- Empowerment;
- Working with groups;
- Building communities;
- Building networks;
- Engaging with conflict;
- Implementing a social mandate – working with involuntary clients;
- Providing long-term care.

We have argued that social work should be directed by its purpose. In our practice frame-work the purpose of social work is to resolve the tensions between people and their social arrangements, which are partly constructed by the wider context of social welfare politics and policies. Social work's purpose is further conceptualized as promoting equitable relationships and helping people gain more control over their own life in a non-oppressive manner. Social work practitioners put this purpose into practice through their assessment (how they understand a situation), the outcomes agreed in relation to that situation, and the interventions selected to achieve these outcomes (how they respond to a situation).

Thus, having considered assessment in Chapter 4, in this and the subsequent chapter we turn to intervention. In Figure 5.1 intervention is incorporated into our practice frame-work. There are many approaches to intervention. They vary by modality (interpersonal, family, group, community and so on), by duration (short, long or medium term) and by whether 'help' is voluntarily sought or mandatorily imposed. Often interventions are por-trayed as if the practitioner engages in only one strategy, for example, care management. In reality, most practitioners implement a number of intervention strategies with any one service user or situation.

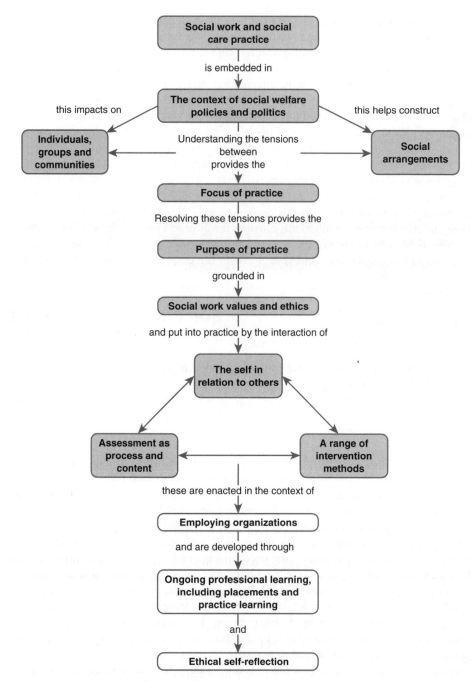

Figure 5.1 Intervention in the practice framework

Social work practice involves the differential application of knowledge and skills to a range of situations. As we noted in the assessment chapter, any intervention requires both general knowledge of change processes and specialized knowledge related to the practice area. Just as assessment is not a content-free process, effective interventions require the development of specialized knowledge, not only of the intervention strategy but also of the practice context.

Practitioners develop a repertoire of intervention strategies which they apply in their practice. We identify 14 intervention strategies that are central to much day-to-day practice. In this chapter we discuss nine of these strategies and in the next chapter we consider five aspects of intervention that are most related to the organizational context of practice. In discussing each of these strategies, we note that each is the subject of detailed theoretical and professional scholarship in its own right. Each strategy will reflect theoretical understandings of people in interaction with their social arrangements and the nature of change and so on. In applying theory in practice we need to be clear about our purposes in assessment and the outcomes sought as this provides the direction for the choice of interventions and use of theory and knowledge. There are a number of choices to be made about intervention and this chapter outlines some of the key dimensions along which choice is made, explicitly or implicitly.

BUILDING RELATIONSHIPS AND THE PURPOSEFUL USE OF SELF

The basic foundation of all social work practice is the process of relationship building and the purposeful use of self. This is as much the case in direct practice with individual service users, as it is in community work and policy work. Relationship building and the purposeful use of self are extensively discussed in Chapters 3 and 4 and are not subject to further explicit discussion in this chapter. However, the rest of this chapter must be read with the material on the centrality of purpose, use of self and relationships in the forefront of the reader's mind.

PROBLEM SOLVING

Problem-solving processes are a part of many models or frameworks for practice (Lehmann and Coady, 2001: 48). As an intervention method, problem solving involves the use of a sequence of rational steps which have the dual aim of relieving the distress caused by the problem and at the same time teaching the processes involved in problem solving so that the service user can apply them in future situations. An associated method, task-centred practice (Reid and Shyne, 1969; Doel and Marsh, 1992), stresses the importance of achieving goals within specific timeframes in order to provide motivation. Both problem-solving and task-centred approaches to practice have influenced the development of care management in Britain (Sheppard, 1995).

Problem solving as an approach to practice has been critiqued as deterministic, mechanistic, and tending to produce conservative, individualistic solutions, in comparison to other approaches perceived to be more radical. Additionally the notion that problems are unwelcome aspects of life and optimism that most problems can be solved if we have the necessary will is a feature of western cultures that may not be shared by other cultures. In the practice framework presented in this book use of theory should be guided by social work purpose, agreed service user-centred outcomes, knowledge of the effectiveness of strategies, the acceptability of strategies to service users, sensitivity to cultural differences and the use of critical reflective questioning of all assumptions and actions. If implemented carefully and with a critical awareness (Lehmann and Coady, 2001), problem-solving and task-centred practice can promote mutuality, partnership and empowerment, particularly in assisting service users to develop strategies to solve intra/interpersonal and socially located problems and to take control over their lives.

Problem solving is the normal process of adaptation to everyday living. We become aware that we have a problem when we cannot readily adapt to the demands made on us. A problem-solving approach operates from a set of assumptions about how individuals, families, groups and communities change, namely:

- People change as the result of a reasoned decision to achieve something better than they have now;
- People change when they accept the inevitable consequences of their own behaviour and see this behaviour as not meeting their needs;
- People change through relationships in which emotional needs are met and their natural resistance to change is accordingly not so inhibiting;
- People change when, through learning and using different ways of behaving, they get more desirable results;
- People change when they see some chance of rewards for the risks they take in making changes.

The primary goal of problem solving is to help with the tensions or problems which have arisen for people in their interactions with social arrangements and may involve change at the individual and wider social level. People usually seek help in gaining some immediate control over their circumstances rather than a total psychological and lifestyle 'overhaul'. They want this help with their perceived problems within as short a time as possible. For most of us, the nearby, reachable goal is the most real. When short-term goals are reached, people can see how their efforts have contributed to an increased feeling of well-being. Constructive change in one area of life also usually has beneficial effects on other areas.

Much of the literature stresses the rational, logical nature of this process. That is, the worker helps the other to rationally think through the nature, causes and effects of a distinct problem. However, this is only part of the problem-solving activity. Clearly all people involved use their own values/stereotypes/agendas to conceptualize the problem, and these can be seen as irrational in that they are not known, acknowledged or declared. Such irrational elements are always present. The onus is on us to attempt to identify our habitual patterns and stereotypes so we do not 'give' other people problems by unknowingly imposing our own framework on their situation and not seeing it in their terms.

It is also important to recognize that a worker may need to use different styles of problem solving such as directive, collaborative and consultancy styles, depending on the needs of individuals, groups and communities, and the nature of problems that are being addressed. For example, the emergence of a crisis generally requires the worker to move from a consultancy role to a more directive style of problem solving. Workers should signal changes in their style of work by discussing with service users or groups the reasons for change. Problem solving is usually conceptualized around a structure consisting of stages of a process which can be applied to most of the intervention strategies discussed in this chapter.

THE PROBLEM-SOLVING PROCESS

The problem-solving process involves the following phases:

- engagement;
- data collection and assessment;
- negotiating agreed outcomes;
- searching for possible ways and means;
- deciding on a course of action;
- investigating the resources available;
- carrying it through; and
- evaluating the outcomes achieved against the agreed outcomes.

In implementing this process, the worker must be aware of the following three principles of working with others to produce change:

1. You cannot make someone else's behaviour change. You can only change your own in such a way that it may produce changes in the other;
2. Because of the systemic nature of change, there is rarely one correct solution to any problem;
3. The whole process is cyclical rather than linear, with constant movement between the different parts of the process, though generally one facet is dominant at any one time.

Different aspects of this process are evident in the examples in this book.

The process in problem solving is as important as the product. Involving service users in all aspects of decision making and sharing our understandings and views are empowering processes. It is also important to make explicit what is happening with all concerned, so that service users can have the opportunity to learn new approaches to the problems that arise in their lives. This facilitates accountability. If we do not make links between the what, how and why of our actions, neither of these important functions can be met. The effectiveness of problem-solving action, in both process and outcome terms, is measured against the extent to which agreed outcomes are achieved.

In some situations, the completion of one phase may trigger further needs. For example, if a group of young mothers meets as an educative/supportive group to do some screen printing, they may, in the process of their discussions, decide they want to tackle the local authority's housing department about its attitude to young parents, or the Department of Work and Pensions because of deficiencies they see in a programme to help young mothers back into the paid workforce (such as the New Deal for Lone Parents). The second agenda isn't directly related to the first, but it is an outcome of the interactive process that went with it. Once specified outcomes have been reached, rather than continuing a cosy but perhaps dependency-inducing relationship, it is important to review progress and plan to finish up in the belief that people can cope without the worker.

EMPOWERMENT

Because the term empowerment is often used indiscriminately in social work and social care practice to describe such varied activities as giving information to improving a service user's self-esteem, it has become somewhat meaningless. Nevertheless, the concept of empowerment is important to our sense of social work purpose. We view empowerment as a generic process that can be incorporated into all intervention strategies. Lee (2001) uses a definition from Solomon that identifies the central concepts of empowerment. It is described as a process and a set of activities

> that aim to reduce the powerlessness that has been created by negative valuations based on membership in a stigmatised group. It involves identification of the power blocks that contribute to the problem as well as the development and implementation of specific strategies aimed at either the reduction of the effects from indirect power blocks or the reduction of the operations of direct power blocks. (1976: 19)

The following principles and activities adapted from Lee (2001: 34) and Sheafor et al. (2000: 481–2) facilitate the change process in empowerment:

- Service users and practitioners work in partnership with each other, especially around outcome setting, where the outcomes agreed upon are owned by the service user;
- Service users develop a stronger and more active sense of self;
- Service users learn problem-solving, communication and assertiveness skills;
- Service users, whether as individuals, groups or communities are supported in developing a more critical analysis of wider social and political issues and the ways these may be disempowering, and strategies that may reduce their negative impacts;
- Service users' strengths are identified and built upon;
- Provision of resources and increased access to resources are needed for much empowerment practice.

From these principles it is clear that what makes a process more or less empowering is the extent to which service users acquire a psychological sense of themselves as being in control over their circumstances, build skills to enable them to effect control over their environment and have access to needed resources. Many practitioners would argue that this is what has always constituted good social work practice. However, it has also been demonstrated that the rhetoric about practice does not always match the reality (Schon, 1995) and that many empowering strategies, such as user involvement processes, often merely maintain the 'status quo' by 'substituting appealing rhetoric for substantive change' (Heumann et al., 2001: 15). Alternatively, empowerment strategies may be misperceived as encouraging an individual to take control not just over their own life but to also over other people's. Care must be taken to ensure that the empowerment of one person does not lead to the oppression of another. In our practice framework we emphasize the dual purpose of social work: helping people take more control in their own lives and promoting equitable relationships – and both purposes are equally important. In the next section we examine one strategy for facilitating individuals' empowerment: group work.

WORKING WITH GROUPS

Groups are integral to human survival. It is through groups that we feel connected to one another and learn how to work cooperatively. Most people have experiences of being members of naturally formed groups, such as the family, and of being members of groups formed for a specific purpose, such as sport, recreation, work and perhaps therapy. Basically, a group is a collection of individuals who come together for a limited time for a common purpose. Groups can be distinguished from communities in that groups terminate when their purpose has been achieved, and are more specialized, homogeneous and intimate than communities (Lee, 2001: 254).

Working with people in groups has a long tradition in social work as a method of facilitating positive personal and social change. Much of community work involves working with a range of groups that comprise communities. Culturally sensitive and empowerment-based group work practice is used to build communities that increase individuals' power and control over their life circumstance, increase access to resources for marginalized and disenfranchised groups and produce more equitable social structures and processes (Gutierrez and Lewis, 1999). Organizational concerns to promote cost-efficient social work practices, the team-based nature of human services and the potential for technology to connect people in groups across time and space suggest that the demand for skilled group work practice will increase. In this section we discuss the knowledge and skills required for effective group work.

WHY GROUP WORK?

As with all decisions about intervention methods, the choice of group work requires a comprehensive assessment of service user needs, agreement about outcomes sought, knowledge of the efficacy of group work and discussion between worker and service users of the acceptability of this approach. The starting point is to consider the range of purposes that groups can accomplish for participants. These can include one or several of the following:

- mutual support and self help;
- exchange of information;
- opportunities to learn and test social skills and behaviours;
- a source of power to change social conditions and influence policies;
- a safe context in which to explore the impact of factors such as gender, 'race' and sexual identity;
- increased social networks, reduced isolation and inclusion;
- improved emotional and social well-being.

The perceived advantage of group work as a change process over individual work is that each participant potentially has access to the multiple perspectives and skills that individuals bring to the group, to meet the particular outcomes sought. However, reports also suggest that some individuals may be damaged by group work, through rejection, confrontation, insensitive challenges to their value systems and their own disclosure of highly personal information (Brown, 1992: 33). Where the outcome sought is to improve the emotional coping capacities of extremely vulnerable service users, individual work may be preferable, or a prerequisite to participation in a group.

KNOWLEDGE AND SKILLS FOR GROUP WORK INTERVENTION

There have been many attempts to develop a typology of groups which links the purpose of a group with a particular approach, for example, a remedial approach to produce individual change, an interactional approach to encourage mutual aid and interpersonal growth and a social goals model to produce social change (Papell and Rothman, 1966). Some writers distinguish between groups that are primarily task oriented and those that are process oriented. However, such neat categories tend not to match the complexity of people's needs and the corresponding need for a combination of aims and approaches. A group may intend to achieve both individual and social change (Cohen and Mullender, 1999) and depending on the specific aims, several approaches, such as social action, education and mutual aid may be employed. In all group work intervention it is important to pay attention to both task and process.

Group development is commonly described as progressing through a number of stages:

- preaffiliation/inclusion/trust/forming;
- power and control/autonomy/storming;
- intimacy/closeness/affection/norming;
- differentiation/interdependence/performing;
- separation/termination/mourning.

This linear model of group development helps the practitioner predict what behaviours to expect over time and how to address relationship difficulties associated with each stage in line with group goals and expected outcomes. However, it is important to acknowledge that there are alternatives to this model. Schiller (1997) and Sternbach (2001) highlight the ways in which women's and men's groups may diverge from this pattern, particularly in relation to the levels of trust needed to support conflict within the group.

Knowledge regarding leadership is also needed for effective group work. Once again attempts have been made to conceptualize leadership in terms of styles, namely, democratic, *laissez faire* and autocratic, and to list attributes of effective facilitators. These ideal types can help the worker to identify their 'natural' style and develop their ability to use different styles when appropriate. The democratic style is most congruent with social work purpose and values. However, there may be times when the group process suggests a different style is needed, for example, an authoritarian approach to halt potentially damaging behaviour and a *laissez faire* style when the leader thinks the group could gain from experiencing a lack of structure.

Group facilitation draws on the range of skills common to all social work practice as well as skills specific to the interactional dynamics that take place when a number of people come together in a purposeful way. Practitioners new to group work tend to communicate as if in a one-to-one interaction, interacting with each group member in turn (like the hub and spokes of a wheel). They may initially have most difficulty with the skill of simultaneously analysing and responding to the multiple interactions occurring. The communication needs to shift away from the leader as the central figure, to cross-participant communication so that the multiple perspectives and skills of participants can emerge.

Benjamin et al. (1997) suggest the analytical skills involved in group work centre around:

- checking communication patterns;
- checking that the group is moving towards its purposes;
- reflecting on the appropriateness of leadership style;
- assessing the climate of the group;
- checking for understanding of group goals.

This ongoing analytic process requires corresponding group maintenance skills, including encouraging equal participation among members and members taking responsibility for problem solving and conflict resolution, focusing on and renegotiating agreed outcomes, and using exercises to further group development. Such exercises include role plays, drama, guided fantasy, diaries, posters, cartoons, painting, photography, play mime, dance, crafts and recreational outings (Doel and Sawdon, 1999: 131). These activities should serve a purpose within the group, for example, to facilitate inclusion, to energize the group, to develop members' awareness of dynamics within the group, to teach problem solving and to resolve conflict. They should be appropriate to group members' attributes, such as their age, culture and physical and cognitive abilities.

PHASES OF GROUP WORK

We prefer to discuss group development in terms of phases: pre-planning, beginnings, middles and endings. This highlights both the development of relationships within groups that occur over time and the notion that issues of inclusion, power and control may arise at any time in the group and may require attention throughout the life of the group.

PRE-PLANNING PHASE

Once purpose and general approach have been decided, the worker needs to attend to pre-planning tasks, particularly membership, leadership arrangements, structure (closed, open, frequency, timing, length of sessions), resources and organizational support (adapted from Brown, 1992). Following general identification of potential members, the worker needs to make specific decisions about membership, taking into consideration factors of age, class, gender, ethnicity and behavioural attributes (where known). These decisions should take account of the need for balance between the level of homogeneity needed to develop group cohesion, and the level of heterogeneity needed to produce the forces for change in the group. As a general rule, no individual should feel too far removed from at least one other member, unless steps can be taken to redress extreme difference (Brown, 1992: 47). Organizational issues need to be addressed before the group can proceed. Important considerations are agency support for the group, resources such as financial commitment for social activities, refreshments and a suitable space where comfort and privacy are available.

BEGINNINGS

The key tasks of the leader and participants in the initial meeting of any group are relationship building and fostering inclusion, setting outcomes for the group, and establishing ground rules. Used sensitively, ice-breaking exercises are an effective means of initiating the process of relationship building, generating energy within the group, relieving anxiety and creating an optimistic, informal atmosphere. Relationship building continues throughout the life of the group as the members work collectively with tasks and processes that arise, each offering opportunities for personal awareness raising, problem resolution and social action.

In terms of setting outcomes, the worker's task in the first group session is to move from the general outcomes based on their assessment of the group's needs to specific outcomes developed by the group members. Explicit agreed outcomes are necessary for member commitment to the group, for member understanding of ends, means and risks involved, and for evaluation purposes. Additionally, group members may identify, either in confidence or openly, personal outcomes that they want to achieve. In the first meeting, the worker also needs to ensure that members openly discuss and agree ground rules for the group, such as confidentiality, respectful communication and respect for difference. This task is both an ethical requirement and a process which has potential to deepen trust, create a safe environment and modify behaviour.

MIDDLES

The middle stage of groups involves continuing to balance task and process, while maintaining the processes of relationship building, development of trust, and dealing with difference and conflict as it arises. Depending on the outcomes sought, for example improved coping capacities to deal with loss and grief, developing therapeutic and self-help processes may be the main task of the group. Where the outcome is a product, for example, a group of parents of disabled children wanting consumer input into disability policy, process issues will still be important, however, the concrete tasks needed to produce a written document will need to be managed within the group.

In the middle stages of a group, the worker draws on their understanding of group dynamics outlined earlier, particularly the potential for multiple perspectives, strengths and skills within the group to be used to achieve the changes sought. The middle phase calls on the worker to clarify communication, build deeper levels of cohesiveness, mediate, confront, identify and value both commonalities and difference (Brandler and Roman, 1999: 46). The worker also needs knowledge of the way in which power manifests itself in interactions within the group. In all groups, the challenge of keeping a balance between process and task requires the worker to renegotiate outcomes, to keep members on track to complete tasks, to encourage members to initiate ideas, to problem solve, and to provide support for change.

ENDINGS

The ending of a group involves issues of both celebration and loss. Depending on how effective the group has been participants are likely to experience feelings of achievement regarding the goals they did obtain and perhaps regret regarding those they did not pursue, for whatever reasons. This is a time when the worker needs to encourage members to reflect on the outcomes achieved in relation to the outcomes sought and the personal satisfaction and dissatisfaction that exists. Review of group outcomes occurs at different points in the life of a group. However, there are always likely to be some outcomes that could not be achieved. Participants should be encouraged to express both positive and negative feelings and to deal with the potential loss of relationships. A group activity dealing with reflection, celebration and goodbyes can be an effective technique to identify and address feelings surrounding endings. For professional development and agency quality assurance, a formal evaluation of the purposes of the group is desirable.

In the following example, Suzanne Mullally writes about her experiences co-facilitating a group for refugee women in London. At the time Suzanne was a final-year social work student and was on placement in a family centre (a voluntary organization) providing individual and group support to children and families.

Practice example: the Refugee Women's Group

During my placement I worked mainly with the centre's service offered to refugee and asylum-seeking families. This includes a refugee women's support group, advice and outreach work, counselling and intensive family support. My focus here is on my role as a co-facilitator of the Refugee Women's Group, an open group, which meets on a weekly basis. I locate my analysis within a systemic understanding of group processes and have also reflected on the meaning of empowerment in society and in group experiences.

Structure and purpose of the group

The Refugee Women's Group has been meeting for the past eight years. Although the group membership has changed throughout this time, the group was initiated and is primarily facilitated by a senior social worker (my practice teacher). The group is co-facilitated when my practice teacher has a student on placement with her. Apart from myself (I am white) all group members identify as black African. My practice teacher is also black and was, herself, originally a refugee. Members mainly self-refer after contact with friends, community groups and social services departments. The group's structure is fairly loose, with a toy library open at the beginning of the session, refreshments and registration, an information exchange, and finally a speaker/topic for discussion. The timing often varies and women arrive and leave at different points during the meeting.

(Continued)

(Continued)

The purpose of the group is to reduce the isolation that women may be experiencing as refugees and to address issues of concern to them and their families. However, because of the open nature of the group, it is often difficult to fix a label on it and at different points in its existence it has achieved different objectives. This reflects the uneven pattern of development that groups with open and changing memberships often follow (Brown, 1997). Sometimes the tasks identified by the group have taken precedence over the process (e.g. in setting up English-language classes or organizing trips). At other times, the process of the group has been more important: when the knowledge of the certainty of the group's existence and its weekly regularity provides a safe, collective experience that might not be present in other aspects of group members' lives. The group does, however, maintain an explicit value base: it is committed to an empowering process that can combat oppression, also an essential component of the systemic model of group work developed by Doel and Sawdon (1999).

While there was considerable difference in the group in relation to religion, culture, status and politics, there were also similarities in terms of bereavement, trauma and the loss experienced as refugees, as well as the racism experienced in Britain. Group members were at different stages in their applications for asylum. The anxieties created by the fears of an asylum application being refused and the increasingly hostile social and political climate towards refugees were important to acknowledge within the group.

Pre-planning and beginnings

When preparing to co-facilitate the group, I had many questions concerning what I, as a white non-refugee woman, could contribute to the process of empowerment within the group. Woodcock (1997) states that working with people who are refugees forces an examination of one's own origins and raises questions about our own experiences of marginality and difference in terms of culture, 'race', gender, politics and religion. Issues of difference and similarity can pose key dilemmas for group facilitators and can cause insecurity in their role (Doel and Sawdon, 1999). Would group members feel inhibited in discussing their experiences of racism with a white worker present? Would my lack of experience in group work undermine the value of my presence? My role would also be transitory and part of a stream of social work students as co-facilitators of the group. How did these changes impact on a group already fluid in terms of membership? Did the group members have choices in who facilitated the group? I was also concerned about co-facilitating the group with my practice teacher, an experienced group worker who shared refugee experiences with group members, and who would also be observing my practice.

I planned with my practice teacher that I would initially take on an observation role, contributing more and more as I and the members got to know each other, with the eventual aim of leading the group sessions. Doel and Sawdon (1999) point out that in group work both members and facilitators can feel on display. In some circumstances this can induce a kind of paralysis in which the person is unable to think or act because of their extreme self-consciousness. However, at one level, the fear I felt in joining a group (which on one occasion was attended by 20 members) had a positive effect. It provided me with some understanding of how new members may feel on attending for the first time. I began to take a more active role in welcoming new members and working with other group members through introductions and making drinks. I began to contribute to the caring and collective ethos of the group (Brown, 1997) and recognized the benefits of listening and 'bearing witness' (Blackwell, 1997) to group members' experiences.

(Continued)

Middles: power and control

Initially I felt that my response to the group was not adequate: that I was not *doing* enough to *prove* my worth. Service users, both in individual and group contexts, can often leave us feeling uncomfortable and with a sense that we should be doing something urgently to 'solve' the situation (Blackwell, 1997). Blackwell also points out that being 'helpful', while a natural response, may easily become exploitative: we use another's vulnerability to fulfil our own need to be helpful and feel good about ourselves. This can actually work against empowering practice as it may increase feelings of helplessness in the service user. My need to *do* within the group could have acted against the real process of assessing my role and may have shielded me from having to listen to, acknowledge and 'stay with' the truth of members' experiences. Through being open about our differences and being curious about the different experiences of group members I began to develop confidence in the value of my role as a co-facilitator. It opened up a dialogue around our perceptions of oppression, linking the personal with the political.

During supervision my practice teacher and I prepared for co-working by discussing our differences and similarities in terms of role, 'race', culture and values. It also helped us process group experiences. For example, in one meeting when we were planning swimming lessons, a group member, Marceline (not her real name), appeared to be rather condescending and sarcastic towards another. She felt that securing a private venue so that no men would be present would unnecessarily delay the start of the lessons. I felt that this was an implicit dig at the women in the group who were Muslim. Neither my practice teacher nor I challenged this comment in the group and we focused on the practicalities of getting the activity organized. We discussed our reactions to the comment in supervision and what we felt had inhibited us from challenging Marceline directly. My practice teacher had not wanted to embarrass Marceline in the group and preferred to talk with her about her comment outside the group context. I felt that as a new worker and, more importantly, as a white worker, I was not confident enough to challenge the remark. However, I was concerned not to collude with any form of discrimination in the group and explored with my practice teacher ways of dealing with the situation. In the next session, I acknowledged at the beginning that there appeared to have been tension in the group about the different religious requirements of group members and I was concerned that people may have felt hurt by this. There was no direct response to this comment, but we spent time talking again about the ground rules and their importance, acknowledging the need to respect individual members' religions.

Middles: working together

Towards the end of my involvement with the group I did facilitate some sessions alone. Although they felt rather chaotic, the task and process of the session seemed to be achieved and I really enjoyed them. I began to develop confidence in my role as a central person. I realized that this does not imply that I had to have authority *over* the group, but rather that I had to acknowledge my position in the group, the access I had to resources, and the emotional strength I could bring to a situation. I also realized that the group members were very adept at working with the different styles of group workers and I had underestimated their expertise in adapting to different leadership/facilitation styles.

(Continued)

(Continued)

Two group members who had attended for a comparatively long time and who were experienced in welcoming new members supported me when I was facilitating on my own. One of these members was Ajaba (not her real name) who I had worked with individually in providing support and advocacy concerning racism she had experienced in contact with a social services department. We had also been working together to set up a self-help group for refugee women (an off-shoot of this group) that would hopefully become politically active in promoting their and their families' rights. Over time it became clear to me that Ajaba provided internal leadership in our group and that these qualities were very much respected by group members (she was later elected chair of the new self-help group). Doel and Sawdon (1999) claim that internal leadership is most effective when it emerges from the group members themselves and when this serves to strengthen the formal leadership or facilitation of the group workers. Following my placement, my practice teacher said that she felt it might be valuable for Ajaba and other group members to take turns in formally facilitating the group. For me, this felt like the fulfilment of the main aim of the group: to commit to an empowering process that can challenge oppression.

Endings

Ajaba also demonstrated to me the importance of endings. I had not really planned a group session around my leaving, perhaps because I had mixed feelings about ending my involvement with people to whom I had become attached and was not really sure how to talk about these feelings in a group setting. Ajaba had arranged a surprise meal with other members. They had each cooked food and brought it to the group. I was overwhelmed by this action because the members had previously used food in the group to celebrate religious festivals and on other occasions to communicate a sense of identity, both as individual members and as friends. Woodcock (1997) expresses how setting groups within the streams of members' cultures stimulates symbolic meaning and creates a new sense of belonging. By bringing food and each saying their goodbyes, I felt a real sense of belonging in the group and an awareness of how the members' experiences as refugees had taught them, and now me, the importance of saying goodbye.

This work with the Refugee Women's Group demonstrates an attempt to tackle oppression in these women's lives. While the group may not have overturned the structures that create and reinforce oppression (e.g. immigration and asylum laws), it was able to create a reasonably safe place for women to share their experiences and seek support from each other. In setting and achieving tasks, it provided a resource for the development of skills and knowledge for managing in British society. It also provided the launch pad for a new self-help group which seeks to have a more political, lobbying remit. The success of the group was due partly to the commitment of the co-facilitators and the group members to forming equitable relationships with each other: ones that acknowledged and respected individuals' power and authority in the group.

Although the group has a much longer lifespan than the time the student social worker spent with it, her involvement in the group reflected many of the common stages of group development. In the early stages of her involvement she wrestled with the nature and meaning of her contribution. This feeling of vulnerability was reduced by taking a more active role in group processes: welcoming and providing drinks for members (a form of ice breaking). She later struggled with her own power and authority as a white co-facilitator working with a group of black women. By acknowledging shared authority and the value of group members themselves exercising leadership functions, the group was able to work together effectively in achieving its aims. The more active role of group members in formal facilitation would change the nature and functioning of the group in the future. For while the group would continue after the student had left it, it had changed shape and her leaving marked the end of a phase in the group's development. For people who may have felt disconnected from British society and from their communities of origin, the experience of sharing and the bonds formed within the group may have enhanced a sense of community and belonging. Group work is an essential part of the process of building communities.

BUILDING COMMUNITY

By building community we mean the processes paid workers use to assist members of a defined community to get a better deal by taking collective action (Twelvetrees, 2001: 1). In terms of intervention the key tasks focus on the basic problem-solving stages of identifying the issue/problem, analysing it from different perspectives within and outside the community, agreeing the desired outcomes and selecting appropriate strategies to achieve them. The tactics adopted will vary with the analysis of the problem and of the willingness or otherwise of those who are seen as part of the problem to change. For example, if powerful individuals or groups oppose that change, the tactics may be to build the capacity of the community to mount a campaign, use education, persuasion through lobbying or cooption, use of the media or large group community action such as demonstrations and lawsuits. It is important to strive to keep communication channels open between community members and those they are attempting to influence, and to maintain a close watch on new opportunities for action, or new challenges to be dealt with as a piece of community work progresses.

Core values in community building reflect a preference for a society based on the values of cooperation and solidarity rather than a society based on values of competition and individualism. However, it is inspired by many different philosophical and belief systems (Plant, 1974) and follows many different patterns or models of practice (Rothman, 1979; Kelly and Sewell, 1988; Kenny, 1999; Ife, 2002). Nevertheless community-building strategies are very much in line with the focus and purpose of social work as we have presented them in this book. They are also strategies that are increasingly acknowledged as important in the regeneration of communities and neighbourhoods seen as 'deprived' and contributing to social exclusion (Gilchrist, 2003). In community building, people are engaged in collective strategies to help gain more control over their own lives and potentially to transform their social arrangements. We will briefly discuss two forms of community building and the links between individual work and community work.

One form of community building is called community development: people, whose lack of control over their own lives leads to some form of exploitation, are enabled to take control through the act of joining with others and increasing their power by developing their skills in working together to change the situation (Kenny, 1999: 11). This style of work can be characterized as 'bottom-up', although as Twelvetrees (2001: 5) notes, care should be taken to identify whether the goals are being driven by the community or by the employing agency, which may require specific outcomes. This approach was advocated by local government workers in the 1980s, but was resisted by the Thatcher governments, leaving voluntary sector agencies as the main sponsors of bottom-up community development activities. Nevertheless, the New Labour focus on regeneration and social inclusion in 'deprived' communities and neighbourhoods has recently highlighted the potential of community development strategies. According to Gilchrist, New Labour has

> embraced many of the values that have become central to community development and incorporated key principles into many of its key programmes and funding initiatives ... The public policy arena reverberates with the rhetoric of economic and social regeneration, of finding 'local solutions for local problems', promoting neighbourhood renewal and enhancing levels of civic engagement ... Apparently, community development skills and strategies are once again being recognized by government and voluntary agencies, but at the heart of many programmes lingers the legacy of Thatcherite thinking in relation to progress couched in terms of externally imposed objectives and an enduring emphasis on individual enterprise and attainment, rather than collective benefit. (2003: 17)

Gilchrist argues that the bottom-up approach that is so important in community development is not well understood by policy makers and managers. The challenge for community development is how it negotiates being coopted into policy initiatives that run counter to its focus on social justice and the power of the collective in developing its own solutions.

A second form of community work, often called social planning, aims to establish linkages between different services or policy makers and the people using a range of services, to inform them of the needs of specific communities and work with them to alter policies or improve services. This style of work may be characterized as more 'top-down'. While government initiatives advocating social inclusion and community regeneration may employ the language or rhetoric of community development, much of it is more accurately described as service planning where ultimate control over the direction and funding of services rests with central government. For example, according to Phillips, 'regeneration remains a process where government tries to change people and places to meet its own demands rather than where government adjusts itself to meet the demands of local people' (2004: 167). Willmott (1989) notes that such top-down initiatives to involve community members can only work if 'bottom-up' initiatives also exist. The choice of approach should be linked to the issues to be addressed and the stages of a piece of work. There may also be a movement from one approach to the other. It is often the case that movement is from individual work to community work when it becomes clear that the issues individuals face are shared by others and require a structural response.

MOVING BETWEEN INDIVIDUAL WORK AND COMMUNITY DEVELOPMENT

Often work in the community, like work with groups, focuses on a public face of private issues. Contact with individuals leads to an awareness of shared issues that need to be addressed; the worker may then facilitate links with those in the community who are willing and able to commit to a community development response to those issues. Unfortunately, in many jobs, moving issues from the private to the public level may not be regarded as a core task, and hence workers may let this work go when they are very busy, or find it hard to justify the time spent on these activities in the context of service agreements. However, not responding at a public level may mean that the work done at an individual level is less than effective. When you think about work with many people in the community on whom governments are prepared to spend money, you realize that much of workers' efforts go into locating appropriate groups or services in the community – and many of these services or groups formed as a result of community-building activities. Working simultaneously across methods requires a clear and shared sense of purpose, a capacity to articulate with others what it is we are trying to achieve together, knowledge and skills appropriate to the task, and a capacity to work with, rather than for, others.

In the example with the group of refugee women, the social work methods ranged from individual work to group work to community building. The group was initially set up by the student's practice teacher because she saw many individuals with what appeared to be common needs. In the development of the group itself, community-building strategies are evident in the way the group was encouraged to take greater control over facilitation and decision making. Although this support group would probably continue to be worker led (given its funding via the family centre), the emergence of a self-help group is an interesting development. This new group has a more political remit and it could develop a valued advocacy and lobbying role in the community. Much of social work and social policy activity is currently concerned with involving service users in partnership strategies. One of the most effective ways to enable involvement is to provide opportunities for service users to meet together and to connect with or even form such advocacy and lobbying organizations.

EVALUATING COMMUNITY WORK PRACTICE

We need some signposts for describing and evaluating our community work practice in the context of our assessment of what might be effective in a given situation. One framework is COMPASS, shown in Figure 5.2. This framework involves assessment, attention to process, skills and roles, but emphasizes particular dimensions of these factors. The COMPASS framework enables a worker to plot his or her position in the community-building process, taking into account four points on two key dimensions (Kelly and Sewell, 1988).

The first dimension is *In/Out*. Here the concern is largely about processes of developing relationships of trust and acceptance with community members. When a worker starts to work with people in a community, he or she is usually an outsider. They do not have a relationship with the people and don't know their situation. Developing a genuine understanding or assessment of people's situations means moving to the position of an insider. Becoming an insider means being with people, listening to them, hearing what they are saying about their situation and responding to what they are saying. Insider status arrives when we begin to work together on what they are saying. Many workers never move from outsider to insider, because they never seek to be with people and hear what they are saying.

The student practitioner and her practice teacher were able to assist people to take control of their own lives because they were willing to be with them and hear their issues. It

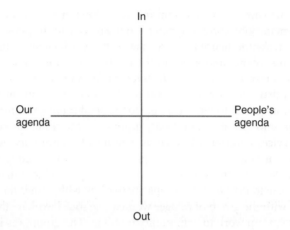

Figure 5.2   Compass

sounds simple to say that we need to be with people and hear them, but it is a complex process. Our professional and societal structures, our own need to have our actions validated rather than to stand in the background, the need for patience and skill all contribute to making the task quite complex.

Our agenda/people's agenda is the second dimension. Here the emphasis is on developing a shared understanding with community members of the differing perspectives that they and we will inevitably hold of the same situation. When we attempt to work alongside people we do not come to the situation as a blank sheet. We generally have some hunches, ideas, feelings or analyses about the situation, as well as some possible solutions. This is our agenda. Throughout history and across most cultures, those who have had some power and who have sought to change the lives of others according to their own agenda have frequently caused tremendous problems. Politicians, bureaucrats, aid workers, missionaries, social workers and political activists have all been guilty of pursuing their own, rather than the people's, agenda. While our insights, hunches or suggestions may be right on target, we should always be aware of whose agenda we are following. If it is not that of the people closest to the situation then they stand a chance of being further disempowered rather than empowered by our actions.

All practice relies on an understanding of the network of relationships around individuals or making up communities. As we have seen, community building relies on the development and/or work with appropriate networks. In interpersonal and group work we also need to pay attention to the structure and functioning of the network of relationships around individuals. Our work with networks is often a key factor in any intervention.

BUILDING NETWORKS

The development of appropriate social networks is an important preventative and developmental task for social workers concerned to enhance people's choices and their control in their own lives. Garrison and Werfer (1977: 109), for example, state that 'the solution to a variety of human dilemmas lies within the collective resources of the individual's social network'. People's social networks are also significant in determining their health and happiness (George and Davis, 1998). This is particularly the case for older people where network type has been demonstrated to be related to morale, loneliness, self-help and use of community services (Wenger, 1994). For many of the writers adopting a network approach to their practice (for example, Germain and Gitterman, 1980; McIntyre, 1986), the interactions between people are seen to be causative of problems and hence the target for change. There are two basic network strategies (Wilson, 1984). These are:

1. Strategies that focus on locating and improving the functioning of existing networks; and
2. Those which focus on creating new networks or linking isolated individuals into what is, for them, a new social network.

WORKING WITH EXISTING NETWORKS: MOBILIZING NETWORK RESOURCES

In this approach, the worker seeks to help mobilize the resources available in existing networks to solve a particular problem experienced by the group or by one of its members. In relation to work with networks on behalf of individuals the worker acts as a facilitator in what Collins and Pancoast (1976) called 'natural helping networks'. This requires the worker to locate the 'natural' care givers in the person's network; plot these on a chart to identify clusters; decide who needs to be consulted; and set up discussions with those people regarded as most likely to be involved – usually neighbours and relatives – as well as with the person whose care needs are central. Wenger (1997), in reviewing research on family support provided to older people, identifies the significant role that partners and adult children play in supporting older people and notes that daughters tend to provide assistance with domestic chores and personal care, while sons assist mainly with household maintenance and financial assistance. Both adult sons and daughters tend to provide considerable amounts of emotional support. Siblings and friends often provide companionship and neighbours are commonly relied on in times of crisis.

Many people are capable of offering 'one-off' types of assistance. A much greater amount of energy is required within a naturally occurring network to maintain an ongoing situation where the rewards are not so obvious – for example, helping an unwelcoming older person remain in their home. Titmuss (1968) argues that the family or network can become overloaded if family care is substituted for professional or paid care without a transfer of resources from the government to the people who are to provide the support. The relationships and the individuals making up the network may be damaged if more is asked of them than they can provide. In Chapter 2 we noted that community care policies have sought to transfer the responsibility for social care and support from government to families and communities. Arguably, this transfer of responsibility has not been matched by the transfer of sufficient resources to develop the required social infrastructure.

WORKING WITH EXISTING NETWORKS: NETWORK SERVICE DELIVERY

Many agencies and their workers make assessments of the vulnerability of people at least partly in terms of their supportive networks. They use this assessment to ration resources as well as to identify how changes in people's networks affect the person and vice versa. In some situations the worker may decide it is better to work intensively with some people in the network – for example, the carers – rather than the identified service user. The Carers (Recognition and Services) 1996 Act demonstrates a commitment to this type of support, although according to Keating et al. (2003), it may unwittingly undermine care networks by directing benefits to individual carers. In targeting a service user's network, networks are seen as mediators of the service the worker is providing and attempts are made to understand the construction the existing network puts on the worker and the worker's efforts.

CREATING NEW NETWORKS: NETWORK EXTENSION

Network extension involves promoting relationships between people who share similar concerns or problems. It is an initial step in developing a group to deal with these concerns and problems. For example, a number of mothers a worker has seen may share common concerns, such as coping with the stress of parenting. Following individual discussions with the worker, they are introduced to each other to decide whether or not they can address some of the issues they face together. This form of networking is called a need–need response, since people with similar needs are linked in the hope that they might be able to generate resources that they do not have alone, such as sharing childcare, providing company and so on. It is important to assess whether people with similar needs do have enough energy to lend to others, even with the support of the group.

Network extension is a key strategy in community work and can facilitate a sense of social trust and empowerment (Gilchrist, 2003). Kelly and Sewell (1988) describe the significance of moving from a one-to-one situation to one in which all the people involved in the issue are talking together, terming this *0–1–3*. When we begin in a community we are one person with no relationships. When one other person shares their concerns with us we are two people with one relationship. But when we assist the two people who have the similar concern to share it with each other, a transformation occurs. Private concerns become public: 'Yes, it is not just me it's happening to, it's happening to you also. Alone I was suffering it, together we can change it.' One relationship becomes three relationships to support and encourage; the move from private to public engenders hope and therefore action; we have 'power' (Kahn, 1970). Bierstedt (1974) suggests that the three sources of power are numbers, organizations and resources: 0–1–3 supplies each of these requirements and is a core process in community building and network extension.

CREATING NEW NETWORKS: NETWORKS AS SERVICE PROVIDERS

This form of network extension aims to link people with specific needs to those who do not have those needs, but do have the resources to meet them. For example, you might try to meet the social needs of young people with a learning disability by linking them to others their age who do not have this disability, using an existing network such as people attending a particular church. The challenge in this form of network extension is to ensure that the links developed do not lead to dependency and control. There are some problems in fostering such relationships. You are, at one and the same time, using people's differences from others as a basis for the right to be treated as if there were no differences. There are also important practical problems in that those in the weaker position can be very hurt if those in the stronger position find they no longer have time in their lives to keep up the contact. Those who drift away can also be left feeling used up and uncomfortable. Care needs to be exercised in extending people's networks so that the most vulnerable person is in control of the process rather than being the wary beneficiary of other people's 'good works'.

TYPES OF RELATIONSHIPS IN NETWORKS

Network intervention depends on an understanding both of the different types of relationships between people and of the structure of the links these relationships make. (The authors wish to acknowledge the work of Colin Peile (1980) in these descriptions of relationships and network structures). Relationships are complex and these ideal types overlap and vary over time. The descriptions listed below relate to perceptions of relationships and do not necessarily relate to what is happening in reality.

1. *Alienation*: A perception held by a person that no relationship exists with another person. The person does not see him or herself as being affected or affecting the other person in any way;
2. *Dependence perception*: A feeling that one is the victim of exploitation by another. The person holding this perception may be conscious of what is happening, but passively accepts that nothing can be done, perhaps even seeing it in positive terms. The dependence orientation may provide a feeling of security;
3. *Control perception*: A feeling that one can control or manipulate another, but is not affected by the other. The person who holds this perception may see it in a very positive light, as doing good, acting for others in their own best interests, or making their decisions for them to lessen the burden. However, such a perception contains an implicit exploitation of others. It implies that the controller knows best and so should be able to manipulate others for everyone's best interests;
4. *Exchange perception*: This involves seeing oneself as being both dependent and controlled, but in different areas and at different times. This perception leads to the view that one just bargains for resources. The value of one's resources to the other will determine that person's bargaining power. If there is equal value, it is seen as a fair exchange. When the resources of one are not valued as much as the resources of the other, feelings of doing poorly or doing well in exchange then arise. In any case, winning is seen to be at someone's expense;
5. *Mutual perception*: A perception which involves seeing oneself in joint or shared control with others in all areas over time, that is, as interdependent. The focus is on trying to create resources in another for their own use only. In the long run, both will benefit by doing this, since in creating resources for another, one learns how to develop one's own resources and the other will have greater capacities to develop resources in others. Clearly such a perception requires a strong and consistent faith in others.

In any one relationship, at a particular point in time, either person may adopt any of these five perceptions of relationships. When all the combinations are considered, we can see there are 15 possible combinations with four stable relationship types:

- alienation–alienation;
- control–dependence;
- exchange–exchange; and
- mutual–mutual.

The other 11 possibilities are unstable because there is disagreement between both people's perception of the relationship. For example, if both people think they can control each other, a conflict is inevitable. This conceptualization provides one way of making sense of the different relationships within a network and alerts us particularly to the power dimension involved in social relationships. The nature of a particular relationship, however, is interdependent with the structure of the other relationships that make up the network.

These relationships or links all have different potentials for work. When they are considered in relation to the different ways in which they are structured, we have a method describing the network structures in which, and with which, we work.

NETWORK STRUCTURE

Density: The degree to which members of one's network are also linked to each other. In high-density networks there is more direct access to all other members of the network to pass on or to acquire information and resources. This avoids the power of the middle person over resources and information.

Density and centrality: More central people will have greater access and control over information and resources, which increases their power in relationship to others. However, the nature of the links must also be taken into account, as people in a number of dependent relationships can occupy a central position (e.g. older service users can be in a very powerless position).

Clusters: Segments of a network of high density are called 'clusters'. The more strategically located a cluster, the more influence it possibly has, even though no one person is centrally located. This position may occur by accident or be the result of a conscious effort to control others. The central position can be maintained by not introducing people, by acting as a go-between or by splitting or breaking up links. It is important to consider the position of those people who form cross-linkages between networks. If the clusters are not conflicting, this person is in a powerful position in relation to both clusters, even if the person does not occupy a central position in either cluster. However, if the clusters are in conflict, then the linking person is in a powerless position, with both groups tending to be suspicious of them and attempting to keep them under control.

Based on this analysis, you could suggest that the ideal structure to avoid exploitative relationships involves high-density, overlapping network clusters. In such a network, it is difficult for any one person to control resource and information flow. Having developed an understanding of the structure and potential of a network, it is appropriate to consider some of the possible dynamics of exchange in networks.

THE DYNAMICS OF EXCHANGE

Individuals cannot satisfy their own interests without taking the interests of others into account, however minimal that consideration might be. But what triggers the decision to become involved with someone else? The answer to this question tends to vary depending on whether the exchange implied in relationships is seen as being between equals or not between equals. Equal exchange is frequently referred to as reciprocal exchange. It is affected by a number of factors which include:

- *Social distance*: The expectations for exchange between socially constructed relationships such as husband–wife, parent–child; neighbour–neighbour and so on;
- *Physical distance*: Kinship or affectional ties may not be enough to overcome the hurdle of great physical distances and, similarly, physical closeness between strangers might create a basis for an exchange relationship;
- *Economic distance*: Disparities in economic resources create differences in access to resources and hence differences in power. Such differences within a reciprocal network may create splits, or cause the relationship to change to that of patron–client;
- *Psychosocial distance*: The kind of trusting relationship established between two individuals. This presupposes a certain amount of familiarity (social distance), opportunity (physical proximity) and compatibility of needs (economic proximity).

In network extension, the norm of reciprocity serves as a starting mechanism. When a family centre worker fosters the coming together of a number of parents with preschool children, the worker makes an assumption that each of these people has valuables that the others seek. In this situation the valuables that they exchange are, first, contact with each other and, second, contact with each other's children. These are valuables precisely because the parents are isolated in the childcaring role and their children are isolated from other children. Our society tends to accentuate social distance, physical distance, economic distance and psychosocial distance between people in general, and network extension becomes a method of lessening at least some of those distances and allowing for the possibility of reciprocity. Experienced social workers become skilled at picking up on those issues around which people are likely to form reciprocal relationships.

In addition to a norm of reciprocity it is also possible to identify a norm of social responsibility which holds that in certain circumstances valuables should be given without return or anticipation of return. The conditions under which this unequal exchange can operate include the following:

- People will help those who are dependent on them. People seek to equalize ratios of rewards to investments both from themselves and for others;
- Altruistic behaviour will be augmented if it has been the person's previous experience that he or she has been helped in a similar situation (an indirect form of reciprocity).

That a person follows the norm of social responsibility does not rule out reciprocal obligation, nor does it mean that some form of return will not necessarily be attached to altruistic behaviour. This notion of social responsibility offers some explanation as to why the method of networks as a resource grouping works. It would be incorrect, however, to assume that the norms of reciprocity and responsibility do not coexist and intertwine. Compliance with the norm of reciprocity over time can develop sentiments such as loyalty and gratitude to those who have kept faith so that if situations develop where they can no longer equally exchange, the norm of social responsibility, or responding to need without expectation of return, comes into effect. According to Wenger (1997) unbalanced relationships in older people's networks are inevitable when confronted with increased impairment and need. This, however, may be tempered by past support provided by that older person. For example, an older woman who has been part of a rural community all her life may continue to receive the material and emotional support from her neighbours even though she is unable to reciprocate in the ways she had in the past.

Network analysis understands people in terms of the collectivity of their relationships – their network. We have suggested that human factors act as starting mechanisms to create new behaviour in existing networks or to bring new networks into existence. Strategies to promote change both within communities and interpersonal networks are often associated with conflict as disrupting the status quo may cut across some people's interests.

ENGAGING WITH CONFLICT

Experiencing conflict is part of being human (Kenny, 1999). Rather than avoiding conflict we need to understand and engage in the process if our work is to be effective. In the practice framework presented in this book conflict is inevitable as we strive to help people gain more control over their lives and as we help develop more equitable relationships.

Conflict is both intra- and interpersonal. Intrapersonal conflict relates to the inner conflict of mixed feelings and desires we may experience with or without interpersonal conflict. In our consideration of interpersonal conflict, in this section, it is important to remember to take intrapersonal conflict into account. Condliffe defines interpersonal conflict as

> a form of relating or interacting where we find ourselves (either as individuals or groups) under some sort of *perceived threat* to our personal or collective *goals*. These goals are usually to do with our *interpersonal wants*. These perceived threats may be either real or imagined. (1991: 3, emphases added)

Italics are used to highlight the three elements that Condliffe considers helpful as starting points in explaining the nature of conflict. Condliffe summarizes Bisno's (1988) sources of conflict in Table 5.1.

What ever the source of conflict, Condliffe suggests there are 'three broad components of conflict: *interests, emotions* and *values*' (1991: 7). Interests, which are both subjective and

Table 5.1   Bisno's sources of conflict

1. *Biosocial sources*	Many theorists place frustration–aggression as the source of conflict. According to this approach frustration often results in aggression which leads to conflict. Frustration also results from the tendency for expectations to increase more rapidly than improvement in circumstances. This is known as 'relative deprivation', and is the reason conflict is often intensified when concessions are made. This tendency can be observed in world conflicts.
2. Personality and interactional sources	These include: abrasive personalities; psychological disturbances; lack of, or poor, interpersonal skills; irritation between people; rivalry; differences in interactional styles; inequities (inequalities) in relationships.
3. Structural sources	Many conflicts are embedded in the structures of organizations and societies. Power, status and class inequities are the underlying forces in many forms of conflict. The civil rights and feminist movements spring from structural sources of conflict.
4. Cultural and ideological sources	Intense conflicts often result from differences in political, social, religious and cultural beliefs. Conflict also arises between people with differing value systems.
5. Convergence	In many settings these various sources of conflict converge. In other words, they interact to produce a complex dispute. There may be many reasons, for example, why two workers within an agency are in conflict. There may be structural reasons such as differences in power; or different personalities or interactional styles; or the beliefs, cultural and ideological, may differ between the two workers and these may also be contributing to the complexity of the dispute.

Source: Adapted from Condiffe (1991). Reproduced with permission.

objective, are the things that motivate people and are usually the substantive issues in conflicts. Emotions are always present in conflict as in all human interaction. Values are the deeply held beliefs about the right way to behave (p. 7). Condliffe comments that 'emotional components of conflict should be dealt with first followed by management of the values and interests components' (p. 7).

Acceptable levels of disagreement and ways of responding to it are culturally defined. Culture also discriminates between women and men in prescribing acceptable behaviour in the face of conflict. For example, physical violence is typically a less acceptable method for women than it is for men. Conflict can be thought of in terms of disagreement, a desire to destroy or opposition. It is a necessary part of life, but we are not all equipped to handle it in a constructive way. Yet conflict can also be beneficial in a situation. Challenging others when there is some form of disagreement can be an important strategy in practice, for example when challenging discriminatory attitudes towards a particular service user.

Conflict is often experienced as draining, disruptive and destructive. It can occur within or between organizations, between workers, between communities, groups, family members and with those who work with them. Conflict can be dealt with by denial, avoidance or 'giving in', which may be effective strategies in minor outbursts. In most situations it is better dealt with by solving the cause of the problem, or by accepting or resolving the conflict (Kenny, 1999). The position the social worker occupies (for examples, as employee, care manager, supervisor) will have an important bearing on their capacity to be neutral, to see and deal with contradictory viewpoints, or on the bargaining capacity they may or may not have.

Conflict usually passes through a number of stages. Understanding the process of conflict assists the worker to separate the message the person is attempting to communicate from the structure in which the message occurs. The stages of conflict are broadly defined as:

- *Articulation*: saying that there is a conflict and what that conflict is;
- *Mobilization*: seeking out others or other information to support your point of view;
- *Personalization*: picking on attributes of the person that discredit them. Anger motivates the accuser to use language that defines the other as a non-person and hence as not entitled to normal courtesies. This escalates the conflict to the point where some change is required;
- *Redefinition*: rethinking your options, which may lead to one party accepting defeat, to a decision to separate or the acceptance of some form of conciliation process;
- *Institutionalization or resolution of conflict*: this instance of conflict either sets the pattern for future conflict, or it is resolved, in the sense that both parties feel they have gained.

Any particular instance of conflict does not necessarily follow these stages in a step-by-step manner. Political debate is often marked by a personalization of the conflict and little attention paid to the pros and cons of the issue at stake. The expression of emotion is part of the process of conflict but the successful resolution of conflict does require the rational consideration of the issues involved. Conflict resolution is usually achieved in one of three ways:

1 *Negotiation*: the parties involved talk to each other without any outsiders involved;
2 *Mediation*: a third party is invited in to mediate the discussion process but has no other power in the situation;
3 *Arbitration*: a third party is given the power to make a judgement between conflicting parties and has the power to enforce that judgement.

The basic principles of conflict resolution, from a social work perspective, derive from a commitment to social justice values, our understanding of the difficulties that arise between people and their social arrangements and our belief in the value of all human beings. These principles suggest that our objective in conflict resolution is to achieve a 'win–win' rather than a 'win–lose' outcome as far as possible. To achieve this, the worker must:

- identify and describe the ground rules for interaction;
- stick to the issues at the heart of the conflict rather than focus on the personalities involved;
- stick to the issues in a process sense rather than try to achieve a predetermined outcome;
- recognize that there are multiple solutions to a conflict.

All of these processes can be linked to the earlier discussion of problem solving, empowerment and group work. Twelvetrees (2001: 66) links success in dealing with conflict as a community worker to careful listening, assertiveness and focusing on issues rather than personalities. The processes of conflict and the principles that generally underlie its successful resolution are of particular importance in work with many service users who are forced into contact with social workers by their life situations.

IMPLEMENTING A SOCIAL MANDATE – WORKING WITH INVOLUNTARY CLIENTS

In situations where the service user is compelled to see the worker, such as when a person with complex mental health needs is 'sectioned' to hospital, the political dimension of the interactive process is predominant. In this case we refer to the person receiving services as a 'client' because the term 'service user' suggests a degree of autonomy and choice over the service delivery that is not present for involuntary clients. The person who is forced into contact with a social worker may not be the sole client, as the beneficiary of the work is also the wider community or those who are or will be allegedly at risk of harm. In this case the purpose of social work intervention, as conceptualized within our practice framework, is not just about helping the involuntary client to gain a greater sense of control over his or her life (where this does not oppress others) or to help them establish equitable relationships. Our purpose is also directed towards helping those affected by the involuntary client to maintain control over their own lives and to ensure they also experience equitable relationships.

Trotter (1999: 3) points out that the worker has a dual role, one part being legalistic/surveillance and the other a helping or problem-solving role. He notes that coming to terms with this dual role is an important practice task if work is to be effective. The following actions are associated with success in working with this dual role:

- Clarifying with the client just what your role is in terms of how these competing agendas are balanced and how that fits with any other workers involved. This includes explaining your role in any statutory procedures, the client's rights in these and the support/advocacy services that might be available to them;
- Giving clients as clear an idea as possible about what your intervention will involve, how long it might take and who will know what about the work done;
- Being clear about your expectations of the client and what areas are or are not negotiable, given the issue that has brought him or her in contact with the authority you represent;
- Understanding the client's expectations of the intervention and being explicit about which of these expectations might be met in this relationship (pp. 47–59).

An important dimension in all practice is the extent to which individuals, groups and communities are compelled, in a range of ways, to engage with different health and social care practitioners, including social workers. People are forced into contact with workers because they have broken some law (prisoners, probationers, young offenders), or because they are alleged to have breached minimum community standards (for example, child neglect/abuse), or because of their status (for example, as patients in a hospital), and they are powerless to refuse it. The distinction between volunteering for services and being compelled to use services is not always clear. People may appear to be volunteering, but may feel coerced by a range of threats into accepting assistance – for example, you may agree to see a university student counsellor for assistance with personal issues because you understand that your request for an extension for an assignment may be rejected unless you seek such assistance. In this section we are discussing intervention relating to practice where it is clear that the person/s receiving the service have not sought contact with your service.

The status of 'involuntary' is associated with clients being seen as 'resistant', 'manipulative' and perhaps 'dependent'. Different approaches to working with involuntary clients involve different ways of understanding such responses that are generally seen as unhelpful by the worker but may be quite functional for the individual. There is a range of ways of working with involuntary clients. Often in social services work, there is detailed guidance on the appropriate management of the relationship and the tasks that should take place. Two approaches, that may well interact with each other, are briefly outlined here. The first takes a social conflict perspective, and the second is solution focused. Both approaches must take into account the social mandate that brought you, as a worker, and the client together.

CONFLICT RESOLUTION WITH THE INVOLUNTARY CLIENT

'The central assumptions of the conflict perspective are that the client is in conflict with some powerful aspect of the social context and that interaction between the social worker and client will deal directly with this conflict' (Cingolani, 1984: 444). The roles that the worker takes, Cingolani argues, have an impact on the relationships that develop. Different relationships have different opportunities for client, worker and statutory authorities. Cingolani (pp. 444–5) describes the relationships associated with two roles at the high-conflict end of the continuum where the focus is on the interests of society: enforcer (the explicit use of the organization's power) and negotiator (representing the interests of the organization and bargains with the client). At the lower end of the conflict continuum she suggests the roles of advocate and coach, which are linked to 'an explicit identification with the client's interests' (p. 445). Practitioners should be aware of the appropriate stance to take in a given situation and where making choices should be as conscious of this as possible.

Imagine you have been asked, by way of an anonymous phone call to the social services duty desk, to investigate the alleged abuse of a child. In line with the relevant legislation (e.g. in England, the Children Act 1989) you are obliged to investigate and report quickly. There appear to be no existing agency records relating to the family so you only have the information provided by the anonymous referrer. In line with agency policy relating to 'first contact' home visits, you arrange to visit with a colleague. You also advise colleagues of your planned visit, record details of the visit and the time of your expected return to the office, and make sure you have a mobile phone with you.

(Continued)

When you and your colleague arrive and explain your reason for calling, the mother seems resentful but passive. The house appears fairly chaotic and the young children are very wary of you. Your first task, after describing the reason for your visit, is to encourage the mother to say what she thinks of the allegations. She may give monosyllabic replies so that you start to feel angry and upset with her. Rather than reacting to your own feelings, you could use these feelings as a guide to how the mother might be feeling. Rather than pushing and prodding to get answers to your questions, it may be more constructive to draw her attention to the fact that she may well be very angry at your visit but at a loss to know how to express that anger. She may well be able then to say what her anger is about. Some of it may be focused on you and some on whoever she believes phoned social services in the first place.

If the conflict with you can be described, there is some hope of moving forward rather than both of you enduring a cat-and-mouse game of evasion. Perhaps this mother becomes very angry with you. She believes she is doing a good job as a mother and that others will back her up. She cannot believe that someone so young and inexperienced, someone who wears jeans to work, can have any ability to assess the situation. You are worrying her and upsetting the children and it's a poor world where councils bully women struggling to do their best with the children. In saying these things, she has quickly moved to personalization in an attempt to take charge of the situation.

The hallmark of successful conflict resolution is to act, rather than react – to continue to value the individual even though we do not value some of their actions. In our example it is important to respond in a way that doesn't trivialize the depths of the mother's anger and anxiety in the situation by saying obvious things like, 'I can see you are upset!' This sort of response fuels the emotional fires and distances the other person from you even more. It might be more appropriate to respond with a statement along the lines that you are both concerned to ensure the children are not under too much stress, but that looking after children brings its own stress and to inquire whether she has any support. Here you are attempting to move to a redefinition of the issues and perhaps setting up a relationship based on negotiation. If the client accepts your attempts to join with her in this way, you are both in a better position to begin a more honest exploration of the difficulties that are present in the situation.

Despite our best efforts to process anger and resentment and find common ground, the client may reject our attempts. One strategy for the woman may be to maintain her anger with you, refusing to be drawn into any discussion about the alleged abuse. This generally doesn't happen. Most people realize that their best interests are served by at least appearing to comply with the social worker's agenda. In this situation, the client may take a more passive outward stance, while inwardly remaining angry and distrustful, in an attempt to try to satisfy the worker that there is no cause for further contact. The client is usually responding as best she can to survive and retain control over what is a threatening situation involving many potential risks to whatever style of life she may be leading. Inwardly, clients may well be feeling extremely vulnerable in relation to authority, although their external behaviour may not reveal this. This example highlights the importance of social workers complying with the agency's safety procedures so that the risk of harm against the worker is minimized. In this situation it is important that there were two workers visiting and that they were able to stay in communication with their office and emergency services if needed. Unfortunately social services departments are often so stretched that they do not have the time to follow through on the effects of these visits, which are stressful and may indeed precipitate worse family conflict than existed before the visit.

When students role-play such situations, they often appear one-dimensional – as very authoritarian or very placating. This results, as Jordan (1979) suggests, from the worker splitting off their contradictory reactions to the situation and is a way of coping with the intra-personal conflict they experience in the role. It is difficult to stay natural in unnatural, worrying or threatening situations. At least some of the problems we have in resolving conflicts in these situations are that we have not come to terms with our authority and that we are therefore less flexible and spontaneous in the use we make of ourselves. This means we are constrained in making full use of ourselves at a time when we want to be most competent.

Reflecting on what has happened and recognizing our internal reactions to the situation are prerequisites to successful conflict resolution. Once we stop listening with all of ourselves, it is difficult to hear what the issues are or to imagine what it might be like to be the other person. If it is possible to resolve the conflict so that both people feel they have gained, it may be possible to move to a helping relationship, in that there is a desire to work together and not just compulsion forcing the client to keep in contact.

People who are characterized as involuntary clients may also be seen as resistant, vulnerable and perhaps dependent (Brill, 1995). Nelson (1975: 587) noted that the term 'resistant' is often seen as pejorative and places responsibility for intervention failures on the 'resistant' and the 'unmotivated', when these may well be appropriate responses to significant stresses. Such assessments have a cultural lens. Ho and Chui (2001) argue that youth workers in Hong Kong were more likely to link resistance to missing appointments and being unwilling to discuss problems, than to disarming and proactive behaviours such as superficial compliance and telling lies, as had been identified by Pipes and Davenport (1990) in the USA. In addition, the perspective of involuntary clients is likely to be different to the views of the workers. For example, Diorio's (1992) report of interviews with 13 parents receiving mandatory protective services highlights the vulnerability, fear and inherent abuse experienced by these parents.

If any overt conflict can be resolved to the point where it is possible to identify acceptable outcomes for intervention, a solution-focused approach has been shown to be an effective way forward.

SOLUTION-FOCUSED WORK WITH INVOLUNTARY CLIENTS

This form of practice can be regarded as a form of the strengths perspective outlined by Saleeby (1997). Workers in statutory agencies negotiate between attempting to empower and cooperate with the people with whom they come in contact, and being obliged to use positions of authority to ensure the safety of individuals and community members at large. Durrant (1996: x) argues that this 'either–or' stance is self-defeating: '(I)t *is* the cooperative, non-adversarial relationship (which values what families say they want rather than what workers think they should want) that is the key to fulfilling our statutory obligations to ensure children's safety.' Given the political nature of most involuntary work, it is not surprising that the literature indicates that work with people who do not want contact with social work services is most likely to break down during the initial stages, when workers and clients seek agreement on what will be done (Ivanoff et al., 1994). A solutions-oriented approach values individuals and families; looks at behaviour that may be seen as 'difficult' or 'manipulative' in terms of what it accomplishes; and cooperates with individuals and families to identify what they would like to achieve and how that may be done as a basis for building a working relationship. The basic work process resembles the stages of problem solving described earlier.

The solution-focused approach gives pre-eminence to the issues identified by the person called the client or service user, even though these may have significant consequences for them. In involuntary work, De Jong and Berg (2001: 364) suggest 'inviting the client into the role of expert', asking for their perceptions of the situation that has led to the current interaction and what they hope for in the future. The client's successes and strengths, rather than their problems, and their hopes for the future are elicited as a base for further cooperative work. Of course, if people make choices that harm others and perhaps themselves, they will be faced with the consequences. The point made here is that people's right to make choices needs to be respected and we need to continue to try to find ways of understanding with the other person so that cooperative work is more likely to be constructive for all concerned.

A number of authors suggest other specific behaviours that are likely to be useful, particularly at the initial stages of contact with involuntary clients. Brodsky and Lichtenstein (1999: 219) suggest using statements instead of questions. Asking questions tends to exacerbate the power imbalance in the relationship more than a 'reciprocal and cooperative working together'. By making statements (without the rising inflection) about your own reactions, what you can see and hear and about possible choices the client is given the choice about responding, rather than being prodded to answer within a framework that you have determined.

Work with involuntary clients is usually structured by government legislation and guidance, as well as by local authority procedures. However, social workers in a range of situations, including mental health and child protection work, still exercise considerable autonomy in the way they form relationships with involuntary clients. We argue that it is important for workers to be open and honest about the tensions in the relationship and allow clients the opportunity to express their frustration and seek support (probably from another source). While the nature of the work, the possible outcomes and people's rights should be explained clearly, it is important to recognize clients' strengths and expertise in their own experiences.

PROVIDING LONG-TERM CARE

The appeal of social work undoubtedly lies in achieving change and removing the barriers to greater autonomy and social fulfilment. Such activities are usually time limited. They allow the worker to demonstrate the efficacy of their skills and the power of their knowledge base. However, much practice is concerned with maintaining the interactions that people already have with their social arrangements. Change may be directed towards restraining the forces which will make things worse for people who face chronic strains in living because of, for example, their physical or mental health.

Unfortunately these basic activities of caring and supporting have tended to be valued less by the profession and society as a whole than those activities which are perceived to be more change oriented. Incorrectly, the skills of those involved in long-term care are often seen as being akin to 'common sense'. It is not surprising that this form of general long-term care usually has gender overtones: it is associated with women caring, and contrasts with the male image of dynamic, go-getting (and high-status) change agent. In contrast, we argue that long-term care work is a highly skilled activity. It involves supporting people through periods of loss and grief and times of relationship conflict. It also involves evaluating the risks presenting in a person's circumstances and acting to minimize these while promoting the person's self-determination. Maintaining an effective and empowering relationship with the service user over a long period of time is a complex task. The importance of social care has recently been articulated by the New Labour government, which stresses the need for workers who combine 'the right human qualities as well as the necessary knowledge and skills' and who are 'open, honest, warm, empathetic and respectful, who treat people using services with equity, are non-judgemental and challenge unfair discrimination' (DoH, 2005: 14).

In line with Davies (1985) we argue that caring is central to social work practice as it is expressed in relationships and as it takes place on a day-to-day basis. For most people in ongoing contact with social workers, 'it is the day in day out routine that truly identifies the nature of social work' (p. 34). Caring is described by Fisher and Tronto as 'a species activity that includes everything we do to maintain, continue, and repair our 'world' so that we can live in it as well as possible' (1990: 40). Sevenhuijsen (1998: 1–2) comments that we would all like to receive dedicated care if we were in a position that required such care, but most of us hope we will never be in this position and hence we can find it difficult to really value the care we provide. Davies goes so far as to argue that the central focus of social work is not change, but maintenance – that is, it is concerned with maintaining both the 'individual and society as a whole and with negotiating the interdependent relationship between each individual and society: it is a policy of reconciliation' (1985: 31–2).

Caring is staying with people through the ups and downs of their lives. This involves helping them improve their living conditions, finding ways around obstacles, finding and using new resources, spending time listening to what people think, feel and do about their situation, and encouraging and supporting them to live the sort of life they want. This demands the creative use of self, outlined in our section on building and maintaining relationships in Chapter 3. Long-term supportive work may be a frustrating process for workers who wish to achieve 'cures' rather than be involved with others in the business of living their lives. Many of those marginalized in our society, such as frail older people and people with mental health needs, live their lives conscious of the extra pressures created by living on the margins. Working with them means sharing the hurt and frustration of discrimination as well as the joy in achievements and a recognition of strengths greater than those we have ourselves.

Where people are conscious of specific issues in their lives, or where the authorities have identified some issues, it is relatively easy for the social worker or social care worker to maintain a focus for work. Other people referred for a social work service may not have, or may not wish to identify, a specific problem, though the worker may assess their situation as beset by significant unmet needs. While we may see their situation as far from satisfactory, they themselves may feel that they have made an adjustment to their circumstances that best suits them. They may simply not agree with our assessment of their situation or may feel that the risks involved in change do not warrant the effort. We need to be aware of the ideologies that inform normative expectations about what is right for people when we seek to understand their situations. Experts often insist that older people, for example, should be as independent and active as possible and avoid an isolated existence in order to lead a healthy old age. It is important to be aware that social workers, like other professionals, have tended to stereotype older people as incapable of change and have consequently tended to offer limited services based on practical assistance (Phillipson, 1982; Bowl, 1986). It is essential to offer them the full range of opportunities that we would offer any other group of people. It is also equally important to accept that people may choose to live their lives in their own way and that they would like some contact with us, but on their own terms. Older people living alone are a frequent target for other people's concerns and the worker may keep in contact to monitor the situation – to be available at the time when an undefined 'something' happens.

In these contexts, people may be very happy to spend time with the worker, but do not give them the satisfaction of providing a 'problem'. Rather, the person would like to discuss ideas and issues, talk about the past, go out and generally try to relate as a person and not as a service user. Students and workers may characterize practice activity in this situation as 'friendly visiting' and not 'proper' social work. Perhaps it is more accurate to say that, as social workers, we are not always sure how to best help in these contexts, rather than saying that we should not get involved. We have limited knowledge about how to be effective when faced with diffuse social needs that refuse to be defined as problems.

One effective approach is to locate people who need long-term support in the context of their networks, their community and their resources. The form of intervention then develops as one of co-worker in the task of living rather than worker and service user in the task of solving problems. According to Payne (1986) social care means meeting the needs of particular individuals, families or groups by enabling them to use resources which exist or can be created in the most effective way.

The process of resource creation by building community networks, or questioning the accessibility and relevance of existing services, 'stimulates political and personal resistance among relatively powerful people in agencies and in service users' lives' (Payne, 1986: 7). For the social care worker adopting this approach, it is important to develop their own support structures to provide them with the energy to keep going through the inevitable rough patches. And for social workers (e.g. as care managers) who are not directly providing this level of long-term support, it is essential that they consider the impact of the work on other social care workers and, with their local authorities, ensure that resources are provided to enable them to carry out their job well (e.g. training and appropriate payment). We will be discussing the processes of care management in the next chapter.

CHAPTER SUMMARY

In this chapter we have considered a number of intervention strategies: working with groups, problem-solving processes, conflict resolution, long-term supportive care, community building and networking. Each of these can assist us in pursuing the purpose of social work – to improve the interactions between people and their social arrangements – that we have outlined in our practice framework. It is clear that any intervention has a starting point, sustaining period and some form of terminating phase. We have described these phases in working with groups, and in problem-solving and conflict situations. It is interesting to observe the similarities and differences in structuring interactions across approaches.

Assessments and interventions by social workers take place in organizational contexts. Social work and social care personnel work in, with, for and against organizations, and the organization may encourage or restrict the worker's creativity in intervention. Understanding organizations and issues for social workers in organizational work is the focus of the next chapter.

NOTE

In this text, we provide a simplified version of the original COMPASS framework. For a more comprehensive description, see Kelly and Sewell (1988).

FURTHER READING

Lehmann, P. and Coady, N. (eds) (2001) *Theoretical Perspectives for Direct Social Work Practice: A Generalist-Eclectic Approach.* New York: Springer Publishing Co.
This American book provides an overview of different theories and models of social work practice with individuals, families and groups. The editors make use of a problem-solving approach in reviewing these theories and models.
Doel, M. and Sawdon, C. (1999) *The Essential Groupworker: Teaching and Learning Creative Groupwork.* London: Jessica Kingsley Publishers.
Drawing on a model of group work training used within a local authority, this book examines critical issues in group development and, importantly, issues of power and oppression in group experiences. The book engages the reader through a series of activities that assist in understanding the role of the worker in setting up, planning and maintaining groups.
Twelvetrees, A. (2001) *Community Work,* 3rd edn. Basingstoke: Palgrave.
This well-established text introduces readers to a wide range of issues in community work, including urban regeneration, and articulates the values that underpin different approaches to community work. There is also a valuable discussion of survival strategies for practitioners.

USEFUL WEBSITES

Access Funds: www.access-funds.co.uk.
Barefoot Social Worker: www.radical.org.uk/barefoot.
Black Information Link: www.blink.org.uk.

Charities Information Bureau: www.cibfunding.org.uk.
Communities Online: www.communities.org.uk.
Refugee Council: www.refugeecouncil.org.uk.
Rural Community Network: www.ruralcommunitynetwork.org.

REFLECTIVE QUESTIONS

1. Think of a situation in which you have been confronted by a problem, either on placement, at work or in your own life. Describe the processes you used to deal with this problem. Identify the similarities and differences between what you did and what the problem-solving approach might suggest as appropriate action.

2. In dealing with conflict situations, how do you commonly respond? What makes it harder or easier for you to manage conflict? Identify the principles you apply in conflict situations.

3. What do you see as the similarities and differences between long-term and short-term work with individuals? When is long-term work appropriate? What issues might you have to deal with in your relationship with the person, in your agency and with explaining your work to colleagues?

6 INTERVENTION AND THE ORGANIZATIONAL CONTEXT

In this chapter we examine:

- The nature of organizations that employ social workers;
- Gender issues in social work organizations;
- Questions to help map an organization;
- Practice principles for working in organizations;
- Working together with others (including teamwork);
- Case management and care management;
- An example of hospital-based care management;
- Records and report writing;
- Advocacy;
- Developing policy.

Social workers are employed, directly or indirectly, by organizations. In our practice framework we have highlighted the focus of social work practice as understanding the interactions and tensions between people and social arrangements. In addition to recognizing the context of social welfare policies and politics as partly constructing these social arrangements, it is possible to see the organizational context of social work and social care delivery as contributing to people's social arrangements. At the very least they determine the range of resources that might or might not be available to service users. In social work practice the purposeful use of self through assessments and interventions is also mediated by the organizational context. How social workers can use themselves, what assessment processes they are able to engage in and what range of intervention strategies are available are all influenced by their organizational roles and, in turn, the role their organization plays in society. However, organizations do not have to be seen solely as a constraint to social work practice. Social workers utilize the resources of organizations to assist others to achieve their goals and they target organizations as objects of their interventions. Just as it is necessary to develop the knowledge and skills to engage with people, effective practice requires organizational knowledge and skills.

Social work practice is shaped by and shapes (albeit sometimes reluctantly and hesitantly) the organizations which employ us and with which we interact. There are inevitable tensions between practitioners and organizations because:

1. Organizations control access to social resources. They are, therefore, a site of conflict over the distribution and redistribution of social and material resources;
2. Social work is frequently practised in contexts where knowledge and practice is contested not just by other professional groups (such as nursing, medicine and so on), but by service users and the community;
3. Social work and social care organizations are often the targets of our own or other workers' intervention. The manner in which services are delivered/not delivered is itself the cause of the tension between people and social arrangements;
4. The organizational context is where we each experience ourselves as workers and hence confront the issues of autonomy and control over our own work, responsibility for work and the ability to work with others.

It is because of these tensions that we highlight in our practice framework the importance of having a good understanding of organizational processes in order to work strategically within the organizations that employ us. The National Occupational Standards (NOS) for social work and Scottish Standards in Social Work Education (SiSWE) also emphasize the importance of social workers being effective and accountable organizational workers. Competence in organizational work involves being able to manage a workload, contribute to the management of resources, prepare organizational records and reports, and work effectively in teams and networks.

This chapter aims to assist you to understand the organizational context of practice and to develop a repertoire of intervention strategies and skills to successfully work in and influence organizations (and survive!). To this end, this chapter is made up of two parts. The first part explores conceptualizations of organizations and their relations to practice. We argue that when practice is conceptualized apart from the organizational context, difficulties result for practitioners. The second part of this chapter explores five aspects of intervention and the organizational context: working with others, case and care management, report writing, advocacy, and policy development. In selecting these aspects of organizational practice to focus on we recognize that we have not examined in depth the human resources context and the experience of social workers as employees. To assist your reading in this regard we direct you to Coulshed and Mullender (2001). In Figure 6.1 we incorporate the organizational context and related interventions into our practice framework.

SOCIAL WORK PRACTICE AND THE ORGANIZATIONAL CONTEXT

Organizations have been conceptualized in terms of functions, types, goals and structures (see Heraud, 1979: 147–56). For our purposes, it is sufficient to conceptualize them as groupings of people, processes and structures established to achieve certain goals through

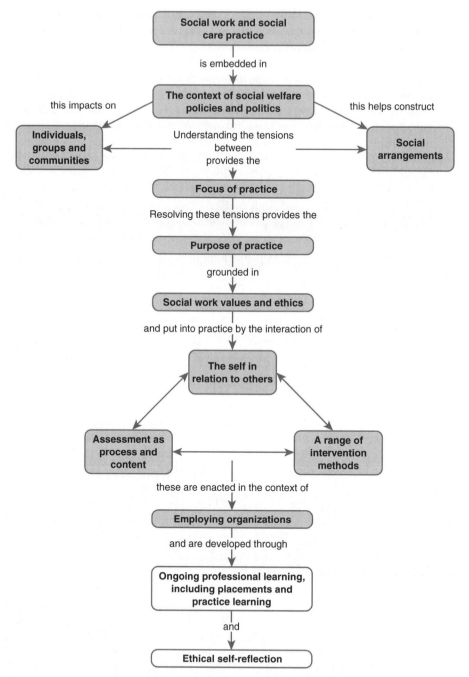

Figure 6.1 Interventions and the organizational context in the practice framework

programmes of activities. Such a definition seeks to encompass many organizational forms, from the small community centre staffed mainly by volunteers to the large bureaucracy. It does not assume that organizations are monolithic in terms of structure, goals or internal norms. Indeed, organizations can be thought of as arenas of conflicting interest (Collins, 1975: 289) in which participants attempt to pursue their own purposes. While the term 'organization' or 'agency' is often used as if it had a will of its own, agencies are in fact the people working for them, and organizational decisions are always the result of individuals interpreting and expressing decisions in accordance with humanly constructed procedures.

The notion of 'organization' explicitly and implicitly embodies elements of routinization and structure necessary for the delivery of services and/or the achievement of goals. Such routinization may reflect an explicit methodology of practice by which the organization seeks to achieve its goals (e.g. a family centre which advocates a particular approach to practice). Alternatively, it may extend only to the provision of the physical supports necessary to undertake the task at hand (e.g. a home care agency). It may involve compliance with a detailed protocol or, on the other hand, reporting irregularly to a loose collection of confederates who constitute a 'management committee'.

Social work and other social care occupations exist only in, or in relation to, some form of organizational context, which in turn is part of the social arrangements with which the occupations, workers and service users interact. The form of practice influences, and is influenced by, the organizational context. This is, of course, a source of tension. Social work practice transcends a particular organizational context, but practice cannot exist apart from the organizational context. Just as we need to understand communities, helping processes, human development and so on, we need to understand the nature of the organizations which employ us and with which we interact.

UNDERSTANDING THE ORGANIZATION: WHAT DOES THE AGENCY EXPRESS?

To practise effectively, it is necessary to understand what the agency expresses both explicitly and implicitly. Each agency has its own history. Many practitioners are prepared to criticize their own and other organizations at the macro level but are far more defensive about criticisms of the effects of their own practice or that of their immediate work group. This is not really surprising. On the whole, people enter social work out of a desire to help (O'Connor and Dalgleish, 1986), to 'do good', and this can blind us to the damage that sometimes results from our actions and the actions of our agencies (see O'Connor and Sweetapple, 1988; O'Connor, 1989, 1993).

Critiques of social care agencies and practices in the media and in some educational programmes are often oversimplified; for instance, emphasizing the coercive and repressive aspects of statutory child protection services. Yet students and practitioners entering such services see the dedication of overworked colleagues seeking to do the best job they can, and to maximize the positives of their interventions and minimize the negatives.

However, agencies don't simply express the sum total of the actions of the people working there. They express their history and their contradictory functions within the context of the state. For example, there is a long residue of bitterness and suspicion directed at social work from its service users and potential service users. Many mental health service users identify themselves as survivors, not so much because of their survival of their own health issues, but because of their survival of the 'system'. The stereotyping of young black men as aggressive and their over-representation in the more coercive end of the mental health system (Takei et al., 1998), already impacts on how black people experience white organizations as oppressive and institutionally racist. The legacy of this oppression will continue to affect the delivery of mental health services and social work for many years to come.

Agencies also express and reinforce wider divisions and patterns of inequality in society, particularly those based on gender, 'race', ethnicity and disability. The tendency for organizations to perpetuate gender inequality has, for example, received increasing attention in the last decade. Two interrelated issues are significant here. First, it can be argued that organizational structures, particularly bureaucratic forms, structure the delivery of social services and caring relationships in ways that have special implications for women as service providers and service users. Second, gender relationships impact on organizational life.

GENDER AND SOCIAL WORK ORGANIZATIONS

Social work and social care are traditionally equated with 'women's work' – women are over-represented as workers and service users (Dale and Foster, 1986: 96). However, men are over-represented as managers and they appear to reach these positions much more quickly than women. Providing care to people is one of the main purposes of the health and social care sector (Baines et al., 1991: 27). The activity of caring is traditionally associated with women but the way in which that care is delivered reflects patriarchal norms of the wider society (Camilleri and Jones, 2001: 26). Care is often delivered in the context of hierarchical structures, routinization and partialization of tasks, vertical decision-making processes and distancing of those people involved in direct service user contact from those who hold most control over decisions about organizational policy and procedures. Through the 'caring' professions of social work, social care, nursing and teaching, women have been able to transfer caring ideals and skills developed in the domestic arena into public life (Baines, 1991: 37).

Feminists such as Finch and Groves (1983) distinguish between 'caring about' and 'caring for'. Both forms of caring may be done in conjunction with each other, but one tends to be more dominant at any one time. 'Caring about' is characterized as an intellectual activity that is linked to objectivity rather than friendship, a sense of professionalism, while 'caring for' is linked to personal relationships with people and the actual tasks of physical and emotional care (Hugman, 1991). Camilleri and Jones argue that the relationship between these discourses of care account for the divisions within social care services where men are more likely to end up in positions of power:

> (T)he discourse of 'care' provides for a reading of 'caring for' as essentially a defining dimension of women's identity, a reading that serves to lock them into patriarchal structures and into a prescribed identity as natural carers. It is a discourse that appears to exclude men. Men on the other hand are identified with 'caring about' where judgements are made on the basis of male 'rationality' and 'logic'. (2001: 29)

McMaster concurs, adding that the 'historical roots of gender inequality are alive and well within social work today' (2001: 111). This is fuelled in western cultures by the competitive, hierarchical and individualistic nature of society, characteristics generally associated with male identities.

From this perspective it is suggested that men who choose to work in direct caring roles challenge dominant models of masculinities (Connell, 2000) and construct a different discourse on practice (Camilleri and Jones, 2001: 30) and the organization of services. But they may also have to confront a stereotype of male care workers that is linked to sexuality. 'For masculinity in this culture, "real" men do not do "women's work". Those who provide care have to be accounted for' (p. 30). Identity for men is largely bound up with being a worker and while this might mean, as Camilleri and Jones argue, that men have privileged spaces in the public arena, a career in caring is problematic within the dominant discourse on masculinity.

Although paid work in social work and social care professions has enabled many women to gain some measure of independence and autonomy, societal definitions of women have continued to shape and control women's experiences of paid work. 'Identity for women workers is typically meshed with being partners, mothers, daughters and so on' (Camilleri and Jones, 2001: 29). Women have had to demonstrate that paid work did not destroy their feminine attributes and virtue. This is demonstrated very clearly in the entry of women into occupations such as nursing (Reverby, 1987) and social work. These professions enabled women to perform socially useful work while remaining subordinate to male professionals and conforming to prevailing social norms about the role and nature of women. For many women, then, human service work involves ongoing struggles for greater autonomy.

Recent developments in Britain have emphasized the importance of social care work. These include the development of the Code of Practice for Social Care Workers, the increased take-up of National Vocational Qualifications (NVQs) in social care and in the workforce initiatives in the government's Green Paper, *Independence, Well-being and Choice* (DoH, 2005). We have yet to see if these will substantially improve the status of social care work and the predominantly female workforce that carries out this work. What is needed is support from governments and social services organizations for social care workers to be involved in holistic care activities. Ideally social care work occurs in the context of personal relationships, where there is flexibility, tolerance of uncertainty and scope for adaptability to changing needs. Unfortunately bureaucratic forms tend to cut across such relationships (Abel and Nelson, 1990: 13). Standardized techniques, performance measures that focus on outcomes while ignoring processes, and record keeping that fails to capture the nuances of care work can stifle connectedness, mutuality and personalization in care relationships.

Our individual interventions cannot be totally separated from past processes and outcomes and current patterns of inequality, based on gender, class, 'race', sexuality, age and disability. We need, therefore, to stand back and subject the practices and processes of any agency to scrutiny in order to understand their changing functions in terms of their histories, their intended and unintended outcomes and the perception and experience of the agency's services by its service users and potential service users. It is necessary to understand the differing levels of your agencies – the committees, the teams, the internal lines of authority, the external lines and so on – in those terms.

ORGANIZATIONS ARE NOT MONOLITHIC

The fact that agencies and organizations express far more than the actions of individual workers does not mean that the nature and consequences of individual practices are pre-set by the functions of the agency. To take such a deterministic approach to practice is to assume that:

1. Organizations are viewed as givens (i.e. they are stable and are not an appropriate focus of intervention);
2. Organizations are coherent wholes with common goals, shared values and a unity of purpose; and
3. Common goals and values exist across the social work and social care sector.

These assumptions are contradicted by research on organizations and the lived experiences of workers in agencies. Organizations are conflict ridden. Despite what might be dictated in government or organizational policy, many social work organizations have no central value system and multiple vague goals. Frequently there is also conflict over organizational goals between external as well as internal actors.

In addition to vague and conflicting goals, the nature of social work practice results in newly qualified practitioners exercising considerable functional autonomy and discretion in their practice. This discretion is not unlimited, but it does exist, and practitioners exercise it constantly.

These conflicts, contradictions and autonomy are of importance to practitioners and service users. Conflicts within and between organizations are negotiated and resolved in everyday life: in the office, in hospital wards, on the streets and in the service user's home. The contradictions create spaces that allow practitioners to exercise their discretion – that is, they provide room to move. Workers can make use of the contradictions and influence the organization. Workers can deviate from organizational norms for or against the service user.

MAPPING THE ORGANIZATION

Successful social work practice depends on a detailed understanding of the organization in which you work, in addition to the organizations which you seek to influence. To achieve such an understanding it is necessary to understand the relationship between the history of the organization and its current structure and function, as well as the organization's relationship with the socio-political context. In essence, developing such an understanding involves 'mapping the organization'. The following questions will assist you to map your organization:

1. What were the organization's original goals and charter?
2. a) What are its current stated goals and charter?
   b) What goals are currently operating?
3. What is the source of its right to operate (e.g. formal state auspice, church auspice and so on)?

4. What are the sources of financial, political and professional support?
5. What are its primary areas of concern?
6. What statutory mandate does the agency exercise and what are its legal responsibilities?
7. How is the agency organized administratively and professionally?
8. What are the formal and informal lines of authority? Who are staff formally responsible to? Who decides who does what in the agency?
9. How do service users perceive the agency?
10. To what extent does the organization define or determine the nature of service user problems?
11. Who makes, and what are, the processes by which key organizational and professional decisions are made?
12. a) Who decides what social workers do in the agency?
    b) In what areas do social workers exercise discretion in the agency?
13. How do staff relate to each other?
14. How do you relate to other staff?

PRACTICE PRINCIPLES

From our discussion of practice and organizations, a series of principles can be derived to inform our practice. These principles are developed in line with our practice framework and are intended to assist social workers to put into effect social work's purpose: to improve the tensions between people and social arrangements by helping people take more control in their lives and by facilitating equitable relationships. The principles for organizational practice are as follows:

1. *Determine if the organization is a target of, or ally in change.* In assessing presenting situations, it is important to scrutinize the agency in as much depth as service users' lives for causes of and solutions to problems. The agency should be conceptualized as an ally in and/or target of change;

2. *Exploit your autonomy.* We have previously noted that newly qualified workers have a degree of autonomy and scope to exercise formal and informal power. As front-line workers, newly qualified practitioners often have most direct contact with service users and must deal with complex and competing demands from three main sets of relationships: with supervisors, co-workers (in their own and other agencies) and service users. In dealing with these complexities in day-to-day practice, you can exercise discretionary power in a number of areas:

    a) Decisions about how you use your time.
    b) Choices about how you present and share information: Where there is a lack of congruence between service users' needs and wants and the needs and wants of the agency. Here there is a choice of whether to resolve that conflict by leaving the issue as the service user's 'problem' or by pressuring the agency – that is, whether you pass the pressure down the line, or send it up.
    c) Interpretation of policy and choice of action: You can interpret policy creatively and act on the basis of your autonomy. It is often a tactical decision whether, in blurred areas, you should seek definite rulings on policy or not. The advantage of seeking a definite ruling is that a positive decision binds further decision making and hence influences the treatment of others. If the 'test case' fails, however, the discretion to act in favour of individuals is removed.

    d) Developing your own power base: Your own power base can be developed by gaining detailed knowledge of areas of relevance to the organization and of who has control over local resources. In so doing, you will alter the informal lines of authority in the agency.

3. *Develop networks of support in the agency.* It is useful to seek to promote the development of work groups based on openness and sharing. This can enhance the tendency towards work group autonomy and the development of collective work structures;

4. *Separate self and agency.* It is important to be able to stand outside the agency. Over-identification blinds workers to issues of justice;

5. *Develop external supports.* This can be achieved through networking with workers in other agencies and through membership of special-interest groups, professional associations and unions;

6. *Perform a monitoring/watchdog role.* Use the Codes of Practice to monitor the organization's sensitivity to issues of justice. Facilitate service users' development and use of external 'watchdogs' (e.g. complaints mechanisms, advocacy services, lobby groups). Raise justice issues inside and outside the organization. Be prepared to act as a 'whistleblower' if your agency is acting illegally or unethically and is not responsive to change.

7. *Develop an understanding of how the law can be used to promote service users' rights.* The law (including legislation, case law and guidance) can be used not just to restrict individual freedom and access to services, but to enhance people's rights and ensure that these are met (Dalrymple and Burke, 1995). It is important for social workers, particularly those in social services departments, to be aware of the duties and powers of local authorities in relation to service users and of the power and relevance of other legislation, such as the Race Relations (Amendment) Act 2002.

These principles should underpin our approach to practice. As we gain experience in working creatively to influence the organization in which we work, we develop first-hand knowledge of how policy is actualized in everyday practice and impacts on the lives of service users. For example, the policies of our agency or broader social policies may be inequitable, may be based on inaccurate or outdated information, or may be ineffective in achieving stated organizational aims. Where these circumstances exist, we need to understand how to influence policies. This will often require a planned change effort.

In the remainder of this chapter we consider five intervention strategies that are very much defined by the organizational context of the social work practitioner. In striving to achieve the purpose of social work, the organizations themselves may be as much a site for intervention as are the individual service users.

WORKING TOGETHER WITH OTHERS

Many practitioners may only spend a small proportion of their time in direct contact with service users. The rest of their time is spent in activities such as meetings and report writing, and in following through contacts on behalf of others. As Stevenson notes, the actuality of social work practice 'is as much to do with seeing about clients as seeing them' (1981: x). This 'seeing about' activity involves contact with other people in our own agency, in the person's group or community network, or in other agencies. The processes involved are variously called conferring, cooperating, partnership, consulting, advocacy and working in teams. Before discussing teamwork and advocacy, we briefly consider the processes of conferring, cooperation, consulting and partnership. These are activities which involve 'working with others', but which don't occur exclusively in teams.

Conferring implies a respect for each other's opinions and a reciprocity between colleagues. It is a common collaborative process and may well involve non-professionals, such as a service user's carer. It may be a group effort when two or more professionals (and hopefully the individual or family concerned) are involved and the meeting is focused on the most appropriate course of action. Such a group is not a team, since each person remains autonomous and the purpose for the group's existence is short term. Workers also confer with colleagues within their organization to explore the need for new services or new ways of functioning, to generally discuss their work or to seek support and direction.

Cooperation may emerge from these different forms of conferring. From a recognition of the issues raised by conferring about a particular situation, those involved may agree to cooperate to resolve the issue or work through a particular task. These groups tend to be time limited, or else become established as ongoing teams (see next section).

Consulting is less reciprocal than conferring or cooperating. It is usually a matter of worker choice, with the person seeking the consultation selecting an 'expert' in the area under consideration. The expert may be inside or outside the organization, but the consultation process functions outside the structural hierarchy. The consultee is free to accept or reject the advice. Consultation is an advisory process to delineate and explore possible options and hence it enlarges the consultee's understanding. It assists the worker in gaining a different or enlarged perspective on his or her work without having options for practice limited by the process of seeking this advice. The focus is on the problem as presented by the consultee and not on the persons with whom the consultee is working. The challenge for students and new practitioners is knowing who to ask, and how to recognize the need for consultation as distinct from supervision (see Chapter 7).

Partnership is similar to cooperation in that it relies on a degree of reciprocity in the relationship. In organizational terms, it often refers to relationships between agencies or individuals in separate agencies or to relationships with service users, either individually or in groups. Partnership implies an ongoing commitment to achieving common goals and involves all parties taking responsibility for achieving those goals. Such partnerships may remain informal, although they may also be formalized in contracts or agreements between individuals or agencies, or in new organizational arrangements (for example, the partnership between health and social services in the formation of Care Trusts and between a range of services for children and young people in Children's Trusts). Mutual respect and a willingness to cooperate over an extended period of time are essential for partnerships to work. Thus, while government policy initiatives may often talk about the need for partnership between various agencies and with service users and may provide structures to enable partnership, if there is not a genuine commitment from all parties the partnership is unlikely to be successful. While partnerships may occur outside of teams or between different teams, for effective teamworking a sense of partnership is essential.

WHAT ARE TEAMS?

The existence of a team implies an organizationally sanctioned basis for people to work together. Not all people who work together form teams. Some people are brought together in a work situation but do not share work or cooperate to help each other. The 'ideal type' of team is a group made up of equals who have developed common goals and strategies to achieve more together than they could alone. Such teams are concerned with more than the specific tasks at hand: they consider the development of team members' skills and the context in which they work – whether that is the community and/or the organization. The leadership of the team aims to enhance the capacity of others to cooperate in reaching decisions. Members feel comfortable in challenging the ideas of others. Conflict is over issues, not personalities, and there is the time and energy to discuss these varying viewpoints. Of course, many teams do not meet these criteria (Payne, 1982; Brill and Levine, 2002). Often the relationships between different team members are not equal. This inequality is generally organizationally defined. Teams may be characterized by the process by which they develop and make decisions, by the disciplinary base, the structures they set up, the type of leadership and the work environment (Payne, 1982: 10).

TEAM DEVELOPMENT

The work environment is a significant factor in determining how teams develop. The development from a work group to a productive team has been considered in two different ways. One approach equates team development with group development. Thus it involves a process of moving through stages – in Brill and Levine's (2002: 213) terms, orientation, accommodation, negotiation, operation and dissolution. Obviously not all work groups move along this continuum. The reasons for this include the conditions under which people work, the amount of leadership effort put into fostering such cohesiveness and the personalities of those involved. A second approach interprets the development of teams as a product of the forces affecting the team. A developmental approach to teamwork requires consideration of the opportunities and the pressures which affect such development. Fatout and Rose (1995: 62–7) suggest that four forces of concern to work teams, generated by people interacting in a group, are communication, cohesion, control and culture. You could use these four categories to understand the health or otherwise of your team's functioning and to identify what action might be appropriate to ensure the team works as well as possible.

TYPES OF TEAMS

Social workers may be members of single-discipline teams and/or multi-disciplinary or multi-professional teams. *Single-discipline* teams are constituted by members of the same occupational group. *Multi-disciplinary* or *inter-disciplinary* teams are constituted by workers of different occupations. In the normal course of their work, workers may be part of both single-discipline and multi-disciplinary teams. Thus a hospital social worker may be a member of the social services team and a series of multi-disciplinary teams within the hospital. Teams may be constituted within a single organization or across organizations. The Local Safeguarding Children Board is an example of an *inter-agency* team, involving members from each of the main agencies responsible for safeguarding children: for example health services, the police, probation service, education and social services. Multi-professional or multi-agency teams bring together representatives from a range of services to address service user needs in a comprehensive way.

Teams do not exist in an organizational vacuum. The operation and functioning of multi-disciplinary or multi-professional, single-discipline and inter-agency teams should be considered in terms of the links between teams and the overall organizational structure. In the management of teams there is a crucial tension 'between achieving the organization's objectives and facilitating participation' (Payne, 2000: 346).

TEAMS AND THE ORGANIZATIONAL STRUCTURE

SINGLE-DISCIPLINE TEAMS

The most common organizational form involving single-discipline teams is the hierarchical structure. In this arrangement, teams (perhaps composed of the leaders of the next level down) control the activities of several other teams. The main advantage of this structure is that links of responsibility and accountability – at least within the organization – are clear. It is quite possible in this organizational form for leadership of the team to be shared among different workers, although the ultimate responsibility still rests with the designated workers. (This may be threatening to higher levels of the administration who do not feel they have as much direct control as they think they need.)

In a hierarchical organization, each person links two different organizational levels. The social worker is between the service user and the organization, their senior between the team for which they are responsible and the more senior levels of the organization, such as service managers. Those in boundary positions experience the stress of choosing between conflicting demands. However, as they have access to data on service user needs and gaps in service delivery, these boundary positions are also potential leverage points from which change in organizational structure or procedure that may benefit service users can be negotiated.

MULTI-DISCIPLINARY TEAMS

Most multi-disciplinary or inter-disciplinary teams operate with a matrix structure, where workers come together in teams according to their professional group. Examples of such a structure are clinical teams in hospitals and community mental health teams. Lines of responsibility are usually professionally to each profession's senior member and administratively, in terms of decisions about service users, to the designated team leader. This structure has both strengths and limitations. The drawback of this form of teamwork is that workers are left to negotiate the boundaries between their professional team and work team (and possibly their inter-agency team). Potentially it facilitates flexibility in formulating the most appropriate response to service users' needs by maximizing and coordinating the contributions of the different disciplines (and perhaps agencies). Leadership of multi-disciplinary teams in many health settings is determined by occupation, and not necessarily by the centrality of the tasks for which one profession may have responsibility. Payne (2000: 346) notes that doctors may see teamwork as a way of effectively implementing their treatment, while other professions may see it as a way of influencing medical decisions.

INTER-AGENCY TEAMS

Social workers have always worked with people from the same or different disciplines who are employed in different agencies. Inter-agency teams tend to work well when the task is clearly defined, there is energy and commitment for the task, the group is adequately resourced, members trust each other and are able to develop a collaborative work style. The focus is on encouraging the participation and cooperation of the required services to achieve the best outcome for a specific service user or to address a community issue, and there may be no hierarchical structure.

INFORMAL AND FORMAL LINES OF AUTHORITY

All organizational groups have formal and informal structures. Individual team members may exercise considerable power, which is acquired through their informal networks rather than their formal positions. What happens in the tearoom or in informal social gatherings after work may have more impact on outcomes than deliberations at formal team meetings. Lines of authority can also be influenced by control over information and communication resources. The person who types the minutes of a meeting can influence how that meeting (and decisions made in it) is represented. Similarly the person who controls use of the sole laser printer, photocopier or fax machine can influence the work patterns of others.

DEFINING AND ALLOCATING WORK

Regardless of the organizational structure within teams, decisions are made about the focus and allocation of work. In this decision making, Payne (1982: 23) points to the importance of distinguishing between tasks, which include the components of the workload allocation, and the roles and expectations of a particular worker. Roles are defined by clustering a set of tasks. Tasks may be decided:

- by considering the work currently undertaken, dividing that into jobs and designating the organizational level to which they belong; or
- by considering the goals and the organization's aims, deciding what needs to be done to achieve the goals and allocating tasks (and hopefully resources) on the basis of this analysis.

The first method is concerned with maintaining the status quo and is organizationally less contentious. The second is organizationally more threatening because existing arrangements are challenged and, generally speaking, some will have to lose out to free up resources so others may gain.

Assuming that the team has decided on the tasks it should tackle and has organized these into a series of roles, how are these roles allocated? The allocation of roles is influenced by status issues as well as by qualifications. The development of post-qualifying training may mean that in the future certain types of work (e.g. child protection investigations) are reserved for social workers with more advanced training. Those with further qualifications may be paid more or find promotion easier to achieve. This can cause tensions in the team. Not all professions are accorded the same status in the wider community and this is generally reflected in the team. High-status professionals such as doctors may feel competent to prescribe what the social worker should do and may unilaterally cut across their work by, for example, discharging a patient with little consultation. It is not surprising that lower-status professionals, such as nurses, social workers and teachers are predominantly female and the higher-status professionals are still predominantly male. The organization and its teams are a reflection of the society that sanctions them. The team structure may continue to maintain inequalities existing in society.

FUNCTIONING IN A TEAM

Effective work with colleagues, whether professional or non-professional, has the same requirements as any other part of practice. Respect for others, an appreciation of their individuality, good listening and communication skills, adequate knowledge of the area and an ability to convey to others what you are thinking, what you are able to do and what you have done are all important. Again, as in any form of social work practice, this behaviour takes place within the context of a set of structural and personal relationships, which affects the ease, or difficulty of working together effectively. The processes and issues associated with functioning in teams are influenced by the context of the team. Before considering issues relevant to all teams, the particular issues faced by workers in community work, in residential work and in secondary settings – primarily hospitals and other health settings – are highlighted.

In *community work teams* there is more linking of roles between the worker and those with whom he or she works. Indeed, those with whom he or she is to work may employ the worker. The team structure here may include the management committee or the local community group, as well as a loose collection of employed staff from a variety of local agencies. The values and objectives of community work encourage the development of groups of people who share common concerns and wish to act on them. A significant amount of the community worker's time will be spent in encouraging, educating and helping to focus the activities of this team without taking over the leadership role which is fostered for a community member.

The same close involvement with the service user group is evident in *residential work,* but generally this is within a hierarchical work structure. The question of who is the 'team' and who are the 'service users' is much more political in an institutional setting than it is in the wider and more open community. Most residential settings (with the exception of prisons) aim to create an environment that is 'therapeutic' or 'homely' or 'caring'. This may only occur when workers and residents trust and support each other. However, to manage the strains and tensions of long-term personal contact, it is tempting for organizations to establish hierarchies and rules which distance staff from residents. In consequence, the social workers in these settings who generally aren't engaged in primary care may feel forced to choose between the residents and the paid work group. It is possible to alter hierarchical structures in these settings so that residents share more responsibility, but generally only with the support of either the senior administrator or their superiors.

In a *secondary setting*, teamwork for social workers may be more difficult because of the different training and values of other professional groups and – particularly in hospital or other settings – because of the status of the dominant profession, usually medicine. Status issues may also compound the organizational difficulties workers experience:

- in obtaining appropriate access to service users;
- in affecting the overall assessment of service user needs; and
- in obtaining the necessary cooperation from service users and their families as well as from staff to carry out their work. People, after all, come to settings such as hospitals for a variety of reasons which do not necessarily include seeing a social worker.

As we have noted previously, the reconfiguration of children's services outlined in *Every Child Matters: Change for Children* (DfES, 2004) and the provisions of the Children Act 2004 mean that working in a secondary setting (education) is going to become a much more common feature of practice with children, young people and their families so may be subject to some of the tensions and difficulties outlined earlier. These tensions are not inevitable and a lot will depend on the nature and quality of the relationships between members of the host agency and their new colleagues.

Team development and team functioning are always influenced by the organizational opportunities for, and constraints on, working together effectively as a team. Yet some teams seem to flourish in spite of, rather than because of, their organizational demands. This is usually the result of good team leadership and committed staff who feel confident that they are offering a quality service to others.

In all teams, regardless of setting, the practitioner has to balance the interests of individual service users and the groups he or she works with against the interests of individual team members and of employers. This balance poses a number of questions. How do we balance the demand for service user confidentiality with the need to share information in the team? How can you time your work with service users so that you don't overrun other team members? How can you handle conflict in the team? How can you involve the agency service users in team decision making?

BALANCING SERVICE USER CONFIDENTIALITY AND THE TEAM'S NEED TO KNOW

Teams, especially multi-disciplinary teams, rely on the sharing of information and assessments by different team members. As the tragic outcomes of the Climbié case showed, this is necessary for a holistic understanding of the situation and for the coordination of responses. Practitioners are sometimes torn between a commitment to service user confidentiality and a commitment to the processes of the team. One response to this dilemma is to assert that workers don't practise alone and hence cannot assume the right to withhold information from other team members. If we work from this premise, good practice requires that the service user group understands that information is disclosed to other team members so that they retain the choice of how much information to share. At the same time, of course, the worker is encouraging people to share the particular details of their lives that are considered to be important for other team members to know.

Confidentiality is as concerned with the control of the use of information as it is with its disclosure. It is therefore important that the way in which the worker makes use of the information is discussed. What sense has the worker made of it? Is this the sense the service user wants conveyed? If they cannot agree, both points of view should be presented in a way that does not belittle the service user as 'difficult', 'manipulative', 'lacking in insight', or present them in other judgemental terms. If information is processed in this way, the worker, the service user and his or her family will all remain involved in the assessment process and will retain some control over that process.

TIMING AND WORKING IN TEAMS

This issue has two manifestations. The first is the frustration of waiting for the team to meet before any decisions can be made. The second is the frustration and anger resulting from decisions made without reference to other team members, but which affect their work. On the whole, teams make a reasonable fist of assessing situations and formulating intervention plans. Much harder is timing consultations to keep up with changes in the situation. Team members tend to act first and inform others later, or perhaps consult with one other team member. There isn't a simple way of achieving an appropriate balance. Organizationally, the team should decide on a structure to review work in hand. This structure needs to be flexible and not take up an inordinate amount of time presenting information on which no new action will be taken. How do you know when to consult with others? Is there such a thing as too much consultation? From the organization's point of view there probably is. They are caught in the bind of wanting maximum work done, which would suggest restricting the amount of time in meetings, and wanting effective control over what happens, which would increase the time in meetings.

From the worker's point of view, the answer again probably lies in the processes which are used. If the social worker is the team leader, then he or she should try to ensure that all team members share the same goals and attitudes to their work so that the decisions they may have to make independently are likely to take account of the pace and content of colleagues' work. In teams where there are trusting, supportive relationships, team members can generally cope with abrupt changes of direction. Where this is not the case, the same behaviour may give rise to conflict and the destruction of the team's potential for cooperative work.

LIKING AND CONFLICT IN TEAMWORK

'Teamwork promotes close relationships and so liking or conflict can easily arise' (Payne, 1982: 74). When people like working together, they usually do a better job. However, if everyone in the team doesn't feel equally liked, they may feel excluded and less able to influence outcomes. This can be one source of conflict in a work group. If this becomes an issue, it is important for those who feel excluded to raise it for discussion with one of those whom they see as being exclusive.

Conflict in teams can be constructive or destructive. Conflict is beneficial in helping team members clarify their goals and preferred work methods. It can stimulate thinking and creates opportunities for new ways of doing things. When conflict is not resolved, however, it can be destructive, alienating workers from each other and reducing the amount of energy available to do their job. Depending on your position in the team, you can cope with conflict by trying to control flare-ups – for example, by keeping warring parties at bay – or by confronting it. Conflict resolution in teams is the same as that in any human situation and the discussion on conflict in Chapter 5 is relevant here.

INVOLVING PEOPLE IN DECISIONS MADE ABOUT THEM

In the past, some teams have not directly involved those most concerned – service users – in deciding which services will be offered. However, as indicated in the NOS and SiSWE, social workers should provide clear information to service users and carers, involve them in decision-making processes and offer them different options. This is congruent with social work's emphasis on self-determination and is in line with the purpose of social work outlined in this book. It acts as a barrier to the formulation of secret assessments which aren't shared with the subject of assessment. Further, it empowers service users by extending their control over their lives.

Yet such involvement doesn't always happen, for a number of reasons. Hornby and Atkins suggest that attending to the needs of a collaborative team for 'sustainable cohesiveness can lead to team members becoming self-absorbed and unduly focused on team relationships, putting these ahead of the need of users' (2000: 183). A further argument is that the actual mandate of social work organizations is to control and not to empower the service user group. Certainly the arguments against the involvement of the service user in the team are most fervent when the control function is most apparent (for example, in child protection where it is asserted that the rights of the child must take precedence over the rights of the parents). Other reasons are that some professionals do not feel comfortable involving the person concerned in discussions with other professionals. Traditionally, participants in medical ward rounds in teaching hospitals have stood around a patient's bed and discussed not them but their medical condition in their presence. On the whole, patients find this worrying and offensive, and rarely educational or empowering.

There are also logistical problems in getting a number of staff and a service user together at the one time. These problems increase when the person is in the community and the team is made up of staff from several agencies. Nevertheless, the benefits of overcoming these problems to share information and to arrive at decisions together are enormous in terms of the service user's sense of well-being, and in terms of the coordination and implementation of interventions. The involvement of service users is an attainable goal in many more team situations than is currently the case. The question that should be asked is why not involve the service user rather than why involve the service user in the team.

TEAM PROCESSES AND SERVICE USER RIGHTS

The underlying push in teams is 'the development of the value of co-operation and the push towards consensus' (Mailick and Ashley, 1981: 132). Consensus allows a unified plan to be agreed upon and each person to carry out their specific function. The push for consensus and the desire to avoid long and conflictual discussions may become the primary goal (Mailick and Ashley, 1981) and lead to compromise and decision making based on incomplete information at the expense of the rights of the service user.

Alternatively, the functioning of the group may be undermined by the dominance of one theoretical formulation and the submergence of all material into that frame of reference. The difficulties experienced by social workers relate to the fact that there is not an equal pressure on all members towards consensus. The relative autonomy of the members is connected with their status and power and that of their profession and its relative centrality to the group. Those with a strong or powerful profession or group identity external to the group are able to remain relatively independent of the group culture. On the other hand, members with lower status are more vulnerable to pressure and less often feel able to take an independent stance. For social workers, this is complicated by the fact that they are frequently in the position of trying to encourage inter-professional cooperation from a position of weakness. Having achieved some semblance of cooperation, they seek to consolidate it.

To be effective within a team or work group, the practitioner should be close enough to it to promote cooperation, but must maintain sufficient distance so that group norms do not overwhelm. This can be achieved through one or all of the following strategies:

- in the absence of powerful status, developing supportive coalitions inside and outside the group;
- actively taking risks in the group by being willing to articulate alternative plans. While creating considerable work for the individual, this also serves to develop an educative base for future influences;
- being sensitive to and encouraging others to be sensitive to human rights issues;
- involving an external advocate.

Successful work in teams requires an understanding of the processes of influencing the actions and decisions of team members and the organization. Teamwork requires collective commitment to effective service delivery to people who often require a number of services from different agencies and workers. These services are often provided in forms that are called case management or care management. It is to these processes that we now turn our attention.

CASE MANAGEMENT AND CARE MANAGEMENT

Case management normally refers to the method of providing extended, continuing care from a diverse range of providers to people with chronic life problems in community settings. In the UK the most common form of case management is referred to as 'care management' and is usually, although not exclusively, practised by social workers employed by social services departments, often in community care or adults' teams. In our discussion we will reflect on case management processes broadly as many British social work agencies are adopting these ideas even if they do not refer to their work as case or care management. We will also examine the more specific approach of care management that has developed in the UK context.

Whether the field of work is unemployment, ageing, people with a range of disabilities or child welfare, there are similarities in case management's approach to the task and the reasons for its adoption as a method of service delivery. According to Rothman (1992) case management is characterized by long-term work, involving multiple helpers, with the goal of enhancing people's ability to develop coping skills that enable them to maintain themselves, at a satisfactory level, in the community. To achieve this result, assistance is offered with a range of needs and the worker attempts to give the person as much control as possible in deciding what help is required. The need to work with a large number of service providers is also said to dilute the practitioner's control and authority.

Social work has had a long history of being involved in various forms of 'case management'. Casework, a less common term nowadays, involved a systematic approach to working with individuals often drawing on therapeutic ideas, such as psychodynamic and cognitive-behavioural approaches. Bowers's definition of casework (cited in Plant, 1970) emphasizes the mobilization of the capacities of the individual and the resources of society to promote better adjustment of the individual to society. The value of individualization – respect for the unique qualities of individuals and rejection of the assumption that individuals should fit certain types – was seen to be central to casework (Plant, 1970). While Rothman (1992) claims that case management is a new practice paradigm, its emphasis on the assessment of individual needs, the tailoring of services to meet these needs and the goal of enhancing individuals' coping skills are reminiscent of traditional approaches to casework.

Ideologically, case management fits the current trend towards individualism, the rhetoric of the family as a core social institution (by relying on informal care) and the determination of governments to reduce the scope of government service delivery and expenditure (Farrar and Inglis, 1996: ix). The case management approach is associated with a move from supply or service-based funding, to demand side funding where resources are tied to individuals rather than services. This can mean that agencies are encouraged to compete for packages of care, rather than cooperate to offer the best possible services. The provider workforce can become highly casualized to enable provider agencies to respond to the fluctuations in demand. The resources and knowledge (e.g. through training and supervision) of service-based models may be lost and the overall quality of the service offered to service users may decline as the erosion of services may reduce their choice of competent service providers.

Care management emerged as a modified form of case management and was initially developed in the UK by the Personal Social Services Research Unit (PSSRU) in Kent (Challis and Davies, 1986). This model was, in turn, based upon a 'social entrepreneurship' approach (Payne, 1995) developed in the United States, which focuses on the interweaving of formal and informal care by a worker who acts as an 'entrepreneur' in getting the system of care working for the service user. This is contrasted with a 'service brokerage' approach in which the worker acts as an advocate for a service user who has already identified gaps in their care (acting more like a travel agent) (Payne, 1995). The PSSRU research involved both the development of a model of case management (referred to as enhanced case management) and the restructuring of local policies and procedures in order to facilitate this model. It targeted frail older people who were most at risk of entering residential or nursing home care. In their evaluation of the implementation of the model Challis and Davies (1986) identified that a lower proportion of older people had been placed in residential care and in some cases the new approach was more cost-effective than the usual pattern of service delivery. There appeared to be a more accurate matching of services to needs and, according to quality of care and subjective well-being indicators, older people and carers directly experienced benefits from the scheme. For social workers the new model provided a more clearly defined and valued role as the coordinator of care. Social workers also appeared to be more sensitive to informal networks of care in their intersection with formal services. Service users experienced more varied care packages and new needs (beyond those defined by 'basic' services) were identified and met.

The success of the PSSRU research was reflected in the promotion of case management in the Griffiths Report (Griffiths, 1988) as a means of implementing a series of community care reforms, including the separation of the roles of purchaser and provider of services. However Griffiths appeared to be more interested in the way the model helped manage resources and effectively arrange services, than in its focus on service user involvement and control in decision making (Payne, 1995). Case management was reframed by the Department of Health (1991a, 1991b) as 'care management' partly because consultations revealed that the term 'case' was thought to be demeaning for individuals. Subsequently care management has taken on a life of its own and now mainly refers to practice within the context of the NHS and Community Care Act 1990 and associated community care legislation and guidance. The ideals of the enhanced case management model developed in Kent appear to have been undermined in the implementation of care management by a concurrent reduction in funding, resulting in care managers being overly concerned with restricting access to resources (gatekeeping) rather than developing flexible and creative care packages.

A more intensive version of case management in the UK can be found in the model adopted by the Sainsbury Centre, which was funded to establish and evaluate four case management services targeting adults with mental health needs in different parts of England (Ryan et al., 1999). The Sainsbury Centre's case management services target those with severe, long-term mental health problems. Engagement with the service user is crucial for the success of the scheme:

> It is through constantly seeking to engage with the service user, on the user's own territory, that an ongoing trusting relationship is achieved. It involves being highly responsive to individual needs; seeking wherever possible to assist the user in achieving the lifestyle in the community that they themselves define as being what they want. (Ryan et al., 1999: 107)

An analysis of the services revealed that they prevented service users 'falling through the net' and linked them to responsive community services, although these were more costly when compared with standard mental health services. According to Ryan et al. (1999) this model of case management has been reframed as 'assertive outreach': an approach to mental health work that is increasingly becoming adopted. It is worth noting that the Sainsbury Centre's model of case management is more intensive than some of those developed in countries such as the United States and Australia where, like care management, case management schemes have been used alongside strategies to reduce expenditure.

CARE MANAGEMENT PROCESSES

As noted by Sheppard (1995) and Fisher (1992) the components and stages of care management reflect those of problem-solving and task-centred approaches to practice (discussed in Chapter 5). In the PSSRU research, Challis and Davies (1986) compared the involvement of older people and carers in shared problem or need definition to task-centred practice, although they recognized that not all older people, such as those with high levels of dependency, would be able to fully engage in these processes. While the stages of care management, as set out in the Department of Health's Managers' and Practitioners' Guides (DoH, 1991a, 1991b), reflect those of task-centred practice, the language of 'wants' in task-centred approaches is replaced by one of 'needs' (Sheppard, 1995).

The care management stages outlined by the Department of Health are as follows:

1. *Publishing information*: making public the needs for which assistance is offered and the arrangements and resources for meeting those needs;
2. *Determining the level of assessment*: making an initial identification of need and matching the appropriate level of assessment to that need;
3. *Assessing need*: understanding individual needs, relating them to agency policies and priorities, and agreeing the objectives for any intervention;
4. *Care planning*: negotiating the most appropriate ways of achieving the objectives identified by the assessment of need and incorporating them into an individual care plan;
5. *Implementing the care plan*: securing the necessary resources or services;
6. *Monitoring*: supporting and controlling the delivery of the care plan on a continuing basis;
7. *Reviewing*: reassessing needs and the service outcomes with a view to revising the care plan at specified intervals. (1991b: 10)

The Department of Health (1991a, 1991b) presents the stages in a circular fashion: the review of needs and service outcomes (stage 7) might lead to a reassessment of need (stage 3) and a new care plan may be set up (stage 4), and so on.

The separation of assessment, planning and purchasing from direct service provision or intervention is at the heart of care management and, indeed, the restructured mixed economy of welfare introduced through the NHS and Community Care Act 1990. However, there remain tensions around this 'purchaser/provider split'. For many care managers, forming a relationship with the service user and communicating with them about their needs represents a type of intervention or 'service' in itself. Through this intervention, service users' situations may be changed by, for example, identifying and resolving areas of unacknowledged need, family conflict or communication problems. It may also help service users to think about alternative strategies for resolving problems in their life without a care plan necessarily having to be set up. Similarly, providers (e.g. home care agencies) often find it difficult not to engage in some form of assessment activity with service users, at least on a small-scale, day-to-day basis. Take, for example, the situation of an older woman who lives alone and receives three home care visits per day for assistance with dressing, washing, meals and getting in and out of bed. On the occasions that her son visits from out of town and assists her that evening with her meal and getting into bed, it is unlikely that the home care agency would have phoned the care manager to request a reassessment of need on the basis of changed circumstances. They or the worker themselves would have reassessed the need and altered the service at the time of delivery. Although in this situation presumably the home care agency should not charge the service user or local authority the same as agreed in the care plan if a reduced service was provided. If the changed circumstances were to continue over an extended period of time, a review might also be necessary. An open acknowledgement of the blurring of assessment/ purchasing functions and provider functions is important and where possible, care managers, service users and providers should agree on the boundaries of their roles and the communication and decision-making arrangements in the case of changed circumstances.

In the following scenario, Diane Aldridge, a final-year social work student reflects on her placement experiences in a care management team in a London hospital. The team comprised 15 care managers, eight of whom were qualified social workers. In general the hospital-based care management team would hold its cases for four weeks following the patient's discharge home, after which the case was transferred to the community-based team.

Practice example: hospital-based care management

Referral and determining the level of assessment

Mr David Harris was an 80-year-old white British man who was suffering from dementia. He was admitted to hospital as a result of a chest infection. He was also dehydrated. He lived with his wife, Mary, who had been his main carer. They have an adult son and daughter, both of whom are married.

   Mr Harris was referred to me at the multi-disciplinary team meeting, which was held on a weekly basis. This was my second meeting and I was anxious about my role and student status. Early in the meeting the consultant physician commented on dementia, noting that 'there is nothing worse than losing your mind'. When discussing the patients, the consultant explained that Mr Harris had been referred to hospital by his GP. She had had concerns about his physical health, and had questioned Mrs Harris's ability to continue caring for her husband as she had also been recently diagnosed as in the early stages of dementia. The consultant felt that Mrs Harris 'cannot look after him' and he needed to be placed in a nursing home. He explained that he had already spoken to Mr Harris's son, who was in agreement. The consultant gestured to me, indicating for me to arrange the placement. I explained that I would speak to Mr Harris and feed back next week.

   During this meeting I experienced a range of feelings. I was angry that dementia had been discussed in such a negative way and that Mr and Mrs Harris's needs and capabilities had been dismissed. I felt that they had been excluded from the decision-making process. I was aware of my own powerlessness, in terms of my student status and inexperience. I felt conscious that I had limited knowledge of dementia and its

(Continued)

(Continued)

effects on individuals and carers. I also thought about how the team members viewed the care management role: that I was just there to arrange services. I decided to discuss my feelings with my practice teacher. I felt this was important in that supervision gave me a safe space to explore my anger and my sense of powerlessness in the face of 'experts'. Supervision gave me the opportunity to voice my concerns. Nevertheless, it also helped me to value the input of other professionals, ensuring that I would not go about the assessment in an independent or cavalier way. It gave me the opportunity to value the social work role in a multi-disciplinary setting while also practising ways to challenge others constructively.

Mr Harris was entitled to an assessment under section 47 (1) (a) of the NHS and Community Care Act 1990. This places a duty on local authorities to carry out an assessment of those who appear 'in need'. As a result of being in hospital, it appeared that Mr Harris was in need and consequently he did not need to go through the initial screening process. His case was formally allocated to me and I began a level two (medium) assessment.

Assessing need

An assessment that takes place in a hospital often occurs when a person is particularly vulnerable due to illness, disability or a breakdown in a social situation. On a practical level, there is also little opportunity for privacy. Older people make up a large proportion of hospital in-patients and are sometimes viewed as 'bed blockers'. I feel that this is a particularly negative term which individualizes the issue and does not take into account some of the external factors (such as shortages of community-based services) that can result in delayed discharges. In my role as a student care manager, I had to balance the tension between ensuring throughput and providing a thorough and holistic assessment.

I approached Mr Harris on the ward, introduced myself and explained my role. I told him that I would help to make plans when it came time for him to leave the hospital. I also contacted Mrs Harris and asked if we could meet the next time she visited the hospital. She became quite anxious and asked me to contact her daughter, saying that 'she will know what to do' and 'whatever she decides will be for the best'. When I contacted Mrs Harris's daughter, she explained that she worked full-time and asked me to meet her husband on the ward. I felt unaccustomed to negotiating with such a range of people in a family system. I felt it was important to clarify the lines of communication between family members and professionals, remembering that the consultant had mainly been in contact with Mr Harris's son not his son-in-law.

When I met with the son-in-law, he seemed very articulate and confident. He was clear about what information he needed and he asked about financial assessments and nursing home placements. As well as these things, I talked with him about the emotional impact a placement might have on Mr and Mrs Harris, as well as the implications of Mr Harris continuing to be cared for at home, including Mrs Harris's ability to provide care. It seemed important to not just talk about the choices available but also the costs – including emotional costs – these choices might involve. I suggested that they needed to spend time with the rest of the family discussing the options available to them. I was aware of how comfortable I felt in working with him. He was a professional who quickly understood concepts like home care, care planning and means tests. I realized how quickly the person being assessed can be lost and how collusive alliances can be formed between generational peers (Biggs, 1996). I resolved that I would involve Mr and Mrs Harris more.

I saw a joint home visit with an occupational therapist as an opportunity to talk with Mrs Harris more fully. I had spoken to Mrs Harris many times on the phone and wanted to meet with her face to face. I felt that a joint visit would be fairer to her as she wouldn't have to answer the same sorts of questions on two

(Continued)

separate occasions. In particular, I wanted to explore Mrs Harris's ability to provide care and her views on receiving support services. During the visit Mrs Harris indicated strongly that she wanted her husband to return home to live with her, although she felt she could no longer meet her husband's needs without assistance. She indicated that she had difficulty helping him get dressed and bathed, and sometimes she could not get him to eat. We talked about various services that might be able to assist with this.

As part of my assessment I also needed to work in partnership with other agencies. I contacted Mr Harris's GP, who told me that she had reservations about sending Mr Harris home because his wife 'couldn't feed a parrot'. She explained that his wife's difficulty getting him to eat and drink contributed to his dehydration. I acknowledged her in-depth understanding of the situation and noted that Mrs Harris wanted him to return home. I asked if she thought Mrs Harris was able to make such a decision. The GP explained that she was and that they had a very strong and loving relationship. As I explained the sorts of services that might be available, the GP became more open about the possibility of Mr Harris returning home. I also got in touch with Mr Harris's Community Psychiatric Nurse and a Care Manager in the community-based team. They both indicated that they would be prepared to support Mr and Mrs Harris when he was discharged.

I was aware that one of the key concerns expressed by the multi-disciplinary team was the level of risk Mr and Mrs Harris would be exposed to if Mr Harris were to return home. Risk assessment seems to be part of everyday language in social care. Nevertheless I feel it is important to think about what is meant by the term risk. Often risk is only thought about negatively – in terms of harm – with little reflection on the positive outcomes of taking a risk, such as a feeling of independence and achievement. I was aware that the professionals' concerns about risk were possibly limiting the way in which Mr and Mrs Harris were involved in decisions about Mr Harris's long-term care. I used the principles endorsed by Hughes (1993: 358) and asked myself 'How can Mr Harris's quality of life be maximized and how can the level and nature of the risk be minimized?'

Mr Harris needed assistance with most aspects of daily living. Often this was provided by Mrs Harris, although there were some specific tasks that would need to be provided by informal and formal supports: washing, dressing, toileting, and monitoring of food and medication intake. Mr and Mrs Harris were financially secure and their living environment was practical and in a good state of repair. Their relationship was strong and they received company and emotional support from their children and grandson. After much discussion with Mr and Mrs Harris and the family, it was agreed that Mr Harris should be returned home with a package of community care services. Initially Mr Harris felt he didn't need support services and that his wife had been managing okay. However, after more detailed discussion he acknowledged that his care had been 'a bit much on her' and recognized the views of the multi-disciplinary team.

Care planning

The care plan set up for Mr Harris was intensive: two carers, four times a day, seven days a week. This would assist in meeting Mr Harris's daily care needs. The plan aimed also to support Mrs Harris and monitor Mr Harris's needs. A hospital-type bed and hoist would be provided. Mr Harris would also be visited by the District Nurse to monitor his skin care, by his Community Psychiatric Nurse, and by a dietician. I was aware at this time that Mrs Harris was not provided with any built-in respite and raised this concern with my supervisor. She suggested we monitor this over the forthcoming weeks. Copies of the care plan were distributed to Mr and Mrs Harris and their family.

(Continued)

(Continued)

Implementing and monitoring the care plan

I worked with a range of professionals in coordinating Mr Harris's discharge and ensuring that services were organized. However, risk situations can change, as quickly became apparent. Mr Harris was discharged without medication or a dosset box (a box that helps people take their medication at the right time), and the District Nurse did not visit as arranged to pump up the mattress on the new bed. This led to considerable distress for Mrs Harris. I contacted the agencies concerned and impressed upon them the need to rectify the situation. I acted as a 'container' for Mrs Harris's anxieties and apologized to her on behalf of the multi-disciplinary team. This made me realize the impact a small detail can have on an individual and their overall confidence. On a positive note, I felt that my role as a care manager was understood by the family and that they had a point of contact if things went wrong.

Mr Harris had only been home a couple of weeks when I realized the need to review his situation. I was contacted by the home care coordinator who explained that his care package was 'too heavy'. That is, the tasks were taking longer than the time allocated in the care plan. The Social Services Inspectorate (1997: 16) has noted that even basic home care tasks provided to people with dementia can be very time consuming. The coordinator also informed me that Mrs Harris had cancelled two of the daytime calls (lunch and teatime). Mrs Harris was finding the timing and frequency of the calls too disrupting. It became apparent that Mr Harris's needs were conflicting with Mrs Harris's preparedness to accept support services.

Reviewing the care plan

I met with Mr and Mrs Harris and their daughter in their home. Mr Harris was in bed during the time of our meeting. After discussion about what had happened, Mrs Harris confided that she no longer felt able to care for her husband at home. This was due to a combination of factors. She felt that his needs were too great, that home care services were too stressful for her, and that the timing of the calls did not meet her needs. I discussed with Mrs Harris possible adjustments to the care plan and the provision of respite services. However I did not want to pressure her. Eventually Mrs Harris said that she thought her husband should go into a nursing home. I tried to encourage her by saying that she still had a role in deciding what happened, such as choosing an appropriate home, sharing information with those who would be looking after him and continuing to be involved in his life at the home. While looking for a home, Mrs Harris agreed for one of the day-time calls to be reinstated. Not long after this Mr Harris's condition deteriorated and he passed away at home.

I learned a lot from working with Mr and Mrs Harris. I had attempted to use my social work role in the multi-disciplinary setting to promote Mr Harris's rights. I was able to make the family aware of the range of service options available. In setting up the care plan I feel I did not pay enough attention to Mrs Harris's expertise. This may have led to her feeling undermined by the workers involved in Mr Harris's care. I also could have ensured that Mrs Harris was given her own assessment via the Carers (Recognition and Services) Act 1995 and that respite services were set up from the beginning. I feel that in hindsight I should have arranged a case conference in order to better coordinate Mr Harris's discharge. Nevertheless, I endeavoured to ensure that Mr and Mrs Harris were fully involved in the decision-making process, even though there were risks involved with the available options.

This example highlights some of the strengths and dilemmas involved in the various processes of care management practice. In assessing Mr Harris's needs, the student practitioner was managing a range of different information sources, while trying to stay focused on the expressed wishes of the service user and his carer. At times it was tempting to collude with professionals and family members to do what seemed best: that option which may have had the least harmful outcome. How much better would the situation have been had Mr Harris been placed into a nursing home directly from hospital? Was the package of care sufficient? How could Mrs Harris have been better acknowledged as a co-provider of services? Despite the problems, the student worked hard to coordinate the different workers involved in Mr Harris's care. Her contacts with the couple appear to have gone beyond the simple role of 'purchaser' of services: she drew on a wide range of social work skills in engaging and supporting them during this difficult time. An important feature of the work was the student's communication with the service user, his family and other professionals. Part of this communication involved accurate recording of events and work carried out, preparation of reports and completion of forms. It is to report writing and record maintenance that we now turn our attention.

RECORDS AND REPORT WRITING

Records are one of the key points where the service user/group, the worker and the organization come together to construct a semi-permanent picture of individuals or groups, and their career with the organization. They are an essential part of effective social work practice. The NOS and SiSWE make it clear that social workers are expected to participate in the management of information in their organizations, as well as maintain up-to-date records and reports, provide evidence for decision making, and share reports and records as appropriately with individuals and organizations. Prince (1996: 180) researched record-keeping practices of social workers in multi-disciplinary child guidance clinics. She concluded that 'records actually occupied a "hot seat" in the power relations between social workers, their clients, managers and consultants (psychiatrists at the clinic), and functioned not only as an index of power but also as a bearer of meanings, codes, resources and emotions' (p. 180). It is important to be aware of the complexity of the recording task when reading and using records as well as writing them. Like other dimensions of organizational practice, record keeping can reflect the purpose of social work – helping people take more control in their lives and promoting equitable relationships – if it is done in a way that is honest, transparent and allows for contributions by service users.

Research suggests that social workers spend one-fifth of their time recording (Prince, 1996: 186), so that apart from negotiating the issues of power imbalances, good recording practices should seek to ensure that the time taken is well used. Good records are an essential practice skill, and recording, like other skills, takes practice if it is to be done effectively and efficiently. Poor recording can lead to unintended but serious consequences. Prince notes: 'Recording in the field of child abuse has been consistently criticised in inquiries into the deaths of children' (1996: 15). Some of the issues noted in these inquiries were that records were 'incomplete, inaccurate, insufficiently detailed and not read by the people involved. There was a failure to separate fact and opinion, to record precise details about the child', to record accurate details of contact by phone or face to face, to make the source of information clear and to provide regular reviews of case notes in large files (p. 15). Bateman (1995: 72) notes that, while it is tempting to treat written records as your own personal property, in law they belong to your employer. Like other records, many social work records come under the remit of the Freedom of Information Act 2000 which enables service users or patients to access information held on themselves by public authorities. Social workers are increasingly called upon to provide access to and explain these records to former service users.

PURPOSE OF RECORDS

When we consider the purposes of keeping records, we can see that each purpose provides opportunities and challenges to the organization, the worker and the people using the services provided. Wilson (1980) argues that records of the work done need to be kept so that

1. there is continuity of the service provided over time;
2. others who may be working with you are informed of what you are doing;
3. workers can be accountable to the agency, the funding body and hopefully service users for the work they do;
4. there is some way of monitoring the quality as well as quantity of the work done; and
5. by recording, you organize your thoughts on what is happening, why it is happening, how it is happening and what might be tried next.

Ife notes that 'community workers will collect a lot of useful information, and need to be able to communicate it in the appropriate forum in such a way that it leads to effective action' (2002: 255). In some contexts agency records may be used in legal actions, either as whole files or reports.

TYPES OF REPORTS

Reports are written for many reasons and this will have an impact on the structure and style of report writing. They may be in the form of letters, minutes of meetings, file notes, a range of reports, submissions, diaries; they may be paper or electronic, they may be your own your work or constructed with others, they may follow prescribed guidelines or be constructed to reflect the needs of the situation under review.

A fairly common broad structure for reports is SOAP:

Subjective data – what the service user/group/community states as the issues;
Objective data – factual data, what can be measured or observed;
Assessment – the conclusions reached from the data; and
Plan – the intervention proposed.

Some agency proformas will detail what specific information needs to be collected and recorded. Social services departments, for example, tend to have fairly consistent proformas, although most also store information in computer databases. Different types of work may require different forms of reporting, though the purpose of records remains consistent across almost all forms of practice.

A range of reports are oriented to summarizing work done or reporting against agreed goals. These may be written for funding bodies or for management committees/managers.

Both these forms of reporting are forms of accounting for the way time has been spent and movement towards agreed goals, as well as a record of the details of situations. Log books/ diaries of the main activities undertaken are a common form of reporting in community work, so that the worker has a record of what was planned and what has been done, can reflect on progress and plan for the future (Twelvetrees, 2001: 191). They might also write progress reports on specific projects. All of these forms of reporting are designed to meet the first three purposes outlined above. They may also relate to the quality control of work, particularly when supervisors or other workers review them. In some contexts they may also be used for research purposes, though often this form of recording is more specialized. Records to meet reporting standards for accreditation agencies, funding bodies or management are also likely to be in place in many settings. Other forms of reports may primarily be for the practitioners' use as they reflect on their practice. We may mainly experience this as students, but this form of reporting is useful for practitioners in challenging situations.

PRACTICE ISSUES IN REPORT WRITING

When considering reporting strategies in line with our practice framework we have highlighted some issues that would need to be addressed. From our perspective these would promote equitable relationships and give people as much control as possible over their own lives. The issues are:

- *Language used in report writing:* language is a site of power and it is important that we use language so that it is accessible to and respectful of others yet captures the complexity of practice. This means using professional language such as 'negotiate' rather than 'chat' and refraining from making personal or discriminatory comments;
- *Identification of 'fact' and 'opinion':* reports should specify the status of the information used, and conclusions should not be drawn unless there is sufficient objective information or evidence that is evaluated against an accepted knowledge base. It is important to present a balanced view of the situation and to try to avoid personal biases;
- *Clear links between information and action:* the usefulness of reports about people or events is often assessed in terms of the clarity of the understanding of the issues in the organizational context. A clear outline of the situation, people's goals for the future and the available resources, should be linked to identifying and specifying the action to be taken to meet those goals;
- *Appropriateness of the content of the report for its purpose:* workers will write a large range of reports for different purposes. Some of these are mentioned above.
- *Level of service user participation in the report:* in almost all situations it is desirable for people whose information is represented in reports or letters to know what has been said, either by reading the material, or by workers providing a summary of the points they will cover in recording the interaction. Often it is preferable for the service user to negotiate a form of words to be included in the report or for them to have space to state their own views. This is particularly important in the event of disagreement;
- *Ways in which reports are used:* confidentiality is a significant issue in relation to records in terms of who gets access to the information they contain and how their physical or electronic security is safeguarded. You should be aware of agency policy in relation to these matters, explain this to service users and take potential audiences into account in deciding just what to include in the record.

These points will apply in most situations, though you will need to be aware of, and take account of specific agency requirements. As a broad rule of thumb, you should record in such a way that you will be comfortable if the people/communities discussed in the report were to read it, both now and in the future. This means that you have reported all the salient points, but not personal information that is irrelevant to the issue; you have recorded the service user's statements as well as your own observations (Timms, 1972: 55) and you have made the record useful for the stated purpose. This is usually assessed in terms of its relevance to future action, and in being succinct without losing important detail.

ADVOCACY

In our practice framework we have highlighted the social worker's employing organization as an important context in which the purpose of social work can be enacted. The organizational contexts of social work and social care also directly and indirectly control access to social and material resources and life chances. Social welfare systems, such as health, social services, probation, education and social security, are centrally involved in the construction and distribution of rights and the enforcement of responsibilities in the community. The planning decisions of local authorities directly impact on the living conditions of communities; policies which encourage gentrification of the inner cities reduce the availability of low-cost housing and fracture existing social networks. Just as important are decisions by schools about students, by courts about sentences, by hospitals about treatment, and so on. In assessing situations and formulating intervention strategies, our attention should be directed at the policies and practices of these organizations. Social workers are in a contradictory position: they exercise some autonomy and discretion in their work in the broader context of tightening welfare expenditure, but suffer because of the marginal position of social work in many of the arenas in which they practise.

It is the front-line workers who are charged with implementing welfare cutbacks. Frequently their employers still maintain their adherence to traditional social care goals while cutting back infrastructure and recurrent support. Workers experience pressure from financial cutbacks and from other professionals (e.g. police, doctors, nurses and so on) who do not share their perspective. There is evidence of differing patterns of response to this pressure:

1. *Rigid adherence to agency perspective:* The pressures and demands of service users are experienced as direct attacks on the self. The individual overidentifies with the organization, perceiving it only as a source of 'good', and denies the legitimacy of any criticisms of the agency (or self). Alternatively, such rigid adherence can result from, and lead to, a process of depersonalization. The individual perceives him or herself as a 'cog in a wheel' and denies responsibility for decisions;
2. *'Industrial sabotage':* The practitioner overlooks certain misdemeanours of the service user, such as the benefit recipient who is cohabiting, or not declaring income, or the parolee engaging in petty theft. Such responses are based on an unstated agreement between worker and service user that the behaviour will be ignored, but if the misdemeanour is discovered and reported by others, the service user is on his or her own (Pearson, 1975);

3. *Practitioner as advocate:* The practitioner defines him- or herself as an active fighter within the agency or team and against the external environment for the rights of individual service users and service users as a group.

Practitioners may find themselves adopting differing variations of the three behaviours at different times. This is especially the case with the last two types. The decision to ignore or actually take up a particular issue is considered to be a tactical one by many workers.

WHAT IS ADVOCACY?

Advocacy is an effort to influence the behaviour of decision makers in relation to another or group of others. Advocacy is a task, a set of techniques and a process. Advocacy, therefore, is not extraordinary behaviour, but the responsibility of all practitioners, and an activity that we engage in frequently in our everyday lives as social workers – its importance reflected, perhaps, by its inclusion within the NOS and SiSWE. It is generally linked to other forms of practice described in Chapter 5. For example, you may move from supportive interpersonal helping to advocacy when this is what the service user, and circumstances require, or you might move from advocacy to social action with a group of citizens who wish to take action an issue of concern. Advocacy emerges from workers' responsibility to service users and from the purpose of practice. It is an effort to enhance the responsiveness of the social care system to people's needs and reflects respect for an individual's human rights. This rights perspective is closely linked to the political, social and civil elements of citizenship:

> Realising one's rights in any of the above areas is to realise one's rights as a citizen, because non-citizens are denied rights. So, it is essential that, where rights are unclear or the opportunity to enforce them is limited, the question of citizenship is addressed to push back the limitations for those affected. (Bateman, 1995: 20)

Bateman argues that the concept of citizenship 'clarifies the basis of advocacy' and that to satisfy the needs of individuals 'in an unequal society, service users must turn needs into rights' and to do this, they may well need the support of a third party as an advocate (p. 21).

TYPES OF ADVOCACY

Advocacy has traditionally been divided into case and class advocacy. *Case advocacy* refers to the process of working with, or on behalf of, an individual or a small group, to obtain services to which they are entitled, or to influence a decision that affects them. *Class advocacy* refers to activity directed at changing policy, practices and laws; hence the outcomes affect a class of individuals. Case and class advocacy can be closely related. A decision in relation to an individual may set a precedent and affect the treatment of many people. Individual cases are also a means of monitoring the system and gathering data for class advocacy.

WHEN TO ADVOCATE

Hepworth et al. (2002: 451) detail a series of specific situations in which advocacy is an appropriate and necessary response. These include:

- when service users are refused a service or benefit to which they are or may be entitled;
- when services are delivered in a dehumanizing manner, such as the treatment of sexual assault victims by police or hospitals;
- in cases of discrimination or human rights breaches;
- when gaps in services cause hardship;
- when agency or government policies adversely affect people in need of services, such as the cultural insensitivity of mainstream social work services;
- when service users are unable to act effectively on their own behalf – for example, persons in institutions such as prisons, nursing homes and residential homes for people with a mental health or learning disability are particularly vulnerable;
- when numerous people have common needs for resources which are not available, such as public housing for the young homeless;
- when a person is denied his or her legal rights; for example a tenant being illegally evicted, a young person being incorrectly questioned by police.

In addition, there are two types of situation where the worker has a particular responsibility to advocate or to ensure that an advocate puts forward the perspective of the service user group:

1. When decisions are made about resources, services, interventions and so on that affect the interest of an individual or group, the individual/group has the right to have their perspective articulated and to respond to the information already considered. In social work, many case conferences perform as hidden courts (Foley, 1977), making decisions on such diverse matters as whether a child will be removed from a family and the placement of older people in residential and nursing homes;
2. When decisions are made about individuals or groups by institutions which are not aware of the totality of individual or group needs, advocacy is necessary. An example is the decisions schools make about students in the absence of a complete understanding of, for instance, the psychosocial background of those students.

It is a basic principle of justice that people should be aware of decisions that affect them and should be entitled to have their position heard by decision makers. In some circumstances, a worker is structurally unable to act as an advocate for a service user or group. For example, a social worker performing the perfectly legitimate action of seeking to take a child into care is clearly unable to argue the parents' case. That, however, does not absolve them from the responsibility of ensuring that an external advocate negotiates on behalf of the parents. Justice is denied when the social worker implicitly or explicitly denies a person their right to be heard.

ADVOCACY, MANIPULATION AND ETHICS

There is a divergence of opinion in the social work literature as to who decides what is advocated. Some argue that the advocate him- or herself should decide (Sosin and Caulum,

1983: 15). Such an approach to advocacy places it within the 'best interest' ideology of social work (O'Connor, 1988) where goals, tasks and processes are controlled by the social worker rather than the service user. This approach also raises the question of when advocacy becomes manipulation – when is a worker using a particular case to pursue his or her own goals? This issue especially comes to the fore when a worker seeks to use a situation as a test case. Rather than create a precedent, organizations will often attempt to settle matters in a way that enhances the situation of one case, but not the class it represents.

Our perspective is that advocacy involves the worker putting his or her skills and knowledge at the disposal of the individual or group. The responsibility of the advocate is to convey to the decision maker, in an articulate and well-argued manner, the perspective of the service user or group. In the process of preparing to advocate, the worker must consult with those instructing him or her, and explain what is possible and what is attainable. He or she must canvass the possible outcomes and consequences of different approaches and different demands. Where workers have particular concerns, they should, if necessary, pursue the issue in other ways. It is inappropriate to use service users as the means to ends.

In Chapter 8 we have summarized broad ethical principles for social care work. In each setting these are likely to be modified to give more specific guidance. Bateman's (1995) ethical principles of advocacy are consistent with our perspective on advocacy and are one example of particularizing these broad principles:

1. act in the service user's best interests;
2. act in accordance with the service user's wishes and instructions;
3. keep the service user properly informed;
4. carry out instructions with diligence and competence;
5. act impartially and offer frank, independent advice;
6. maintain service user confidentiality. (pp. 25–41)

APPROACHES TO ADVOCACY

In deciding the approach to advocacy in a particular situation, it is important to:

- decide what is to be advocated;
- identify the decision makers;
- identify and understand the framework by which the decision makers make their decision. This may simply be the Act or the regulations that they administer and the agency guidelines to interpretation, or it could extend to an identification of the political influences which affect the decision makers;
- decide on what is to be advocated;
- identify the manner in which the decision makers perceive their relationship to the advocacy effort (e.g. are they positive, neutral or hostile?).

The first basic principle underpinning every advocacy effort is to get the facts of the particular situation as clear as possible and to understand the regulatory framework of the issue. The second is to proceed from the position of least contest. The advocate must mobilize only enough force to achieve his or her purpose and to cause minimal damage to future advocacy efforts. This means starting at the lowest possible level in an organization that is consistent with obtaining the outcome you desire. Thus, where a social worker in a voluntary organization is advocating on behalf of a person with a disability whose community care needs have not been fully met by social services, the initial advocacy should be directed at the individual care manager involved in assessing need and setting up the care plan.

In other situations, when the decision makers are hostile to the advocate or what the advocate represents, the lowest appropriate level in the hierarchy may be quite senior (or external to the organization). For example, rather than complaining to the local sergeant about police maltreatment of a young person, it may be more appropriate to proceed to a higher level in the police service or to a complaints tribunal. The third principle is to identify prospective allies. Advocacy work often requires the support of a range of parties to be effective. For example, if you are advocating for better public housing for a family, you are more likely to be successful if your actions are supported by relevant people such as the children's headteacher, doctor, or religious advisor or perhaps the local politician.

The approach to advocacy adopted depends on the decision or processes that you are seeking to influence. It is necessary to identify the level to which advocacy should be directed. Following Sosin and Caulum (1983), three levels are identified:

1. *Individual level:* Advocacy directed at the individual level is concerned with the manner in which a specific service user or group is dealt with in a specific situation. It does not seek to challenge the agency rules or processes. It addresses factual issues. In such situations the advocate's role is one of putting new information before the decision maker and/or pointing out mistakes that have previously been made. For example, where the advocate presents the care manager with more detailed information about an older person's community care needs, which did not come to light during an earlier assessment;
2. *Administrative level:* At this level the advocate is accepting of the basic rules of the agency/organization, but seeks to alter or change the way the agency applies those rules. Thus, in the area of child sexual abuse, advocates have sought to change the way in which the courts treat children through a process of education of barristers and magistrates;
3. *Policy or legislative level:* Here the advocate seeks to change the rules that are affecting the individual or group. A worker may advocate a change in the rules of eligibility for services. Advocacy at this level might involve linking with other political activists. Advocacy strategies initiated with carers' groups were successful in the implementation of the Carers (Recognition and Services) Act 1995, resulting in carers being entitled to an assessment in their own right. Similarly, disability rights activists influenced the formation of direct payments schemes through the Community Care (Direct Payments) Act 1996.

The identification of the issues and the level at which advocacy should be directed are prerequisites for successful advocacy.

STRATEGIES OF ADVOCACY

Advocacy seeks to influence the behaviour of decision makers. Having decided what to advocate, and at what level the advocacy effort should be directed, the appropriate advocacy strategy needs to be delineated. Underpinning all advocacy strategies must be an educative strategy, which seeks to raise the level of understanding in the (specific and general) community about the issue of concern.

Sosin and Caulum (1983) delineate three strategic approaches to advocacy:

1. *Normative strategies* rest upon moral arguments and a generation of a recognition of common values. This is the most appropriate strategy where there is a recognition of the legitimacy of the advocacy effort and shared understanding of the needs and issues involved (e.g. in your own agency or in an inter-agency coalition);
2. *Utilitarian strategies* rely on bargaining and negotiation. They are appropriate where the decision makers are neither favourable nor antagonistic to the advocacy effort;
3. *Coercive strategies* involve the use of conflict and complaint. In adversarial contexts where there is no shared understanding or willingness to hear the perspective of the other, coercive strategies are used to force the attention of the decision maker(s).

STAGES AND TECHNIQUES OF ADVOCACY

The stages of advocacy are a refinement of the problem-solving process outlined in the previous chapter. Bateman (1995: 140) summarizes these stages as

1. Presentation of the problem – the way in which you became involved and decided the situation required an advocacy approach;
2. Information gathering – trying to ensure that all relevant material has been gathered and working with the service user to decide on what the service user wants to achieve;
3. Legal research – comparing the facts you have gathered with relevant policy or procedural documents or legislation;
4. Interpretation and feedback to the service user – come to some conclusions about how the problem presented relates to existing policy/legislation and the options that raises, consult with the service user, perhaps obtain further information, reach a conclusion with the service user about whether to proceed, and if so, whether to go to stages 5 or 6;
5. Active negotiation and advocacy – engaging with those who have the capacity to make the relevant decisions;
6. Litigation – using formal appeal processes, such as tribunals, if stage 5 is not appropriate or unsuccessful.

As in all forms of problem solving, success may be compromised by rushing to action without enough preparation, or without taking enough notice of what the service user actually wants.

The techniques used will flow from the strategy adopted. Many of these skills, such as active listening, appropriate questioning, establishing rapport with the service user, are generic to all practice. Other skills, that may not always be needed in other forms of practice, relate to the presentation of written and oral submissions, practice in relation to petitions and formal appeals, providing expert evidence and perhaps interviewing witnesses, lobbying and different forms of public education. Bateman (1995) suggests that workers engaged in advocacy also need skills in assertiveness and the constructive use of aggression, negotiation (both of which were considered, at least in part in the discussion of conflict management in Chapter 5), and legal research. One outcome of advocacy work, as noted earlier, may be an awareness of the need to change the rules, the final intervention to be examined in this chapter.

DEVELOPING POLICY

Policy change has the potential to bring about structural solutions to difficulties that service users have in common. A planned approach to influencing policy requires us to think politically and strategically. Rees (1991: 104) advocates taking a political economy perspective on organizations and therefore their policies. This involves understanding the interrelationships between political and economic processes within and without the agency; the processes by which power is distributed within organizations; constraints and controls; and individual workers' experiences of all these issues in their day-to-day work (p. 104).

As suggested throughout this book, policy and practice cannot be separated from the wider socio-economic and political contexts. Problems in people's lives must be considered in relation to their social arrangements. Failure to identify the political in individualized problems and to think strategically about their solutions inevitably disadvantages and entrenches service users' problems. Jordan (1988) demonstrates how lack of political awareness of the impoverishment of service users created by British social policy has led social workers in some fields to use more compulsory measures and less adversarial methods against the state, on behalf of service users. Under these circumstances, relationships with service users become more antagonistic and gross inequities created by policies remain unchallenged, either by social workers as a group, or in coalition with service users. This runs contrary to the purpose of social work as we have advocated it in this book: promoting equitable relationships and encouraging people to take more control in their lives.

Warren (1977: 34–56) suggests a model for planned social change based on political and strategic analysis and action consistent with the purpose of practice delineated in this text. The model directs the worker's attention to identifying the outcomes sought, the focus of change, the coalition of forces necessary to bring about the change and the strategies necessary to bring about the change:

1. *The outcomes sought:* What type of change is sought? Are we trying to influence behaviour, relationships, or ideas (or all three)?
2. *The focus of change*: We need to identify the focus of attention for change (individual, organization and society). When considering changing policy, we need to understand the institution through which current policy is expressed; the content of current policy; key players involved in policy formation; power distribution and power relationships; areas of dissatisfaction and satisfaction with policy; and readiness for change within the system(s) concerned.
3. *Identifying those involved in the change effort:* We need to identify the individuals, groups and coalitions who may be involved in strategies for change; their position in the system and their sources of power. It is important to be aware that service users themselves bear the direct consequences of policy decisions made in relation to them. Service user participation in processes of policy change is therefore important not only for ethical reasons, but also to maximize the effectiveness and relevance to consumers of outcomes of policy changes.
4. *Strategies for change*: Change strategies and situations in which they are most appropriately applied are summarized in Table 6.1.

Table 6.1   Strategies for change

Change strategies	Situations	Methods	Mode of control
Cooperation	Where there is fairly substantial agreement as to the general nature of the outcomes sought and the problem is to develop the best course to achieve the objective.	Rational planning; research action; consensus decision making; group dynamics; community development; community and organizational self studies; fact-finding studies.	Primarily utilitarian
Campaign	Where there is no consensus on the need and will to move towards objectives, but it is believed agreement couid be achieved by persuasion of some sort.	Advocacy research; educational and propaganda campaigns; proselytizing; consciousness raising; rational persuasion; emotional appeals; lobbying.	Utilitarian and normative
Contest	Where there is basic disagreement about the outcomes sought and those who oppose it must somehow be defeated.	Organizing contest groups; coercion; appeals to third parties; disruption; violence/non-violence.	Normative and coercive

Source: Adapted from Warren (1977: 49).

CHANGE–RESISTANCE AND STABILIZATION

Strategies to change policy may be met with resistance for a variety of reasons, such as workers' preferences for safe, habitual ways of working; fear of disruption to a 'known' system; loss of power; and threats to ideological beliefs that policy changes may bring.

Social workers sometimes tend to locate resistance to change in other groups of workers, while showing less enthusiasm to scrutinize these same tendencies in their own work. As well as being aware of our own difficulties with change, we need to be sensitive to the possibility that we are mistaken in our beliefs that there is need for policy change (Warren, 1977: 51). Resistance should be seen as an opportunity to hear important information, not just an obstacle to overcome.

Strategies to change policy must take into account problems of stabilizing and maintaining changes. Warren (1977) suggests that, generally, changes are more likely be enduring when:

- the change process does not centre on the involvement of one person, but involves a range of people;
- there is a high level of readiness to change within an organization;
- the change process itself is oriented to democratic participation, rather than imposed; and
- the change process is gradual rather than abrupt.

Social workers should not be bystanders in their organizations or in the social care systems in which those organizations are located. In trying to achieve social work's purpose, we have responsibilities to work strategically – for example, through advocacy or through developing policy – to improve the interactions between people and their social arrangements.

CHAPTER SUMMARY

This chapter has focused on the organizational context of practice. It sought to enhance understanding of organizations to facilitate the ability to work in and influence them. An understanding of the organizational context and its ramifications is a necessary part of any assessment. The processes of working in and influencing organizations are constituent elements of interventions.

Students directly experience the organizational context during their education while they undertake practice placements. The placement and practice learning experience is the focus of the next chapter. Working in organizations involves us in making day-to-day decisions about how we will act with service users. Workers are constantly faced with sets of choices, often involving different and conflicting values. It is crucial that we are aware of the ethical and value assumptions that underpin our practice if we are to make choices that are congruent with our purposes. Ethical issues in practice are considered in the final chapter.

FURTHER READING

Hornby, S. and Atkins, J. (2000) *Collaborative Care: Interprofessional, Interagency and Interpersonal*, 2nd edn. Oxford: Blackwell Science.

This book examines the complexities of inter-professional and inter-agency working and suggests ways of working collaboratively in different organizational contexts and across organizational hierarchies.

Sheppard, M. (1995) *Care Management and the New Social Work: A Critical Analysis.* London: Whiting and Birch.

Sheppard examines the ideological underpinnings of the development of care management in the UK and highlights the role of managerialism in producing a limited and routinized approach to care management practice. Important links are made between social work theories and care management processes and the potential of social work to inform care management is highlighted.

Bateman, N. (1995) *Advocacy Skills: A Handbook for Human Service Professionals.* Aldershot: Arena

Bateman provides practical guidelines for successful advocacy in health and social care settings. The ethical principles underpinning advocacy are examined and specific skills and strategies, such as negotiation and assertiveness, are discussed.

USEFUL WEBSITES

Better Caring (nursing home resource): www.bettercaring.co.uk.
Citizens Advice Bureau: www.citizensadvice.org.uk.
Disability Alliance: www.disabilityalliance.org.
Disabled Living Centres Council: www.dlcc.org.uk.
Directory of Care Homes: www.carehome.co.uk.
Online Social Care: www.socialcareonline.org.uk.
Freedom of Information: www.dca.gov.uk/foi.
Personal Social Services Research Unit: www.pssru.ac.uk.

REFLECTIVE QUESTIONS

1. Using the questions set out in this chapter, map an organization with which you are familiar (e.g. through placement or agency visits);
2. Identify from your placement or agency visits a problem or issue experienced by a service user with that organization and

   a) develop a case advocacy strategy for the individual;
   b) develop a class advocacy strategy to address the issue.

3. Consider a situation with which you are familiar where you might think case management would be appropriate (e.g. from placement, from your understanding of the needs of particular groups in the community, from your own experiences). What might be the structural and personal tensions in implementing this approach and what might be its benefits?

7 PLACEMENTS AND PRACTICE LEARNING

In this chapter we examine:

- Contextual issues relating to placements and practice learning in the UK;
- Roles and responsibilities on placement;
- Issues in preparing for and beginning placement;
- Learning on placement, including learning styles;
- The practice assessor/student relationship, including supervision;
- Assessing competence and learning on placement, for example in relation to the National Occupational Standards (NOS) or Scottish Standards in Social Work Education (SiSWE).

Of all the learning experiences available on a social work course, the ones that students cite as being most memorable are their practice placements, largely because they are 'doing the real thing'. Placements provide an opportunity to learn from others – service users, carers, social work colleagues and other workers – as well as a chance to practise the skills gained from prior learning. Gradually and with careful supervision students are encouraged to take on more responsibility so that by the end of their final placement they are able to operate as a newly qualified social worker would be operating in that particular organization. The mix of working alongside professionals, taking greater responsibility, experiencing the difference that can be made in a social work role, and realizing that you do know something about the issues and how to address them are experiences that can excite and motivate, and admittedly sometimes also worry and threaten (Rogers et al., 2000: 2). Placement, and first placement in particular, may be a time to think carefully about whether or not a career in social work really fits with your interests and abilities. It is also an important time for others – particularly practice assessors and tutors – to evaluate if you are suited to social work and have the capacity to work competently and safely.

In the practice framework that we have presented throughout this book, we emphazise the importance of social workers understanding the tensions between people and their social arrangements and the need for social workers to assist in resolving these tensions by using themselves and their professional relationships in assessment and intervention activities. The social work purpose has been further clarified as enabling people (individuals, groups and communities) to take more control in their lives and as encouraging equitable social relationships. In Figure 7.1 we incorporate the role of ongoing professional learning (including placements and practice learning) into our practice framework. Professional learning involves developing both a deeper understanding of social work purpose and a greater capacity to implement this purpose through improving skills and knowledge. While in this chapter we focus on social work students and their experiences on placement, professional learning will continue long after students finish placement and indeed their social work degree. Over time they will engage in continuing professional development activities and post-qualifying education and will themselves perhaps act in the role of practice assessor. For social work practitioners we would encourage you to remember your own placement experiences, reflect on how your professional learning has developed since then and consider the contribution you could now make to a student on placement. Taking a student on placement and setting up practice learning opportunities can help develop a culture of learning in social work organizations and reinvigorate an awareness of social work purpose, values, knowledge and skills. We believe that student placements should not be a marginalized activity; rather they should be at the centre of social work both in the university or college and in the social work organization.

ISSUES IN PLACEMENTS AND PRACTICE LEARNING

Placements are structured educational opportunities that require students to be located and carry out tasks in an organization that provides social work or related services. Placements are one form of practice learning that takes place on a social work programme. Other forms of practice learning include skills labs, observation of service users and/or social workers in practice, and research activities. In many respects placement might seem like working in the organization, though you notice quickly that there is no pay attached! The similarities with work are that you are required to adhere to organizational policies, including exercising due care, being diligent, keeping agreed hours, dressing and behaving in a manner appropriate to your placement setting, and adhering to the Care Councils' Codes of Practice. They are different in that the primary objective of you being in the placement is not the product of any work that you might do, but your learning. Thus your main task on placement is to learn. You are not an unpaid worker to do whatever is required.

When setting the framework for the honours degree, it was decided that about half of students' experience would be in a form of practice learning (a principle also in place under the Diploma in Social Work). While the allocation and make-up of practice learning days vary between the different countries of the UK, generally students undertake at least 200 days of practice learning (you should refer to the Care Councils' guidelines in each country for specific details). In each country students are required to have had experience in at least two practice settings, with at least two service user groups, and with

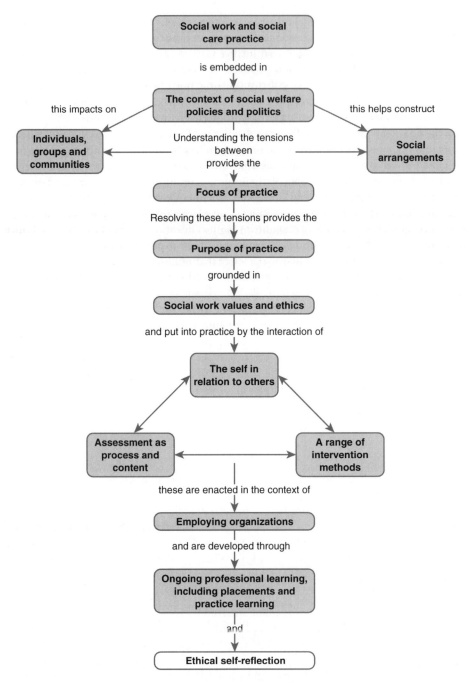

Figure 7.1   Ongoing professional learning, including placements and practice learning, in the practice framework

statutory social work tasks, including legal interventions (e.g. DoH, 2002a; Northern Ireland Social Care Council, 2003; Scottish Social Services Council, 2003; Care Council of Wales, 2004). In line with the increased involvement of service users and carers in social work education across the board, it is expected that users and carers would be involved in many aspects of placement-based practice learning, including the offering of placements in user-controlled services, allowing students to shadow and observe them in different situations, and providing feedback on students' performance (Levin, 2004).

In the final years of the operation of the Diploma of Social Work it was widely acknowledged that the number of placement opportunities had been shrinking due to factors such as high turnover rates for social workers in local authorities, some authorities operating with high levels of vacancies (particularly in some London boroughs), and social workers who gained the practice teaching qualification subsequently moving into management (Kearney, 2003). Thus the increased emphasis on placements and practice learning in the honours degrees puts even more pressure on higher education institutions and social work organizations. As students with (understandably) high expectations of what placements can deliver, it is important to recognize the effect that resource and staff shortages can have on the range of practice learning opportunities available and how they can be provided.

Despite this gloomy picture, attempts are being made to increase the number of practice learning opportunities and practice assessors (Practice Learning Taskforce, 2003). As suggested by a report produced by the Social Care Institute for Excellence (Kearney, 2003) a key strategy is to promote a culture of learning in social work agencies so that practice learning, teaching and assessing become part of the organizational infrastructure. Thus, even when a practice teacher (with the practice teaching qualification) moves into management, she or he should continue to be involved in practice teaching either directly or through supporting and mentoring practice assessors. Having students on placement stimulates this culture of learning and thus their involvement in the organization can be promoted as a resource rather than a burden. Other strategies to improve the number and flexibility of placements include group placements, group supervision, 'long-arm' or off-site practice teaching by qualified social workers, and on-site assessment and supervision provided by non-social work colleagues.

ROLES AND RESPONSIBILITIES ON PLACEMENTS

Any one practice placement brings together at least two different organizations: a higher education institution and an agency providing social work or social care services. Ideally, the relationship between the two should be structured as a partnership, such as we outlined in Chapter 6. They are two (usually) independent organizations joining together for a specific purpose: to provide a student with a unique learning opportunity. Like any partnership between people or organizations, power issues come into play depending on how the organizations can influence each other and what each wants to achieve. For the university or college the priority is to arrange a student placement that provides a good learning experience with quality practice teaching and supervision. Ideally, they are looking for a stable organization that values student and staff learning and that has the resources to both support and assess the student's work. The latter is important because higher education institutions need to place not just those students who are seen as 'high flyers' and who will automatically be seen as a benefit to the agency, but also those students who have had little or no prior work experience or who may not be performing so well and who may need more assistance. From the point of view of the placement agency, the priority might be for support and advice from the university or college in the supervision and assessment of the student's work. They may have particular expectations about the sorts of knowledge, skills and values that a student will display on starting the placement. They may also have expectations about the work the student will do while on placement and the level of contribution they can make to the team. There may be tensions for the agency in determining if the investment of a social worker's time in practice assessing is offset by the contribution the student can make in his or her work. Although we would argue that the benefits are much greater in that student placements can stimulate a culture of learning in an agency.

While the people involved in organizing and delivering any placement will vary, in most cases the key players are the practice assessor, the student and the tutor. As the Quality Assurance Agency for Higher Education (2001: 7) recognizes, students have responsibilities both to the higher education institution and to the placement agency, including its employees and service users. They are responsible for their learning and professional relationships, for recording progress, and for advising of any problems. They have the right to a safe working environment and to be treated in line with relevant legislation. Practice assessors are responsible for helping the student negotiate the organization, assisting them to identify learning needs and priorities, allocating work to them, providing teaching and supervision, and developing opportunities for assessing competence. Tutors evaluate the teaching and learning on placement and make suggestions for how this can be enhanced or extended (e.g. providing advice on useful reading). The tutor becomes an important player when there are disagreements between the student and practice assessor or if there are other problems on placement. Placements work best where there are strong three-way links between the student, practice assessor and tutor. The links between student, practice assessor and tutor are realized through phone contact and 'three-way' meetings held during the placement. The aim should be to develop an open, honest and supportive three-way relationship.

Within the placement agency other people might be involved in the placement. Managers or placement coordinators may be involved in setting up the placement, in negotiating the allocation of work to the student and in negotiating issues if problems occur. Invariably students will find themselves working in a team environment and other professionals, administrative staff, volunteers and service users may assist their learning in different sorts of ways, for example by allowing the student to observe them or by engaging the student in collaborative work. In some cases an off-site practice teacher or assessor (often referred to as a long-arm) may be appointed where the on-site assessor/supervisor is not a qualified social worker or does not have sufficient experience. In this situation usually the on-site assessor supports the student in their day-to-day practice and the long-arm assessor provides input around the social work role in the agency and the student's professional development as a social worker.

Within the college or university a range of staff may be involved in setting up placements and bringing students together in seminars to reflect on their practice learning. Other students are often an important source of support and encouragement. Higher education institutions will have various mechanisms in place for making a final assessment on students' placement performance. This may involve panels of staff, agency and service user representatives evaluating evidence provided by students and practice assessors. There will also be one or two external examiners (academic staff from another college or university) whose role is to determine the quality of student assessment and ensure standards. They have specific quality assurance reporting responsibilities to the Care Councils (see General Social Care Council, 2003).

One issue that is important to consider is the inevitable power dynamics within placement relationships and, in particular, in the relationship between the student and the practice assessor. At an obvious level students appear in a less powerful position than practice assessors because of their student role. However, it is also important to acknowledge the impact of socially structured differences along the lines of gender, 'race', age, sexual identity, class and so on. The differences between students and others in the agency along these lines may affect the power relations the student experiences. For example, students for whom English is not their first language may face additional stress in fitting into the agency and meeting its requirements: 'Because I speak English with an accent, the staff don't always try to understand me. But I am expected to know what they say. I struggle with feeling inferior' (Final placement student).

When practice assessors and students can openly explore their differences and highlight gaps between their assumptions and approaches, both are likely to learn and feel valued. While practice assessors may themselves experience marginalization within their workplace (for example, due to being a black worker in a largely white organization), the onus initially is on the practice assessor to raise issues of difference and consider ways difference can be explored and used as a resource within the placement. Furthermore, agencies and universities or colleges should ensure that students are not discriminated against in their choice of placements or their work conditions. For example, the higher education institution should operate in line with the Special Education Needs and Disability Act 2001 and take reasonable steps to ensure that students with disabilities are not disadvantaged in their placements.

When placements are going well, problems in the mix of roles and responsibilities are rarely noticed. However, when there are difficulties tensions between the various parties and organizations quickly appear. These can sometimes be understood as conflicts between different systems and the exercise of power, where the student feels least empowered.

Sometimes a particular element in one of the organizations becomes a scapegoat for placement problems and becomes the target for change by the other parties. Such elements might include a concern that the agency is exploiting the student as unpaid labour, or that the student feels forced to side with or against service users, or that the university or college is out of touch with the reality of practice demands. Placements are fraught with these sorts of tensions. It is unreasonable to expect that as people in human organizations the key players in placement provision are immune to such conflict. Nevertheless when agencies and higher education institutions have clear policies around practice learning opportunities there is usually more chance of addressing these tensions and ensuring that the provision and assessment of student learning remains paramount.

BEGINNING PLACEMENTS

While it depends on the allocation process in place at the particular university or college, invariably students will be asked their views about what sort of placement they would like and, importantly, what would best meet their learning priorities. As a student, you may be influenced by what motivated you to study social work in the first place, interests developed in the course, and the prevailing wisdom in the student body about where the 'good' placements are. You are likely to have a bias towards particular fields of practice and against others. It is not unusual for students to seek placements in areas in which they feel they have prior knowledge. Some fields of practice are seen as less glamorous than others and your interests may reflect these biases. It is helpful to keep as open a mind as possible about where you would consider doing placement and remember that a placement that is in a different setting or with a different service user group may still allow you to develop knowledge and skills that can be transferred to your preferred work situation in due course. Other students might express a preference for placements that will maximize their employment opportunities. The location of the placement and amount of travelling time required, the standard of dress required, the amount of childcare required may also influence students' preferences. You may be quite idealistic about your requests for placement or be more pragmatic, trading ideals for the reality of other demands.

From the agency's point of view, getting you started involves getting to know you and familiarizing you with the agency procedures. Even though students will have undergone a period of preparation for practice, as per the degree requirements, the agency will also be concerned with evaluating when and how you will be ready to work with service users in that context. Practice assessors and managers have a responsibility to ensure that service users will not be at risk through their contact with you. The practice assessor may need to observe your initial interactions with service users. He or she will also draw on observations of you interacting with other staff and may gain feedback from them as well. The practice assessor will also rely on their sense of the relationship they are developing with you and the information provided on you by the university or college. The aim is to assess if you are 'safe' to start work. This assessment will be influenced by everyone's level of trust. You need to ask if you are not sure what is expected of you. Getting started, from the student's point of view, is linked to getting to know the agency and its community environment, setting appropriate boundaries between you and your practice assessor (and learning about appropriate boundaries between you and the people you work with), and understanding how you learn best and what you want to learn.

It's not so unusual for students to feel a little overwhelmed walking into their agency on day one. All sorts of things can seem like difficulties. Do I take my lunch? What will I wear? What sort of material should I take with me?

I was going on a placement with older people and I did wonder about my nose rings. I decided to start off by taking them out, and letting them get to know me. (First placement student)

Most of these questions get answered very quickly and you are able to move on to developing an understanding of your agency. The information provided to you by your university or college may set specific tasks that help in this orientation. Some topics it could be helpful to think about at the beginning of placement are:

- the structure and history of the agency;
- its location and mandate within wider social policies and legislation;
- its funding base;
- its policies;
- its organizational structure – and where you and your practice assessor fit in that structure.

Many of the agency's rules and routines will be explained in the first few days. Take the time to read the written material that is available and discuss your understanding of how the organization works with your practice assessor. This is particularly important in agencies that have a statutory mandate as so much of the work is directly linked to legislation and government guidance. Some important rules or policies may be informal; for example, the use of coffee mugs in the kitchen. A good general rule of thumb is 'When in doubt, ask!' As you develop an understanding of the agency you will see that it is part of a network of community services. It is important to make contact with at least some of these services and to critically reflect on the way they do or do not link, do or do not meet needs and who is accessing available resources.

An important issue to consider when beginning placement is your personal and professional boundaries: appropriate ways of behaving in your placement relationships. There may be clear agency policy on appropriate personal boundaries between workers, and their students, and the people who use the service provided. Some issues that may arise include difficulties maintaining confidentiality, concerns about personal safety and strong feelings of liking or disliking a service user and the repercussions. Invariably there will also be boundary issues in students' relationships with practice assessors. These include what personal issues you could, or should, raise; the differences between therapy and supervision of your practice; and what differences between yourself and your practice assessor could or should be explored (Cochrane and Hanley, 1999: 14). For example, in what circumstances is it all right to disclose that you have had personal experience with the mental health system? When is such disclosure mandatory? What personal and practice information is confidential to the supervisory relationship and when and how should information be shared? Practice placements are characterized by learning across difference. Some of our different attributes will have an impact on what is considered appropriate boundary keeping. For example, you may consider that the way you are being treated is culturally insensitive and hence crosses your personal boundaries, but does not appear to worry others. Such matters need to be raised, with a focus on the issues at stake. Including guidelines that help in resolving such issues in a clear agreement about your placement with your practice assessor will provide a framework for these negotiations.

At the beginning of placements students will be introduced and be expected to contribute to different documents that will support and monitor practice learning. What form these documents take will vary between higher education institutions. Examples include learning agreements or contracts, placement curricula, learning plans, and supervision contracts. We believe that it is important that in each placement the following information is clearly written and agreed to:

- practical information (e.g. contact information, hours of working, travel arrangements, overtime arrangements);
- the student's learning needs;
- placement goals;
- information about agency policies (e.g. anti-discrimination policies, occupational health and safety policies);
- statements outlining the responsibilities of student, practice assessor and tutor;
- an indication of how difference and anti-discrimination issues will be negotiated;
- supervision and teaching arrangements;
- assessment arrangements (e.g. strategies to assess competence in relation to NOS or SiSWE);
- procedures when students are at risk of failing placement;
- procedures for the management of conflict and complaints;
- key tasks to be completed during the placement and timeframe for completion.

It is our view that students, practice assessors and tutors should be partners in developing such documents. Students bring an awareness of their existing skills and capacities, as well as an understanding of their own priorities for learning. Practice assessors usually have a good understanding of what a person needs to know (e.g. in terms of professional skills and organizational and policy knowledge) in order to be an effective social worker in the agency. College or university tutors have a sense of the student's wider learning across the degree and how practice learning on placement links to practice and other learning elsewhere on the course. All parties should have a good understanding of the NOS or SiSWE and, in part, structure the learning opportunities on the placement so that the student has had opportunities to demonstrate competence in relation to these standards.

LEARNING ON PLACEMENT

The central purpose of placement is to learn from being engaged in practice. We say we have learned something when we can make new connections in terms of how we understand and behave in our environments. Learning involves the whole person and is associated with change. Placement is concerned with learning how to learn as well as what is learned by engaging in practice, reflective conversations with practice assessors, and direct teaching in the form of role plays, and observing and imitating others. Such learning may mean that we can see the application of a broad idea in a particular situation, or perhaps that we identify principles that can be applied generally in a particular piece of work. It may mean that we learn new sets of behaviours, methods or skills that can be effective in designated situations. It may mean that we develop more knowledge about how systems (be they families, communities, organizations and so on) work well or what can go wrong and we learn to use that information in our work with such systems. Whatever the focus of our learning, we will learn more about ourselves as human beings, what we value and why and how we can affect others. There are a range of theories about learning as such (see Cooper, 2000) that help in understanding the learning process. In this section we will focus on learning how to learn, learning styles and tools to help structure learning on placement.

INTEGRATING THEORY AND PRACTICE ON PLACEMENT

It is often said that placements provide the opportunity and the requirement to integrate theory and practice. The frequent repetition of this phrase elevates it to 'article of faith' status, and many students and practitioners are left with an uncomfortable feeling that their integration of theory and practice is lacking. Others dismiss the topic and argue that they are theoretical agnostics or atheoretical. But such a suggestion implies that we act in a mental vacuum. In all aspects of our lives, including being a social worker, our actions reflect our personal theories organized into a framework: the personal sense that we make of a particular situation. These frameworks may act as filters to the other knowledge we need to be competent learners and practitioners. They are not sufficient in themselves to guide practice since they have not been explicitly articulated or subjected to our own and others' critical scrutiny. Placement is a time to enrich our frameworks with knowledge that has been articulated and tested by others.

When we state that social work practice is theory – or knowledge – based, we are asserting that it is a purposeful activity: that it is planned, directed, and that the actions reflect the central purpose of this practice. The application of knowledge and theory provides a basis for an active approach to practice rather than simply serving as *post hoc* explanations of events. We may be consciously using a particular theory to direct action, such as the strengths approach. We may be drawing on knowledge gained from research, such as an understanding of the effect of social networks on attachment. We may have a theoretical idea of what to do in a particular situation and we may develop theories that explain what occurred. Reflecting during an interaction, or with hindsight, provides an opportunity to articulate the theories that seemed to be operating in a particular situation and to make links between the ideal we planned for and the reality of what occurred.

We are asserting the need for a critical and informed approach to practice, in which one's actions reflect more than a personal quirk or the guidelines of an organization. For students, placement facilitates the testing of classroom material in the real world: it provides the context where public and personal theories are put to the test of practice and are subsequently revised, modified and/or confirmed. Schon (1995) argues that the practitioner has to transform theory in light of learning from past experiences (reflection-on-action) and through improvization during the course of tackling a task (reflection-in-action). Practitioners are engaged in knowledge creation. Gould (1996: 5) notes the apparent paradox that the 'creation of personal knowledge is a very social process'. Different theoretical perspectives can inform how personal and social understandings interrelate. For example, feminist theories provide insight into the connections between personal and public knowledge.

Praxis, or the integration of the theory and practice of social work, does not result from the simple addition of theory to practice (or vice versa). Rather, the integration is experienced as a conceptual leap. This may involve recognizing that a particular event can be seen as an example of a broader principle or that a specific direction can be deduced from a broad principle. It occurs when a new comprehensive sense is made of elements previously considered unrelated:

> It sounds so simple once you see it, but I remember recognizing that two situations where I seemed to go off the track were related. In my work with [a community group] and with Mrs W, once I realized that a common issue was my wanting to 'tidy them up' and that I was not really listening or moving at their pace, there were new ways for me to try that linked to what they wanted rather than what I wanted to achieve. (First placement student)

Such integration is dependent on the identification of both what we wanted to achieve and what we actually achieved. Being able to put words around our real and our ideal worlds is the first step in linking theory and practice. What we are actually doing in this process is identifying relevant knowledge, value and skill concepts and linking them in the context of our assessment in a particular agency context. By making cause and effect-type statements, we are linking our understanding of the here-and-now situation using broad concepts gathered in other contexts. When we have a collection of such statements we can look for patterns in what we 'know', that is, we can identify our framework and compare this with related literature.

Drawing on Bateson's proposition that learning occurs at a number of different levels, Reay (1986: 55) argues that social work students need to 'move through the stage of attaching theoretical labels to pieces of intervention or parts of situations', to the stage of recognizing a higher-order rule which governs the process of learning. This process of moving from making conditioned responses to mastering the process of learning, Reay argues, has to be taught; she suggests this learning is more likely to occur if 'a limited selection of theories is assimilated and rigorously applied' (p. 63). This would suggest that on placement you should try to become well acquainted with a few relevant theories, including those underpinned by research findings, and test this written theory with your experienced theory.

Bogo and Vayda (1998) suggest an Integration of Theory and Practice Loop, an adaptation of Kolb's (1984) work on learning cycles, as one way of conceptualizing the process of learning. Figure 7.2 represents a slightly expanded view of their loop. The authors make the point that the starting point for learning is the retrieval of a particular practice experience. This contrasts with other approaches to practice learning, which take a specific knowledge base or the impact of the situation on the worker as the starting point (Wijnberg and Schwartz, 1977).

In summary, the process of linking theory and practice involves the identification of gaps between what was done and what we think should ideally have been done. The person engaging in this process seeks to understand why the gap occurred and subsequently tries to move the real and the ideal closer together. Each review of a specific situation affects the person's general framework: strengthening, modifying or enlarging that framework. To be able to

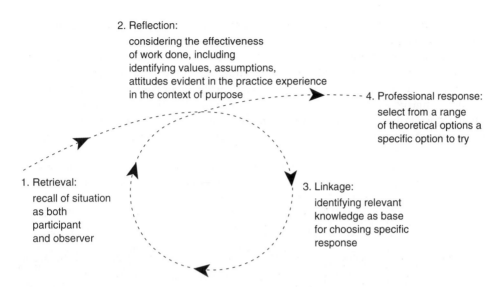

Figure 7.2   An adaptation of Bogo and Vayda's Integration of Theory and Practice Loop

engage in this process, students need to experience and understand it – that is, they need to learn how to learn. One strategy to support this is to learn more about our own preferred learning style.

LEARNING STYLES

Learning styles, or learning patterns, refer to our characteristic ways of approaching and assimilating new experiences. The way you learn best can be described in terms of learning environments, preferred structures around learning, cultural influences, and reasoning patterns. For some writers (Towle, 1954; Shardlow and Doel, 1996) the learning style may be regarded as a relatively stable attribute of personality, holding that our characteristic responses to learning needs are similar to our characteristic responses to life demands. While we would not want to be too deterministic, it does seem to be the case that who we are and where we see our strengths are very much connected to how we learn. Inevitably though, a person's preferred learning style will be limited by the opportunities they have to use this style (Cartney, 2000).

Other authors (Knowles, 1972) consider the student's age to be a factor influencing learning styles. There are significant age differences within the adult group who may be studying social work in the UK. Sometimes concerns are raised that young adults may not have the capacity, maturity or experience to study social work. Conversely myths around the inability of older people to learn may lead to assumptions about the capacity of mature-age students to engage in social work learning. We would argue that age in itself is not a useful indicator of learning style, capacity or pace. Insofar as learning involves consideration of the present in a framework of past and future, the learning process incorporates 'unlearning' for all learners, regardless of age.

Kolb (1984) describes four basic styles of learning as convergent, divergent, assimilative and accommodative. A convergent learner relies primarily on abstract conceptualization and active experimentation. A divergent learner makes use of concrete experience and reflective observation. If you learn by assimilation you rely on abstract conceptualization and reflective observation while accommodative learners, in contrast, use active experimentation and concrete experience. A number of authors produce questionnaires aimed at establishing your learning style (Honey and Mumford, 1986). You might reflect on how you approach the task of coming to grips with new material or learning from what you have done. You might seek feedback from others about perceptions of your most comfortable starting point in the business of learning. In these efforts you are trying to identify whether you are more comfortable learning from playing with ideas or from reflecting on what you have seen, done or felt, or from observation or being involved.

Other authors give consideration to the nature of learning in higher education (Biggs, 1991; Ramsden, 1992) and suggest there are two basic orientations to learning among tertiary students: either a deep or surface approach. Deep learners are interested in the underlying principles, make links between different areas of knowledge, actively seek new ideas and spend time reflecting on the whole. Surface learners are interested in what they need to know to get a specific task done, understand the parts rather than the whole, and are not interested in the underlying theories or in making connections to previous learning or experiences. Different situations may call for one type of approach over another; for example, you really only need to know how to fill a form in, not the underlying rationale for each question, so a surface approach is useful. In other situations, relying on surface learning will mean you are unable to understand and move forward in a complex situation. Gardiner (1989) observed learning on placement from the viewpoint of students and practice assessors. He concluded that the student's learning approach is dependent on the approach taken to the learning by the practice assessor and that there were three levels of learning. The first, and most common, focuses on the content of learning and is a surface approach. The second focuses more on the process than content of learning and hence is a deep approach to learning where the student actively looks for the meaning in what they observe. The final stage focuses on learning to learn.

The point in describing learning styles is not to affix a permanent label but to identify a starting point. This is an important aspect of taking some control in our learning and is central to making the most of placements. Discussions of similarities and differences between practice assessors' and students' learning styles and how any differences can be accommodated can be used to stimulate teaching and learning activities in supervision (Cartney, 2000). With the assistance of practice assessors and tutors your learning skills, styles and strategies can be acknowledged in your placement and built into the documents used to support the placement.

TEACHING, LEARNING AND ASSESSING IN SUPERVISION

In the Preface we noted shifts in the use of terminology around the practice assessor's role. It still seems the case that, despite these developments, the dedicated time set aside for meetings between the practice assessor and student continues to be referred to as supervision, probably because they reflect the other sorts of supervision arrangements already in place in the agency. So for our purposes supervision refers to a formal prearranged situation in which the student's work is reviewed and assessed. At a minimum, this is necessary to ensure accountability, but good supervision goes beyond this narrow (if necessary) remit and provides a much broader learning experience. Salient principles are identified and linked to make sense of situations in relation to an overall framework. Support is offered by the practice assessor in the learning task and plans are made for future work. Specific teaching and learning strategies may be used to assist with this. Supervision is also an opportunity to reflect on your growth as a professional social worker and how your current learning experiences contribute to this growth. Supervision should usually encompass educative, supportive, administrative and assessing functions.

In formal supervision sessions, you may be asked to discuss work done or literature read, to present various written reports, or perhaps to present audio or video tapes of interviews (with service users' permission of course). Sometimes it is useful to use role plays of anticipated or past pieces of work. It is often helpful for you and your practice assessor to draw up an agenda for each supervision session. Agendas are useful devices in helping share the power inherent in making decisions about what is discussed in supervision. Each agenda should indicate priority material, the necessary preparation for supervision and who is responsible for what tasks. Preparation for supervision enhances the productivity of the session in that it avoids supervision that only involves 'thinking on the run'. Obviously, the urgent demands of a particular piece of work may mean some rescheduling of the agenda items or require *ad hoc* advice or support outside the formal meeting.

On any placement, both the student and the practice assessor have thoughts and experiences that never get processed in supervision. This occurs because we have to take much of our behaviour for granted in order to function. However, you will gain much more 'portable' learning from the experience if you do process interactions so that you can devise some principles to be tested out in other situations.

On the whole, we are most motivated to consider those parts of work where we were conscious at the time that something – albeit a vague and blurry something – was going on. We might choose to focus on a particular piece of interaction which went well or perhaps one that went badly. We might be half-conscious of a theme repeated somewhere else in our work. Often it will be easier to focus on those parts of work where we were actively listening, where we did process what was happening (however fleetingly) at the time. We do this because by processing interactions at the time we had some notion of ourselves as observers of ourselves in interaction. With this as a starting point it is possible to build out to the part of the interaction that we don't recall so clearly and to consider why this lack of recall may have happened. It is important to have a clear view of ourselves in action if we are to become conscious of the values put into practice and the analysis we have of how individuals and societies function. If we do not know what we do, or why we do it, it is impossible to take more control over how we choose to use ourselves as social workers.

Various forms of student recording are used in supervision. The skill of clearly expressing ideas in written form is important to social work as a whole (it is emphasized in the Quality Assurance Agency's *Benchmark Statement*, 2000) and learning to write clearly and concisely in a practice context should be on the learning agenda. It is a good idea to identify the principles relevant to good record keeping in your particular agency. These principles may include: always state the evidence for the conclusion reached in the report; always write in a style that you would be happy for any other person to read; have a clear structure for the record so others can easily follow your logic; and use inclusive and clear language. For a student, this skill aids the reflective process between what is done and what is known so that the principles guiding practice can be delineated. Written ideas also keep your practice assessor informed in some detail about your work so they can be accountable for your work to the agency and to the people the agency works with. Written records produced while on placement (e.g. reports, case notes, letters) provide a good source of evidence when you and your practice assessor set about assessing your competence to practise. Other written materials frequently used on placement include reflective journals or diaries and logs of work and evidence (to help demonstrate competence).

An ever present element in the practice assessor/student relationship is the assessment of the student's performance over the placement, which may involve the collation of evidence to demonstrate competence in relation to the NOS or SiSWE. Thus a key task of supervision is the discussion of the student's progress in relation to the assessment tasks agreed to earlier in the placement. The provision of feedback (both positive and constructively critical) by the practice assessor will be an important aspect to supervision. Students tend to respond differently to critical feedback. Some accept it meekly and without question, others react defensively and seek to challenge all the points made. How feedback is provided and taken on board has implications for how effectively the other tasks of supervision can be carried out and, more broadly, for the practice assessor/student relationship. From our perspective it is important that practice assessors are honest and open with students in supervision in providing feedback on a particular piece of work and on their progress overall. They should provide that feedback carefully and sensitively and provide plenty of opportunity for discussion and self-assessment by the student. In terms of the student, it is our view that you should think carefully about the feedback provided and talk through the issues with your practice assessor, identifying strategies to redress any problems. Where you have an alternative picture of what happened or your progress this should be discussed honestly with the practice assessor. In this way the assessment of your practice – your practice assessor's assessment and your own self-assessment – is central to your learning on placement. Assessment should be an activity that takes place throughout placement so that feedback on assessment tasks can stimulate new learning.

ASSESSMENT, EVALUATION AND FINISHING UP

While assessment of your practice performance should be a continual process, inevitably it comes into sharp focus towards the end when competence may need to be demonstrated in relation to the NOS or SiSWE. It is important to note though that your broader evaluation of your experiences and learning while on placement – what you got out of it personally and professionally – continues well beyond your final day. As you re-engage with course work, as you prepare for a future placement or as you work in practice as a qualified social worker, it is inevitable that you will revisit your placement experiences and interpret and learn from them in new ways. In this section we will discuss assessment processes and tasks and identify some of the issues involved in evaluating placement experiences and finishing up.

Strategies and tasks in relation to the assessment of a student's performance and collection of evidence to demonstrate competence should be discussed and mapped out early on in the placement. Ideally they should be made explicit in a written document. Students and practice assessors should be able to plan for assessment tasks and it is essential that time is allowed for immediate debriefing after the event and the subsequent provision of more detailed feedback during supervision. For example, a common assessment task is the observation of the student's direct work with a service user by a practice assessor. This task should be discussed in advance and the role of the assessor agreed (for example, if the interview seemed to be going 'off the rails' how should the assessor intervene?). The presence of the assessor during the interview should be negotiated with the service user well in advance and they should be allowed to have some influence over how the observation is to take place (for example, where the practice assessor should sit if the interview is to be in the service user's own home). The recording of the observation needs to be considered. Will the practice assessor take notes? If so, what impact might this have on the service user and the student? How will feedback from the service user be obtained? After the interview is completed the student will inevitably be wanting some direct feedback from the assessor and possibly some support and reassurance too. It is important to allow time for this debriefing, but equally important for the practice assessor not to blurt out all of his or her thoughts at this point. For both parties it is probably best that the practice assessor takes some time to prepare the feedback properly and go through it in detail with the student during a supervision session.

Accounts of such assessment tasks provide vital evidence in demonstrating competence in relation to the NOS or SiSWE. Inevitably the university or college will have a view on the sort of evidence that is appropriate, but it will usually include accounts of:

- the specific outcomes of work carried out by the student;
- observations of the student's direct work with service users, carers and communities (by the practice assessor and by other staff);
- observations of the student's work liaising with colleagues both inside the agency, with external organizations, and at meetings;
- discussions and activities (e.g. role plays) carried out in supervision;
- written work completed by the student;
- process records or audio or video recording of interviews or encounters with service users or carers;
- feedback on the quality of the student's work by service users, carers and other staff;
- joint work conducted by the practice assessor or other staff with the student;
- presentations on their learning by the student;
- the student's own self-assessment of their performance and competence.

The university or college will specify the ways in which this evidence should be demonstrated. A common strategy is to require practice assessors and students to write reports (often at mid-point and end-point) detailing evidence of competence in relation to each of the Key Roles of the NOS or SiSWE. Ideally the responses to the standards should explain not just that the student is able to, for example, 'manage risk to individuals, families, carers, groups, communities, self and colleagues' but explain specifically how this has been demonstrated on placement (for example, by observations of the student conducting risk assessment interviews and using agency safety procedures). In some cases the university or college will request reflections on students' learning and how they have progressed in relation to their competence in each Key Role. The practice assessor will probably be required to state whether or not they believe that the standards have been adequately met and at what level (e.g. intermediate or at newly qualified worker level). The writing up of such reports should be an open process. Neither party should be surprised by what the other writes and both parties may be required to sign to say that they have seen and discussed the other's report. Where the student disagrees with the comments and recommendation of the practice assessor, they are often allowed to provide an addendum explaining this.

Other strategies include students writing an assignment or detailed case study based on their placement experiences and providing evidence of their competence as a result of this work. In some cases students may develop a professional practice portfolio which may be explicitly set up to help demonstrate competence in relation to the standards and which may be added to as the practice learning progresses. For the majority of students, writing up accounts of their practice learning and evidence of their competence should summarize and pull together what they already know about their practice and what they have been writing about in other formats (for example, in a reflective journal).

As students progress through placement, their practice assessor begins to draw conclusions about their overall performance and competence. Where difficulties are identified early on it is important that these are outlined clearly with strategies required to address them well thought through. Such discussions are useful for an early three-way meeting between student, practice assessor and tutor. In this situation students are under pressure to demonstrate that they can pass the placement and this may mean that they find it hard to take the risks associated with learning. Where students initially performed well and then made a series of mistakes the practice assessor's assessment may shift from 'passing' to 'marginal'. In such a situation it is difficult for the student and assessor to hold on to a picture of the student's overall performance. The student may feel compelled to advocate his or her 'good' points while the practice assessor may feel compelled to gain admissions about the 'bad' ones. Again, it is essential to involve the tutor in these assessment discussions so that an overall picture of abilities and limits can be developed. Tasks should be set for the student so that in the future he or she has another opportunity to demonstrate competence at a passing level. The university or college should provide information on appropriate procedures in situations where failing has become a possibility. Failures are usually determined in relation to the NOS or SiSWE and will be based on evidence of students' practice performance. If you are in this difficult situation and do not think you have had a fair hearing you should familiarize yourself with appeal structures within your university or college. Student unions sometimes provide advocates for students in such situations. For practice assessors a recommendation that the student should fail placement is never taken lightly. However, while placement failure is difficult to contemplate, it must be recognized that this is one of the most important activities that a placement agency and a university or college carry out in that it supports the profession's entry standards and the rights of service users to competent practitioners.

As in social work practice, finishing up on placement is an important process. Planned terminations usually involve some evaluation process. This relates not just to the outcomes of assessment processes, but also to your reflection on and overall evaluation of your experiences on placement, such as the relationships formed with service users and staff. It is worth ensuring that there is time to discuss with significant people your experiences and learning before leaving the placement. Finishing up also usually involves some formal leave-taking ceremony: a lunch, afternoon tea or something similar. These ceremonies are important in showing that you were valued, as well as to mark your change of status with the agency. Finishing up also includes the practical jobs of making sure records are up to date, that cases are closed or handed over to colleagues and that all the loose ends are tidied.

CHAPTER SUMMARY

Placements are often recalled by graduates as the most memorable parts of their social work degree. They have such an impact because they demand the student's attention and provide the opportunity and challenge to see whether and how the student can 'pull it all together' and demonstrate competence in relation to the NOS or SiSWE. In this chapter we have considered the way in which we link what we know with what we do in practice. We have suggested that if placements are primarily a learning experience we need to understand our own learning styles as a starting point to feeling in control of the learning process. It is important for you to learn from practice, rather than relying on someone else to point out what areas need attention. There is no perfect placement, but all placements offer a wealth of practice learning experiences for processing at the time and in the future.

FURTHER READING

Shardlow, S. and Doel, M. (1996) *Practice Learning and Teaching.* Houndmills: Macmillan. This is a valuable resource for students, practice assessors and practice teachers. Shardlow and Doel outline in this book (and their related publications) the context of learning on placement, theories of learning, and strategies and methods to facilitate practice learning.
Gould, N. and Taylor, I. (eds) (1996) *Reflective Learning for Social Work.* Aldershot: Arena. This edited collection examines the application of reflective learning and reflective practice ideas (notably from Schon) to social work. The strategies outlined should be of use to students and practice assessors in setting up learning experiences on placement, as well as to social work practitioners and educators more widely.

USEFUL WEBSITES

International Association of Schools of Social Work: www.ifsw.org.
National Institute of Adult Continuing Education: www.niace.org.uk.
National Organization for Practice Teaching: www.nopt.org.
Practice Learning Taskforce: www.practicelearning.org.uk.
Professional Education and Disability Support Project: www.hull.ac.uk/pedds.
Social Care Association: www.socialcaring.co.uk.

REFLECTIVE QUESTIONS

1. Identify the three things you think you will find the most challenging on placement and the three things you think will help you deal with these challenges. Can you identify the structural as well as personal elements of these issues?
2. What are your expectations for placement? How could you make use of your tutor to deal with these expectations yourself?
3. Review the Key Roles of the National Occupational Standards or SiSWE. What sorts of evidence will you need to collect in order to demonstrate competence?

8 TOWARDS ETHICAL SELF-REFLECTIVE PRACTICE

In this chapter we examine:

- The importance of ethics for practice;
- The relationship between ethics and values;
- Broad theoretical approaches to ethics;
- Core professional ethical principles for practice;
- The role of codes of ethics and codes of practice;
- An approach to ethical self-reflection in practice;

Ethical issues are at the heart of a discipline such as social work. (Hugman and Smith, 1995: 1)

In this text we have argued that social work and social care practice are concerned with the difficulties people face in their social lives and hence workers are caught up in the ethical questions of contemporary society. Clark (2000: 10) suggests that because individuals live their lives embedded in a network of social relations, practitioners inevitably confront ethical issues generated by people's potentially conflicting 'practical and emotional needs and interests'. The key issues for social workers include threats to individual autonomy, conflicts of interest within families and between individuals and society, conflicts around ways of life where there is no social consensus (e.g. different ways of being a family), the consequences of pressure on social resources, and issues around the levels of competency of practitioners for the tasks they face (pp. 10–24).

We have suggested in this book that practice should be purpose driven and that, within our practice framework, social work's purpose should be about resolving the tensions between people and their social arrangements by helping them take more control in their lives and by encouraging equitable relationships. This purpose is grounded in social work values and ethics which thus provide a rudder, a way of setting a direction both for what we should be trying to achieve as social workers and how we ought to behave in relation to others, whether they are service users, colleagues or employers. Figure 8.1 identifies the

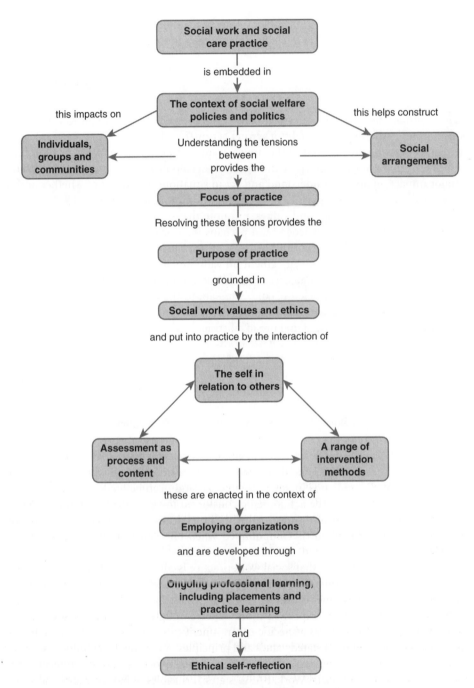

Figure 8.1   Ethical self-reflection in the practice framework

centrality of social work values and ethics in our practice framework. We also incorporate the role of ethical self-reflection in facilitating ongoing professional learning.

ETHICS AND VALUES

Ethical self-reflection involves the systematic exploration of how we ought to act in relation to others: what we see as right or wrong action, or what is good and what is bad in life. *Values* describe the way we put that moral framework into action in our relationships with others, in the way we interpret and develop social policy or do research. Values have a major impact on how we understand and act in situations, regardless of whether or not we can articulate what our particular values are. Compton and Galaway (1994) explore the interaction of knowledge and values and note that some of the greatest conflicts in social work occur where knowledge (and perhaps legal or policy requirements) conflict with a value stance. Furthermore, they argue that values can be understood at both abstract and specific levels, with agreement on values increasing with increasing levels of abstraction. So while we might all agree that self-determination is an important principle in practice, when we are sufficiently concerned about the implications of applying that principle in a specific situation we may become less supportive of the principle. There is a considerable challenge in applying broad, abstract principles in specific, contextualized situations.

Ethics and values provide a basis for making choices when a range of actions is possible. They provide one yardstick against which actions can be evaluated. Ethical understandings must be grounded in the day-to-day demands faced by workers, and cannot be divorced from the standpoint of those involved (Jordan, 1990). For example, if we accept that, as an ethical principle, social workers should show respect for persons then we should be able to locate that statement in the context in which action demonstrating respect occurs, and identify the criteria that may be used in that context to determine whether respect has been demonstrated. That is, ethical standards provide a measure through which the relationships between means and ends in any particular situation can be made clearer (Hugman and Smith, 1995: 2). When the action being considered involves access to resources or to decision making, ethics are also concerned with the exercise of power. This is the case for many professional groups but is compounded when one considers the specific way in which social work is constructed.

We have argued in this text that social work practice is concerned with addressing issues of discrimination and marginalization within a social justice framework. In many countries, such ethical commitments are expressed in professional codes of ethics for social work – though they may be expressed more or less strongly. The British Association of Social Workers (BASW) makes a specific commitment to social justice in both its definition of social work and in its stated values and principles. Adopting the definition of social work issued by the International Federation of Social Workers and the International Association of Schools of Social Work, BASW states: 'Principles of human rights and social justice are fundamental to social work' (www.basw.co.uk). *The Code of Ethics for Social Work*

(BASW, 2002) also identifies five basic values to which social work is committed, and summarizes them in the following sentence: 'Social work practice should both promote respect for *human dignity* and pursue *social justice*, through *service to humanity, integrity* and *competence*.' Such a commitment leads to value-based statements about what is seen as socially desirable that can and will be contested by significant sectors of the community. While social work reflects aspects of contemporary society, not everyone in that society will agree with its goals in a specific situation.

To that extent, ethics and values are inherently 'political', so every exploration of their implications must be concerned also with this contested nature of social work activity (Hugman and Smith, 1995: 1). Justice, for example, may be conceptualized as people achieving their rights or what society views as their 'just deserts', as requiring equal distribution of resources or equality in meeting needs (Banks, 2001).

These different perceptions are linked to different ethical theories, which are explored later. They are also linked to the tensions between care and control functions, and to the underlying ideologies and ways in which work within the welfare state is structured to meet social needs. The contextual nature of social work and social care practice, and of the ethics and values which underpin it means that the 'implications of ethical principles must not only be spelt out but also must be located in the legal, organisational and political contexts in which social work is inevitably practised' (Hugman and Smith, 1995: 5).

The paradigm shifts associated with New Right policies such as the privatization and marketization of social care raise questions about the utility of current professional value bases (Ernst, 1995: 1). After many years of injecting the market into the social care sector, Jordan's (1988) argument that the role of the social worker has become more authoritarian and investigative and the ideology of social workers has become more punitive still rings true, despite the communitarian flavour of New Labour's social policy. Inevitably some workers lost their advocacy role when they became care managers and, in some contexts, what are effectively resource managers (Holman, 1993: 39). While New Labour appears to place much value on developing partnerships with service users, shifts in social work over the last few decades may have reduced the chance of working cooperatively with service users at least until social work establishes closer links with service user movements (Beresford and Croft, 2004). Crimeen and Wilson (1997: 49) argue that 'social work and social workers have always compromised their professional values in order to survive and maintain a position within the welfare state'. They argue that the market ideology of the competitive individual presents particular challenges when set against the values of collective social justice embedded in social work and other social care occupations. By recognizing the challenge as an ethical as well as a political one, a way forward might be found. The choice for workers is not whether there is an ethical dimension to their work, but whether or not they explore these dimensions. It is suggested that if professional ethical dimensions are neglected, they are replaced with personal moral standards and/or uncontested sets of procedural practices determined by employing bodies. Neither of these sources is sufficient in the current work environment.

There are many reasons why we should seek to understand the ethical dimensions of our practice. They include the following:

- We work with limited resources and unlimited demands. We are consequently involved in some form of service rationing. On what basis should those decisions be made? For example, how do social workers in voluntary sector agencies resolve competing with other service providers for service contracts and cooperating with them to deliver comprehensive services?
- The implications of rapidly expanding biomedical technologies which raise questions about privacy, quality of life and even access to life.
- Increasing cultural diversity and more debate about agreed moral positions in society. Different cultures value different understandings of the world and different social arrangements. What constitutes 'good' can only be understood in the context of a particular culture and may conflict with other understandings of 'good'.
- The increasing attention to what constitutes ethical practice as distinct from technically correct practice, especially in contested situations.

While the ethical base of practice is frequently commented on, the empirical evidence supporting the sector's claims about how it implements its ethical framework is in short supply. The questions Clark (2000: 37) suggests as important for future research revolve around practitioners' understandings of the ethical requirements of practice and the ways practitioners resolve ethical problems. Reamer (2001) proposes the use of an ethics audit, a management tool he has developed to manage risk, as one way of addressing these issues.

Ethical factors operate in all aspects of practice. (If you stop and think, you can probably identify ethical issues in almost all situations – even how you allocate your daily work hours.) These factors may be difficult to identify because they are masked by assumptions made about the problem, by funding issues or agency policy issues. We are more conscious of ethical problems. Frequently we recognize ethical problems because they require us to make a decision we would rather not make. For example, when completing a form for Attendance Allowance (the benefit provided to people over 65 who need help with personal care or supervision), a social worker may deliberate about how much to emphasize the impact of a service user's problems to help the claim for the benefit. In this situation the worker is balancing their sense of the importance of the benefit to the service user (and carer), with a sense of duty to stick to the rules and to tell the truth. Such a situation may turn into an ethical dilemma. An ethical dilemma is experienced when two or more ethical principles conflict or when there is an awareness of competing obligations which cannot be resolved simply, such as a situation where there is a conflict of interests between the applicant's needs and a public requirement that laws should be obeyed for the good of all. In any given situation it is possible for different workers to arrive at their conclusions using ethical principles in the professional code, or to use practice wisdom and specific techniques without regard to ethical principles in any conscious way.

We are suggesting that constructive self-reflective practice depends in large measure on an ability to identify the ethical dimensions that underpin any practice, regardless of our level of consciousness of these dimensions. Reviewing the available research on social work ethics, Clark suggests a core theme in the findings 'is the conflict between principles of client self-determination and protection, care and control' (2000: 38). This conflict is reflected in different theoretical approaches to ethics.

To help identify what underpins ethical issues, problems and dilemmas, we turn to a brief overview of the ethical theories linked to the profession's value base; broad ethical practice principles; codes of ethics and codes of practice; and a framework for ethical decision making providing a basis for reflective practice.

AN OVERVIEW OF ETHICAL THEORIES USED IN SOCIAL WORK

There are a number of conceptualizations of what constitutes 'good' and how that 'good' may be pursued in practice. Theories can be grouped into principle-based approaches to action and those that focus on the moral character of the actor (Banks, 2001: 23). Each of these conceptualizations has impacted on the formulations of practice principles described in the next section of this chapter.

A FOCUS ON RIGHT ACTION

This group of theories focuses on different approaches to developing general ethical principles that should guide action. These theories understand ethical reasoning to be 'a rational process of applying principles and derived rules to particular cases' (Banks, 2001: 24). They are also used to justify action.

KANTIAN ETHICS

Kantian ethics, summarized as 'do unto others', have been very influential in focusing the ethical attention in social work on how people ought to be treated. This is a form of what are termed deontological (from *deon*, a duty) ethics. We work out what is our duty, as distinct from our inclination, by a process of logical reasoning (Banks, 2001: 25). Kant, an 18th-century German philosopher, argued that people are intrinsically worthy of respect regardless of how they have behaved or the position they find themselves in, because they have moral agency. A core feature of Kantian ethics is the emphasis on rationality and the importance of the will (p. 25). The principle of the fundamental respect and dignity owed to every individual as an overriding duty is based in this ethical approach. This belief suggests that people are ends in themselves, not a means to an end determined in any other way. In social work practice such an approach to ethics is associated with respect for the individual person as a self-determining being (p. 27), and has been used to develop a set of general principles about how a worker ought to treat an individual user of services. These principles were explored in Chapter 3 in the discussion on relationship development. Until quite recently, much of the social work literature on values and ethics has concentrated solely on such principles. Banks (2001) notes that there has been a movement away from this 'list approach' and from focusing the ethical debates solely on the worker in relation to the user of social work. By paying attention only to the worker–service user relationship, the focus is on individual rights and liberties rather than questions of welfare, social justice and responsibility, which the agency context and society in general raise (p. 30). She argues for a more systemic framework, which identifies the status of varying principles in relation to each other to aid in settling conflicts between principles and in decision making.

Utilitarian ethics are a form of teleological (from *telos* 'an end') ethics associated with philosophers such as J.S. Mill and Bentham. This approach directs us to act to bring about the greatest good, or happiness or pleasure, or the least amount of pain or harm in the world as a whole. The focus is on the overall happiness of the community and not on that of any particular individual and thus utilitarian ethics are said to have a focus on welfare or justice (Banks, 2001: 30). This approach introduces the agency and societal context of practice and focuses on utility, promoting as much good as possible. Justice is seen in procedural terms and relates to distributing goods as fairly or widely as possible.

Both Kantian and utilitarian approaches have been influential in the way workers think about ethics. Disagreements about situations often reveal the tension between these approaches. For example, if a community worker is working for a community that is threatened with a toxic waste dump which it does not want for a range of reasons, including threats to health and land values, action that developed strategies to help this community to succeed in its aims even though it seems very clear that this is the best site, geologically, and the dump will have to be built somewhere, has a Kantian base. In the earlier example about Attendance Allowance, to support the applicant and overstate their incapacities might reflect a Kantian base because the principle that the individual's welfare should be maximized is adhered to. Where a worker insists on sticking to the rules this may reflect a utilitarian base because the rules are there to promote the fair distribution of resources within society. Banks suggests that both the Kantian and utilitarian theories are limited in their usefulness in providing direction because they are both based on an ethic of justice and a system of individualized rights, duties and an impartiality and rationality not necessarily reflected in the day-to-day world of practice (pp. 34–6).

RIGHTS-BASED THEORIES

Rights-based theories were developed by philosophers such as Rawls (1973) and Feinberg (1980), both modern North American writers. The theories vary from duty-based Kantian ethics and rule-based utilitarianism in that they assume there are widely differing views within a society about what is good and about what sort of society can best achieve that good. Society is viewed not so much as a community of common interests, but as a battleground of different interests where the individual's freedom and interests must be balanced against those of others. The only common value is freedom itself, though this begs the question about how far justice is based on equality with respect to basic goods as well as to freedom itself.

RADICAL FRAMEWORKS

Radical frameworks of moral thinking were developed by Marx (1963) and later by other writers, such as Jagger (1983) using a feminist perspective, and Jordan (1990) and Rees (1991) who suggest that our actions must be directed at recognizing the ways in which we are divided against each other and consequently made powerful or powerless. They focus on social change and on more reciprocal relationships between worker and service user, more democratic decision-making processes and more resources for the poor. Justice is conceptualized as equality in meeting needs and utility as equating collective good with individual good. Jordan (1991) points out the contradictions between social work's traditional Kantian values which promote the rights of the individual and statements about structural oppression in its broad statements of goals which would challenge those same individual rights. These frameworks have 'the inverse problem of rights-based theories which are explicit about their ethics claims but leave unstated many of their equally important political and social assumptions' (Rhodes, 1986: 36).

A FOCUS ON THE MORAL CHARACTER OF THE ACTOR

Two approaches, virtue ethics and the ethics of care, attempt to redress what is seen as an imbalance in understanding moral reasoning solely in terms of rationality and action, by focusing on the moral character of the actor, the context and relationships between people (Banks, 2001: 42). Both approaches stem from the work of Aristotle.

VIRTUE-BASED ETHICS

Banks (2001: 43), quoting Statman (1997), notes that in virtue ethics the basic judgements in ethics are judgements about character, where a virtue is 'a character trait that a human being needs to flourish or live well'. What characterizes a virtue may change over time, and may change between cultures. A virtuous person is honest, for example, because they want to be an honest person, rather than because they wish to obey an abstract principle to that effect, or to gain what being honest may achieve in this particular situation. In the context of social work, such an approach to ethics would lead to a discussion of the virtues needed in a worker. Textbooks suggest virtues such as compassion, detached caring, warmth and honesty – the list perhaps ought to include a kind of moral courage, hopefulness and humility. Codes of ethics often describe virtues essential to practice in conjunction with an outline of ethical principles. For example, the BASW *Code of Ethics* (2002) notes that 'honesty, reliability, openness and impartiality' are essential components of integrity (Value 3.4), one of the five key values identified for social work practice. Beauchamp and Childress, ethicists in bioethics who rely heavily on a principle approach to ethics, acknowledge: 'Often what counts most in the moral life is not consistent adherence to principles and rules, but reliable character, moral good sense, and emotional responsiveness' (1994: 462), quoted in Banks (2001: 42).

ETHIC OF CARE

The majority of ethicists in this area fall within the tradition of virtue ethics, but focus particularly on the virtues needed to help others. Okin (1994) suggests such virtues may include patience, the ability to listen carefully, and a readiness to focus on the other. An ethic of care emphasizes responsibility rather than duty, and relationships rather than principles. While this approach has been largely credited to the women's movement and the work of Gilligan (1982) in particular, many cultures also adopt a view of the self 'which stresses a sense of cooperation, interdependence and collective responsibility as opposed to the ethic of justice' (Banks, 2001: 47), where the focus is on social contracts, individual freedom, duty and a ranked order of values. The ethic of care can be linked to virtue-based frameworks dating from the work of Aristotle. Rhodes (1986) sees these as particularly appropriate to professions because the ethical issues often focus on the nature of relationships and our responsibilities in those relationships with a range of others.

Morality in social work has had a somewhat doubtful status. Social work has struggled to free itself from an association with charity, deservedness and moralizing about how people ought to live their lives. Pressures towards achieving professional status have attempted to push out moral dilemmas from practice and convert them to matters of knowledge and technique wherever possible. It is relatively recently that the social work literature has begun to address the moral embeddedness of all social functioning. Gray notes that 'morality is an internal sense, within each person, of other people, their value as human beings deserving of respect' (1995: 65). It is important that as social welfare systems are restructured workers maintain this form of moral focus. Banks (2001: 54) argues that a virtue-based approach to ethics is a good counterbalance to a rule-based approach. We want people to respect the rights of others, not just because that is an ethical imperative, but also because it is what morally good people do. Understanding the ethical base to our practice requires 'a process of critical and responsible reflection' (p. 54), on the meaning and implications of ethical principles. We turn now to consider these principles in social work.

ETHICAL PRINCIPLES IN SOCIAL WORK PRACTICE

These ethical theories are all used in social work and broader social care practice to formulate practice principles. Given their differences, it is not surprising that there is no commonly agreed, coherent set of principles for practice. Variations occur not only in the areas covered by such principles but also in the way they are framed and expressed. They may be expressed in very broad terms, covering many situations but being fairly vague on the specifics, or more specifically, covering fewer situations but giving clear guidelines. Further, they may be expressed in terms of 'dos' or 'don'ts'. What is the difference between 'don't lie' and 'tell the truth'? It is possible to satisfy negative principles by not doing what is prohibited, but it is almost impossible to always satisfy universal positive principles. Thus we may not always know the truth, and even if we did, it would be very difficult to tell each and every truth. Similarly we are obliged 'not to kill', but we are perhaps less obliged or less able, to help each and every person stay alive. We are more likely to agree on evils to be avoided than positives to be promoted. Negative principles are usually broad in scope, positive obligations are usually role-specific, for example what parents ought to do.

Banks (2001: 37) provides four basic principles, stated as positives, for social work:

1. respect for and promotion of individuals' rights to self-determination;
2. promotion of welfare or well-being;
3. equality;
4. distributive justice.

These principles are consistent with the purpose of social work practice expressed in this text. Banks is clear that none of these principles are straightforward in meaning or in their implications for practice. In the following sections issues relating to each of the principles are briefly considered in order to identify some of the challenges for current and future practice.

RESPECT FOR AND PROMOTION OF SELF-DETERMINATION

Self-determination was identified in Chapter 3 as being facilitative of the development of the worker–service user relationship in social care. Self-determination can mean allowing people to do as they determine (negative self-determination), or creating an environment which would allow them to become more self-determining (positive self-determination). While self-determination, in both these senses, is a well-established practice principle, the very real limits involved in acting in relation to this principle with people who have very limited opportunities to choose, have also been acknowledged. Loewenberg and Dolgoff (1992) suggest that access to self-determination varies with the reliance of the service user on the benefits he or she receives from the worker. A person's capacity to exercise self-determination is also affected by the availability of real options, the degree of coercion to choose one option, an awareness of available choices and their implications in the short and long term, and the capacity of the person to choose and to act on the basis of that choice (p. 100).

For social care, and social work more specifically, the importance of self-determination is best articulated by service user movements, including the disabled people's movement. Their approach to self-determination extends beyond the consumerist and conservative communitarian approaches that have been apparent in government policy. The challenge presented to social workers by service user movements is to form alliances, individually and collectively, with service users and encourage the development of user-controlled services (Beresford and Croft, 2004). Within traditional organizations social workers have a responsibility to identify the structural, political, economic and personal limitations to self-determination and where appropriate to take an advocacy role to achieve a service user's rights. However, in the interests of justice, it may not always be morally right to promote a particular service user's rights at the expense of those of others (Banks, 2001: 38).

PROMOTION OF WELL-BEING

Within our definition of the purpose of social work, the promotion of well-being is linked to improving the interactions between people and their social arrangements. We have stressed that people act in accordance with their understanding of particular situations. Whether such activities will be judged as promoting welfare will depend on the yardstick chosen, our own or others' views of the service user's welfare, and cultural views on what constitutes basic human needs and a good quality of life. Our codes of ethics stress a commitment to social justice and to work in the service user's interests. Nevertheless in many arenas of practice it is the worker's view of those interests that is given more weight than those of the service user. As with self-determination, in some situations what constitutes the service user's well-being is clear cut; in other situations the worker is also obliged to consider the interests of other people and society at large. That is, in applying both principles there may be a conflict between the Kantian and utilitarian approaches to what is well-being. This potential for conflict reminds us that social workers work on the boundaries between individual and social choices and our ethical frame-work needs to coordinate these two forms of decision making (Jordan, 1991: 28).

EQUALITY

Banks (2001: 44) suggests that equality can be interpreted in a range of ways including: equal treatment – preventing disadvantage in access to services without prejudice or favour; equal opportunity – the removal of disadvantage so that people are given the means to achieve socially desirable ends; and equality of result – disadvantage is removed altogether so people with similar needs get similar services regardless of income, 'race' or class. It is generally easier to achieve equality of treatment, linked to the principle of respect for persons discussed in Chapter 3, than to achieve equality of opportunity or of result, which will generally require structural changes.

DISTRIBUTIVE JUSTICE

Justice and equality are clearly linked, though the application of a concept of justice based on property rights or 'just deserts' may result in inequality. The application of a concept of justice based on need may result in a form of distributive justice. Banks notes that social workers 'are responsible for distributing public resources (whether they are counselling, care or money) according to certain criteria based variously on rights, just desert and need' (2001: 45). She goes on to comment that 'this principle is in operation in much social work decision making and is becoming more central in the present climate as resource alloca-tion becomes a more common role for social workers' (p. 45).

CODES OF ETHICS AND CODES OF PRACTICE

Nearly all professional and occupational bodies seek to delineate their occupational domain and to articulate their moral stance through adoption of codes of ethics and/or practice which bind members to act in the manner described by the codes. Professional codes of ethics tend to be stated as general principles, applicable to a broad range of situ-ations and used as a guide for practice. In the UK, the British Association of Social Workers (BASW) publishes a *Code of Ethics* (2002), based in part on the code of ethics adopted by the International Federation of Social Workers (IFSW). Recently in the UK codes of practice for social care workers *and* employers have been issued by the national Care

Councils. The codes of practice set out a series of standards that practitioners and employers must adhere to. In both codes of ethics and codes of practice the language is of duties and responsibilities. However, it seems that the power to compel particular behaviours on the part of practitioners (and impose penalties when standards are breached) is greater with respect to the codes of practice issued by the Care Councils mainly because they are supported by the authority of the state (through the national regulatory bodies, the Care Councils), rather than the profession. Nevertheless both codes of ethics and codes of practice provide important benchmarks against which practice may be judged.

A code of ethics is a profession's response to the inevitable dilemmas of service provision: it is a statement of ethical standards of behaviour for its members. While based on consultations with members of the profession, the codes of practice reflect more the priorities of government in setting standards. Taken together such codes reflect professional and government concerns and define the guiding principles of professional activities. It follows that their functions are to:

- establish guidelines for professional behaviour;
- assist in establishing a professional identity;
- provide for self-regulating measures (codes of ethics);
- provide for regulating measures by government (codes of practice);
- protect service users from incompetent practitioners; and
- protect workers from malpractice lawsuits.

Codes of ethics and codes of practice explicate the moral stance of the profession, including the obligation to promote and safeguard the dignity, well-being and growth of service users, and to provide an ethical framework that assists in decision making. In addition, a core component of any code of ethics or practice is the obligation on the practitioner to maintain a certain standard of service. Ethical practice is competent practice and requires an ongoing commitment on behalf of the practitioner to attain and maintain the appropriate level of competence.

According to Gaha (1996) a code of ethics is an 'imperfect regulator' of professional conduct for a number of reasons. Gaha criticizes codes of ethics for not going far enough in areas such as observing unethical conduct by colleagues, and for not supporting workers who take action against their organization on ethical or technical grounds. Workers can only be disciplined for ethical breaches of the BASW Code of Ethics if they are members of the Association, currently not a compulsory requirement for employment in almost all cases. However, the introduction of the Care Councils' code of practice may go some way towards addressing these concerns. Agreement to abide by the standards identified in the code of practice is a requirement for registration as a social worker in the UK.

Many social workers are employed in organizations with their own codes of conduct, policies, standards manuals or legislative base. There may be tension between such guidelines and professional codes of ethics and codes of practice. Other workers may have no clear guidelines supplied by their employer and will have to use their codes of ethics and codes of practice in that situation. In spite of these imperfections, dealing constructively with ethical issues, problems and dilemmas, requires a good working knowledge of the codes and clarity of thought about their personal and professional values in relation to the issue under review. The process of decision making using an ethical base is examined in the next section.

AN APPROACH TO ETHICAL DECISION MAKING

In the practice framework we present in this book we identify social work practitioners, who work within social welfare and organizational contexts, implementing social work's purpose through the way they use themselves and in their application of social work values. We argue that social work's purpose should be enacted in all aspects of practice: from record keeping to care management to building social networks and communities. Inevitably though, social workers will encounter ethical dilemmas in their practice and thus, within our practice framework, we need to consider strategies to support ethical decision making and reflection.

What is asked of us, as professionals, is that we carefully consider and define the issues; that we gather the information needed to make an informed decision; that we allow ourselves to be guided by the codes of ethics and codes of practice to which we subscribe; that we recognize and consider the effect of our own values and beliefs and our own life experiences upon our decision-making processes; that we honour the values and beliefs of those impacted by our decisions (service users, agencies, communities and society at large); that we reason and reflect upon the choices available to us; and that we act with integrity in the manner that we believe will be best for all concerned (Rothman, 1998: xvi).

In her book, Rothman develops each of these stages and provides worked case examples of a range of ethical dilemmas. Each of these stages resembles the problem-solving model with which we are by now familiar. A brief summary of each stage is presented below with reference to case studies used in earlier chapters.

DEFINING THE ETHICAL PROBLEM

The first task is to sort through all the contextual and specific information to identify the ethical issue or issues. These are usually stated as a choice between two mutually exclusive courses of action, such as confidentiality versus a duty to warn, or distribution by merit or need versus distribution by equal share. Defining the dilemma provides a focus for the next stage.

In Chapter 6 we encountered a student social worker acting as a care manager of an 80-year-old man (Mr Harris) with dementia who was about to be discharged from hospital. While addressing the concerns of other professionals, his family and his partner, the student had to focus on the needs and capabilities of Mr Harris. In particular she had to determine if he and Mrs Harris could manage if he returned home to live or if he should be placed in a nursing home. The first option (the one advocated by both Mr and Mrs Harris) appeared to be more risky but would promote his independence and self-determination. The second option (advocated by the consultant physician and Mr Harris's son) seemed safer but would inevitably reduce Mr Harris's sense of autonomy. In this case the student social worker sided with self-determination and Mr Harris was returned home with an extensive care package.

This example also illustrates that ethical dilemmas or problems often emerge where two or more people have competing interests and where the worker is required to balance these interests. If we return to the Refugee Women's Group (reported on in Chapter 5) we can see that in being confronted with a group member's (Marceline's) inappropriate and culturally insensitive behaviour, the student social worker was presented with an ethical dilemma relating to individual well-being versus social justice. Should she openly challenge culturally inappropriate behaviour in the group, should she ignore it or should she discuss the issues separately with the individual concerned? Each option represents a differing view of how to maximize the welfare of the individuals involved in the group and the group as a whole, and how to promote social justice in terms of cultural and religious equality. If she ignored what Marceline said and the effect it had on the group she would be promoting Marceline's welfare at the expense of other members of the group and contributing to the stigmatization of Muslim cultures. If she openly challenged her comments potentially (although not absolutely) by embarrassing her, Marceline's interests would become subordinate to that of other group members and to social justice issues. The student's strategy, in managing the competing interests, was to not openly confront Marceline but at the next group meeting to revisit the group rules and prompt a discussion about sensitivity around cultural and religious issues. The way we define the ethical problem provides a direction to the rest of the work, encouraging us to explore some issues and to ignore others.

GATHERING INFORMATION

This refers to the process of gathering more information about the general issues surrounding the situation. Good ethical decision making rests on appropriate research in texts, with colleagues and with the person(s) concerned. In order to prepare a discharge plan for Mr Harris, the student social worker needed to gather a wide range of information from all concerned parties, including his wife, family and other professionals involved in his care. Most importantly she needed to gather information from Mr Harris himself about his own wishes. This was not straightforward given that he had dementia and was not able to fully conceptualize the risks he (and his partner) might face if he were to return home. Thus, she was sifting through lots of information, but was also evaluating, drawing on medical advice, Mr Harris's capacity to be involved in the decision-making process. The student also drew on community care literature and government guidance to assist her understanding of Mr Harris's situation and to take the appropriate course of action. While Mr Harris's eventual discharge home was not successful for long, it is important to note that the student's strategy was informed by a commitment to supporting the individual to maximize power and control their life in a manner consistent with other equitable relationships.

EXAMINING THE ETHICAL THEORETICAL CONCEPTS

This examination relates to the ethical theories mentioned earlier in this chapter. In exploring an ethical theory Rothman (1998) suggests that three important questions are:

1. the *authoritative question* – where does the theory turn for validation of its basic principles?
2. the *distributive question* – whose interest does the theory address?
3. the *substantive question* – what goals are desirable ends within this theory?

In Tina's story (reported in Chapter 3) the competing ethical frameworks for the student practitioner might be seen initially as an ethic of care for Tina and utilitarian ethics that suggest Tina should put her children's needs before her own. These different ethical theories promote different conditions of 'happiness' in these examples, including personal agency, human relatedness and successfully meeting challenges.

Ethical decision making is only possible if there is the ability to make choices between meaningful alternatives and there is an ability to put that choice into effect, that is, to operationalize it. In Tina's situation the student practitioner had little power in the assessment process and subsequent intervention. However, by being able to sit with Tina, and feel her distress rather than react to her treatment of her children, some of Tina's strengths as a parent were able to emerge and a future for Tina with her children could be imagined. And while at times the student social worker felt that she didn't (or shouldn't) have power in the Refugee Women's Group, she was able to use her position to promote equitable group processes by encouraging the group to revisit the group rules at the beginning of the next session. Although there were other courses of action open to her, she was able to follow through with what was for her the 'right' strategy.

MOVING FROM ETHICAL THEORIES TO PRINCIPLES THAT GIVE GUIDANCE

'Principles ensure consistency and justice in the application of theory to specific ethical problems in practice. They decrease the worker's dependence on personal values and biases by providing objective criteria that may be applied in many different circumstances' (Rothman, 1998: 11). In Chapter 6 we outlined the ethical principles Bateman (1995) proposes for advocacy work. These aim to ensure that the worker always puts the service user's needs first and is accountable to the service user, rather than using service users to achieve the worker's ends. A number of writers propose different sets of principles that need to be rank ordered to be of use in guiding action. Gewirth's (1978) *Principles Hierarchy* and Loewenberg and Dolgoff's (1992) *Ethical Principles Screen* are presented in ranked order, while Beauchamp and Childress's (1994) *Bioethics Perspective* is unranked. These three approaches are listed briefly in Table 8.1. The central point is the need to identify for ourselves the set of principles we are using at any one time, and how consistently we apply that set of principles. Different sets of principles will yield different decisions and different outcomes.

In the work with Mr Harris there were apparent tensions between autonomy and well-being, with the option of moving to a nursing home considered the one that would best promote his (physical) well-being. According to Gewirth's (1978) Principle 3 the individual's right to autonomy should prevail over his or her right to well-being. However, the impact of Mr Harris's returning home on Mrs Harris brings into focus Principle 2 and one would need to determine if Mr Harris's autonomy compromised Mrs Harris's well-being. It was this recognition which eventually (after a period of time at home) led to an

Table 8.1 Three ethical decision-making frameworks

1. GEWIRTH'S PRINCIPLES HIERARCHY – RANKED

Principle 1

Rules against basic harms to the necessary preconditions of action (food, health, shelter and so on) take precedence over rules against harms such as lying, revealing confidences or threats to additive goods such as education, recreation and wealth.

Principle 2

An individual's right to basic well-being takes precedence over another individual's right to freedom.

Principle 3

An individual's right to freedom takes precedence over his or her own right to basic well-being.

Principle 4

The obligation to obey laws, rules and regulations to which one has voluntarily and freely consented ordinarily overrides one's rights to engage voluntarily in a manner that conflicts with these laws, rules and obligations.

Principle 5

Individuals' rights to well-being may override laws, rules, regulations and arrangements of voluntary associations in cases of conflict.

Principle 6

The obligation to prevent basic harms such as starvation and to promote basic public goods such as housing, education and public assistance overrides the right to retain one's own property.

Source: Adapted from Gewirth (1978: 978). Reproduced with permission.

2. (LOEWENBERG AND DOLGOFF) ETHICAL PRINCIPLES SCREEN – RANKED

Ethical Principle 1	Principle of the protection of life
Ethical Principle 2	Principle of equality and inequality
Ethical Principle 3	Principle of autonomy and freedom
Ethical Principle 4	Principle of least harm
Ethical Principle 5	Principle of quality of life
Ethical Principle 6	Principle of privacy and confidentiality
Ethical Principle 7	Principle of truthfulness and full disclosure

Source: Loewenberg and Dolgoff (1992) Reprinted with permission.

3. (BEAUCHAMP AND CHILDRESS) BIOETHICS PERSPECTIVE – UNRANKED

Principle 1

Respect for autonomy: individuals, provided they have been appropriately informed, have a right to make decisions about their bodies and health care, even if their decisions may impact negatively on their health, functioning and life.

Principle 2

Nonmaleficence: one ought to do no harm.

Table 8.1 *(Continued)*

Principle 3
Beneficence: obligation to actively pursue the welfare of others.

Principle 4
Justice: available resources should be distributed fairly and equitably without prejudice, bias or discrimination.

Related rules

Confidentiality: recognises the private, sensitive nature of the relationship and encourages trust with personal information.

Truthfulness: requires that the patient have access to all relevant information about his/her care in a sensitive, open and honest manner.

Informed consent: requires health care staff to obtain the patient's express consent to be treated after the patient has been fully informed of the benefits and risks of treatment.

Source: Beauchamp and Childress (1994). Used by permission.

agreement to place Mr Harris in a nursing home (although he died before he was placed). In relation to Loewenberg and Dolgoff's (1992) principles, the principle of autonomy is not paramount and careful consideration would need to be given to the impact of any decision on both Mr and Mrs Harris's physical health. For Beauchamp and Childress (1994) there is much emphasis on self-determination. However, Mr Harris's situation is also compromised by his ability to exercise autonomy. There are questions about his cognitive capacity given his dementia and his ability to understand the implications of a decision to return home. It is important to note that a diagnosis of dementia does not in itself negate individuals' right to self-determination; it just means that in each individual situation the person's degree of decision-making ability will need to be evaluated. In such situations the tensions between self-determination and well-being are particularly complicated but of immense importance. Similar dilemmas can be identified in relation to gendered domestic violence situations where a woman's capacity to decide to continue to stay with her violent partner is questioned because of a climate of fear and control within the relationship. However, taking action against a woman's wishes in such a situation may have serious implications and could serve only to reinforce a sense of powerlessness.

USING THE CODE OF ETHICS

In arriving at a decision, it is important to pay attention to the profession's code of ethics. Such a code provides a sense of identity to the profession and through that sense of identity we are given some direction in difficult situations, although the limits of the use of such codes, described earlier in this chapter, need to be taken into account. The BASW *Code of Ethics* (2002) is built on five core principles: practitioners are required to give equal priority to respect for *human dignity and worth* and the pursuit of *social justice*. The remaining three principles of service to humanity, integrity and competence are the ways practitioners demonstrate this commitment. These principles can be related to the student's work with the Refugee Women's Group. Knowing how to respond in such a situation can be assisted by referring to the principles in the *Code of Ethics*. For example, BASW (2002: 3.2.2, section c) suggests that, when a worker is seeking to promote justice and social fairness, acting to minimize barriers and expand choice and potential for all service users, he or she should pay special regard to those who are disadvantaged, vulnerable, oppressed or have exceptional needs. If the assessment was that Marceline's behaviour stigmatized a group of people and contributed to their marginalization, then the student practitioner was right to take action to promote a more equitable group environment.

SERVICE USER VALUES, SOCIETAL VALUES AND PERSONAL VALUES

These are vital parts of the decision-making process. As in all aspects of practice, the service user's values, world view, cultural outlook and religious beliefs must be integrated into ethical decision making. Similarly, the worker has a responsibility to society at large and is expected to uphold societal values as well as advocate for change. What are these values? Defining such values is a complex and difficult task. In this book we have presented a particular understanding of society and social work practice in that society. The values that often have the most impact on how situations are defined and resolved are those of the worker. These are often the values that come from our own unique life experiences, our professional training and our belief system. They are the screen through which we see the world and through which we present our understanding of ethical issues, problems and dilemmas. Self-reflective practice depends on an ability to reflect on this central dimension of our practice to make it more available to scrutiny by ourselves and others.

DEFINING OPTIONS AND ARRIVING AT A RESOLUTION

Options must be as fully reasoned as possible; they must reflect real possible courses of action that can be implemented by the worker (Rothman, 1998: 20). Options are formulated by deciding on one arm of the dilemma, by developing a synthesis of the options or finding a different solution entirely. These options will reflect our view of what social work should be concerned about, our understanding of the particular issue and our skills in applying relevant knowledge and skills to influence outcomes in the desired direction.

Any practice situation is defined by ethical issues, problems and dilemmas. Identifying them and understanding how these conflicts arise – for example through unequal power relationships with service users or through society's ambivalence towards the role of social workers – is an important component of being a reflective practitioner. By identifying these issues, dilemmas and problems practitioners become 'more confident about their own values and how to put them into practice; they integrate knowledge, values and skills; reflect on practice and learn from it; they are prepared to take risks and moral blame' (Banks, 1995: 140).

CONCLUSION: RETURNING TO THE PRACTICE FRAMEWORK

In the practice framework presented in this book we note the importance of understanding social work within the context of social welfare policy and politics (highlighted in Chapter 2) and the context of the employing organization (highlighted in Chapter 6). These contexts frame the jobs social workers have available to them and provide much needed resources that social workers can use to benefit service users. However, social workers are not mindless functionaries in these contexts; they also seek to enact social work's own purpose through their practice. Within our practice framework we articulate this purpose as resolving the tensions between people and their social arrangements. We see this purpose as grounded in social work values and, in particular, we argue that social work purpose can best be put into practice by helping people gain more control over their own lives (where this does not adversely affect others) and helping people develop and maintain equitable social relationships.

Social workers use themselves in putting this purpose into practice. They draw on their communication skills and capacity to form professional relationships with service users, whether they are in individual, group or community settings (discussed in Chapter 3). Service users tend to value social workers who can recognize and engage with their whole self, as well as with the problems or issues they might be facing. Within our practice framework we argue that the types of relationships that social workers form with service users should be shaped by social work values, such as empowerment, self-determination and confidentiality. These relationships are the basis for developing accurate assessments of people's circumstances, identifying outcomes that need to be achieved, and formulating interventions to achieve them.

We argue that the focus of assessments, as with the focus of social work generally, should be developing an understanding of the interactions and tensions between people and their social arrangements (examined in Chapter 4). We also emphasize the importance of social workers drawing on professional knowledge to facilitate this understanding and to test emerging explanations. Professional knowledge or discourses comprise the social arrangements with which service users interact and thus it is important for practitioners to reflect critically on how their emerging understanding and assessment might be empowering or disempowering for service users. In line with our practice framework and conceptualization of assessment, we identify three stages in a systematic approach to assessment:

1. Identify the key players, their views of the problem and the key aspects of the situation;
2. Integrate information, particularly the nature of the transactions with social arrangements that play a significant role in creating and maintaining the tension or difficulties;
3. Negotiate and establish outcomes with service users or groups and develop a plan of intervention.

Invariably, the assessment processes workers engage in will be framed by specific policies or procedures in place in particular organizations or by statutory requirements. Workers may also wish to assess the capacities of communities and social networks through community profiles and network analysis.

As with assessments, social workers draw on a wide range of professional knowledge when formulating interventions to meet the outcomes agreed with service users (or those imposed in the case of involuntary clients). In our practice framework, we do not specify what this knowledge should be, although we draw on valuable material when articulating different interventions in Chapters 5 and 6. Like assessments, the implementation of these interventions should be guided by our understanding of social work purpose and values and should be subjected to critical analysis and reflection. In some cases the focus of social work intervention is helping individuals resolve personal issues in their lives (for example, by problem solving), by working with people in groups to facilitate support and empowerment, by providing and maintaining their long-term care, or by engaging in care management activities. It might also involve challenging and reforming the nature of the social arrangements themselves by helping build communities or by developing policy or by engaging in advocacy. Inevitably, social workers need a good understanding of the organizational dimensions of practice if they are to successfully implement interventions and to work strategically to change their own and other social care organizations. Central to organizational practice is the capacity to work with others, especially in professional and multi-professional teams, to implement social work's purpose and to achieve the best results for service users. In many situations, social workers need to develop skills for engaging in conflict situations, working with involuntary clients and developing social networks.

We put forward the view that social workers should engage in ongoing professional learning. While this begins before entering social work or social care and continues throughout (and beyond) a degree programme, when students are on their practice placements the learning achieved can be enormous (as outlined in Chapter 7). For many students this is a key time when the ideals of social work as conceptualized in college or university are brought into the organizational arena and are put into practice. Developing an understanding of your own preferred learning style while on placement can assist future learning activities. While such learning may take place in formal settings (e.g. a post-qualifying course), we argue (in this chapter) that social workers should be constantly engaged in a process of ethical self-reflection. This requires an understanding of the ethical principles framed in codes of ethics and codes of practice and a capacity to apply these principles in day-to-day work. Of particular concern are those situations where ethical principles appear to be in conflict with each other (ethical dilemmas).

The framework presented in this book is not designed to be overly prescriptive or deterministic. We emphasize that many social workers will want to develop their own sense of social work purpose in line with the values of the profession. In our framework we articulate a particular purpose that is grounded in an understanding of the relationship between people and their social arrangements. We recognize social work as comprising part of these arrangements and thus acknowledge that social work can be experienced positively and negatively by service users. We see social work purpose as enacted in the day-to-day and sometimes mundane activities of workers who use themselves in their relationships with individuals, groups and communities. While recognizing the power of social arrangements and discourses, we see people (service users and social workers included) as active subjects, capable of facilitating and achieving change. We encourage you to engage with our practice framework and to consider your own sense of social work purpose to guide your professional practice and reflection.

CHAPTER SUMMARY

Social work is inherently a moral endeavour. It not only seeks to alleviate human suffering, but it strives to achieve a better world. Like any utopian project its commitment to a better tomorrow can blind it to the flaws in its current practice or alternatively can lead it to judge and excuse current practice as a means to an end. For many social workers and other social care practitioners their commitment to social justice is tested by the constraints of working within a welfare state that remains dominated by neo-liberal and managerialist ideology and practices, albeit tempered by 'Third Way' rhetoric. That is both the challenge and opportunity presented by social work in contemporary Britain. From our perspective, social workers must ground their practice in critical and ethical self-reflection if they are to engage with these challenges and opportunities.

Professional learning is ongoing and will continue long after reading this book or completing a social work degree or achieving a post-qualifying award. In particular, a critical and ethical self-reflective practice requires openness to learning – an openness to continually re-evaluate ourselves in action, to re-evaluate the choices we make and the understanding we have of the focus of our work. A desire and ability to keep learning from others by reflecting on the experience keeps us in touch with reality and enables us to reach out to others, to imagine how issues might be resolved and to have the energy and courage to begin again.

FURTHER READING

Banks, S. (2001) *Ethics and Values in Social Work,* 2nd edn. Basingstoke: Palgrave.
   This book overviews different approaches to professional ethics and reviews ethical and value issues in recent developments affecting social work practice, including managerialism and user rights. Banks also explains ethical dilemmas and decision making, drawing on case material and presenting exercises to stimulate learning.
Clark, C. (2000) *Social Work Ethics: Politics, Principles and Practice.* Basingstoke: Palgrave Macmillan.
   In a book that poses fundamental questions about social work and its relationship to the state, Clark outlines an approach to social work professional ethics based on respect, justice, citizenship and discipline.
Hugman, R. and Smith, D. (eds) (1995) *Ethical Issues in Social Work.* London: Routledge.
   This collected edition examines the realities of ethical issues in social work practice and the dilemmas social workers often face in their day-to-day work. For Hugman and Smith understanding and deciding on the right course of action must be related to the immediate situation at hand.

USEFUL WEBSITES

CODES OF ETHICS

British Association of Social Workers (BASW): www.basw.co.uk.

Codes of ethics of each national association of social work are available online from their websites (see the list at the end of Chapter 1).

Ethics Updates: http://ethics.sandiego.edu.

International Federation of Social Workers (IFSW): www.ifsw.org/Publications/4.4. pub.html.

CODES OF PRACTICE

Care Council for Wales/Cyngor Gofal Cymru: www.ccwales.org.uk.

General Social Care Council (GSCC): www.gscc.org.uk.

Northern Ireland Social Care Council (NISCC): www.niscc.info.

Scottish Social Services Council (SSSC): www.sssc.uk.com.

REFLECTIVE QUESTIONS

1. Identify an ethical dilemma from your practice, life experience or from the media and, using the decision-making framework outlined in this chapter, identify the ethical issues that emerged, explain how they arose, and justify the decision you reached;

2. Make a note of the values you hold to be important as a worker. Compare your list with the code of ethics for your profession. Can you suggest and defend any modifications to your code of ethics?

REFERENCES

Abel, E. and Nelson, M. (1990) 'Circles of care: an introductory essay', in E. Abel and M. Nelson (eds), *Circles of Care: Work and Identity in Women's Lives*. New York: State University of New York Press.

Adams, R., Dominelli, L. and Payne, M. (eds) (2002) *Critical Practice in Social Work*. Houndmills: Palgrave.

Arber, S. and Ginn, J. (2004) 'Ageing and gender: diversity and change', in Office for National Statistics (ONS), *Social Trends. No. 34. 2004 Edition*. London: HMSO.

Askham, J., Henshaw, L. and Tarpley, M. (1995) *Social and Health Authority Services for Elderly People from Black and Minority Ethnic Communities*. London: HMSO.

Audit Commission (1986) *Making a Reality of Community Care*. London: HMSO.

Baines, C. (1991) 'The professions and an ethic of care', in C. Baines, P. Evans and S. Neysmith (eds), *Women's Caring: Feminist Perspectives on Social Welfare*. Toronto: McClelland and Steward Inc.

Baines, C., Evans, P. and Neysmith, S. (1991) 'Caring: its impact on the lives of women', in C. Baines, P. Evans and S. Neysmith (eds), *Women's Caring: Feminist Perspectives on Social Welfare*. Toronto: McClelland and Steward Inc.

Bandura, A. (2001) 'Social cognitive theory: an agentic perspective', *Annual Review of Psychology*, 52: 1–26.

Banks, S. (1995) *Ethics and Values in Social Work*. Basingstoke: Macmillan.

Banks, S. (2001) *Ethics and Values in Social Work*, 2nd edn. Basingstoke: Palgrave.

Barnes, M. (1999) 'Users as citizens: collective action and the local governance of welfare', *Social Policy and Administration*, 33(1): 73–90.

Barry, M. and Hallett, C. (eds) (1998) *Social Exclusion and Social Work: Issues of Theory, Policy and Practice*. Lyme Regis: Russell House.

Bateman, N. (1995) *Advocacy Skills: A Handbook for Human Service Professionals*. Aldershot: Arena.

Beauchamp, T. and Childress, J. (1994) *Principles of Biomedical Ethics*. New York: Oxford University Press.

Beckingham, A. and Watt, S. (1995) 'Daring to grow old: lessons in healthy ageing and empowerment', *Educational Gerontology*, 21: 479–95.

Benjamin, J., Bessant, J. and Watts, R. (1997) *Making Groups Work: Rethinking Practice*. St Leonards: Allen and Unwin.

Bepko, C. and Krestan, J. (1991) *Too Good for Her Own Good: Searching for Self and Intimacy in Important Relationships*. New York: Harper Perennial.

Beresford, P. (1993) 'A programme for change: current issues in user involvement and empowerment', in P. Beresford and T. Harding (eds), *A Challenge to Change: Practical Experiences of Building User-led Services*. London: National Institute for Social Work.

Beresford, P. (2001) 'Service users, social policy and the future of welfare', *Critical Social Policy*, 21(4): 494–512.

Beresford, P. and Croft, S. (2004) 'Service users and practitioners reunited: the key component for social work reform', *British Journal of Social Work*, 34: 53–68.

Beresford, P. and Wilson, A. (1998) 'Social exclusion and social work: challenging the contradictions of exclusive debate', in M. Barry and C. Hallett (eds), *Social Exclusion and Social Work: Issues of Theory, Policy and Practice*. Lyme Regis: Russell House.

Berreen, R. and Browne, E. (1986) 'Maiden aunt or earth mother: social welfare within the social work curriculum', *Advances in Social Work Education*, 1: 2–9.

Berridge, D. (1999) 'Child welfare in England: problems, promises and prospects', *International Journal of Social Welfare*, 8: 288–96.

Bierstedt, R. (1974) *Power and Progress*. New York: McGraw-Hill.

Biggs, J. (ed.) (1991) *Teaching for Learning: The View from Cognitive Psychology*. Hawthorn: Australian Council for Educational Research.

Biggs, S. (1996) *Understanding Ageing: Images, Attitudes and Professional Practice*. Buckingham: Open University Press.

Bisno, H. (1988) *Managing Conflict*. Beverly Hills, CA: Sage.

Blackwell, R.D. (1997) 'Holding, containing and bearing witness to the problem of helpfulness in encounters with torture survivors', *Journal of Social Work Practice*, 11(2): 81–9.

Bogo, M. and Vayda, E. (1998) *The Practice of Field Instruction in Social Work: Theory and Process*, 2nd edn. New York: Columbia University Press.

Bowl, R. (1986) 'Social work with old people', in C. Phillipson and A. Walker (eds), *Ageing and Social Policy*. Aldershot: Gower.

Brandler, S. and Roman, C. (1999) *Group Work: Skills and Strategies for Effective Interventions*. New York: Haworth Press.

Brill, N. (1995) *Working with People: The Helping Process*, 5th edn. New York: Longman.

Brill, N. and Levine, J. (2002) *Working with People: The Helping Process*, 7th edn. Boston, MA: Allyn and Bacon.

Brill, N. and Levine, J. (2005) *Working with People: The Helping Process*, 8th edn. Boston, MA: Allyn and Bacon.

British Association of Social Workers (BASW) (2002) *The Code of Ethics for Social Work*. Birmingham: BASW.

Brodsky, S. and Lichtenstein, B. (1999) 'Don't ask questions: a psychotherapeutic strategy for treatment of involuntary clients', *American Journal of Psychotherapy*, 53(2): 215–20.

Brown, A. (1992) *Groupwork*, 3rd edn. Aldershot: Ashgate.

Brown, A. (1997) 'Groupwork', in M. Davies (ed.), *The Blackwell Companion to Social Work*. Oxford: Blackwell.

Bussemaker, J. and Voet, R. (1998) 'Citizenship and gender: theoretical approaches and historical legacies', *Critical Social Policy*, 18(3): 277–307.

Butler, I. and Drakeford, M. (2001) 'Which Blair Project?: communitarianism, social authoritarianism and social work', *Journal of Social Work*, 1(1): 7–20.

Butler-Sloss, E. (1988) *Report of the Inquiry into Child Abuse in Cleveland 1987*. London: HMSO.

Butt, J. and Mizra, K. (1996) *Social Care and Black Communities*. London: HMSO.

Camilleri, P. and Jones, P. (2001) 'Doing "women's work?": men, masculinity and caring', in B. Pease and P. Camilleri (eds), *Working with Men in the Human Services*. Crows Nest, NSW: Allen and Unwin.

Care Council of Wales (CCW) (2004) *Raising Standards: The Quality Framework for the Degree in Social Work in Wales*. Cardiff: Care Council of Wales.

Cartney, P. (2000) 'Adult learning styles: implications for practice teaching in social work', *Social Work Education*, 19(6): 609–26.

Cemlyn, S., Fahmy, E. and Gordon, D. (2005) 'Poverty, neighbourhood renewal and the voluntary and community sector in West Cornwall', *Community Development Journal*, 40(1): 76–85.

Challis, D. and Davies, B. (1986) *Case Management in Community Care*. Aldershot: Ashgate.

Chan, C. (2000) 'Chinese culture and values in social work intervention', in Ngoh-Tiong Tan and Elis Envall (eds), *Social Work around the World*. Berne, Switzerland: International Federation of Social Workers Press.

Chaney, P. (2004) 'The post-devolution equality agenda: the case of the Welsh Assembly's statutory duty to promote equality of opportunity', *Policy and Politics*, 32(1): 63–77.

Christie, A. (1998) 'Is social work a "non-traditional" occupation for men?', *British Journal of Social Work*, 28(4): 491–510.

Cingolani, J. (1984) 'Social conflict perspectives on work with involuntary clients', *Social Work*, September: 442–4.

Clark, C. (2000) *Social Work Ethics: Politics, Principles and Practice*. Basingstoke: Macmillan.

Cochrane, S. and Hanley, M. (1999) *Learning through Field: A Developmental Approach*. Boston, MA: Allyn and Bacon.

Cohen, M. and Mullender, A. (1999) 'The personal in the political: exploring the group work continuum from individual to social change goals', *Social Work with Groups*, 22(1): 13–31.

Cohen, S. (1985) *Visions of Social Control*. London: Polity Press.

Colley, H. and Hodkinson, P. (2001) 'Problems with *Bridging the Gap*: the reversal of structure and agency in addressing social exclusion', *Critical Social Policy*, 21(3): 335–59.

Collins, A.H. and Pancoast, B.L. (1976) *Natural Helping Networks: A Strategy for Prevention*. Washington, DC: National Association of Social Workers.

Collins, R. (1975) *Conflict Sociology: Toward an Explanatory Science*. New York: Academic Press.

Combs, A., Avila, D. and Purkey, W. (1978) *Helping Relationships: Basic Concepts for the Helping Professions*, 2nd edn. Boston, MA: Allyn and Bacon.

Commission for Racial Equality (2003) *Towards Racial Equality: An Evaluation of the Public Duty to Promote Race Equality and Good Race Relations in England and Wales (2002)*. London: Commission for Racial Equality.

Community Care (2003) 'Degree of hope', *Community Care*, 3 October.

Compton, B. and Galaway, B. (1989) *Social Work Processes*, 4th edn. Chicago, IL: Dorsey Press.

Compton, B. and Galaway, B. (1994) *Social Work Processes*, 5th edn. Pacific Grove, CA: Brooks/Cole.

Condliffe, P. (1991) *Conflict Management: A Practical Guide*. Melbourne: TAFE Publications.

Connell, R. (2000) *The Men and the Boys*. St Leonards: Allen and Unwin.

Cooper, A. (2005) 'Surface and depth in the Victoria Climbié Inquiry Report', *Child and Family Social Work*, 10(1): 1–9.

Cooper, L. (2000) 'Teaching and learning in human services field work', in L. Cooper and L. Briggs (eds), *Field Work in the Human Services: Theory and Practice for Field Educators, Practice Teachers and Supervisors*. St Leonards: Allen and Unwin, pp. 10–25.

Corby, B. (2000) *Child Abuse: Towards a Knowledge Base*, 2nd edn. Buckingham: Open University Press.

Coulshed, V. and Mullender, A. (2001) *Management in Social Work*, 2nd edn. Basingstoke: Palgrave.

Cox, D. (1989) *Welfare Practice in a Multicultural Society*. Sydney: Prentice Hall.

Cree, V. (1996) 'Why do men care?', in K. Cavanagh and V. Cree (eds), *Working with Men: Feminism and Social Work*. London: Routledge.

Crimeen, K. and Wilson, L. (1997) 'Economic rationalism or social justice: a challenge for social workers', *Australian Social Work*, 50(4): 47–52.

Crimmins, D. and Whalen, A. (1999) 'Rights-based approaches to work with young people', in S. Banks (ed.), *Ethical Issues in Youth Work*. London: Routledge, pp. 164–80.

Dale, J. and Foster, P. (1986) *Feminists and State Welfare.* London: Routledge and Kegan Paul.

Dalrymple, J. and Burke, B. (1995) *Anti-oppressive Practice: Social Care and the Law.* Buckingham: Open University Press.

Daniel, B., Wassell, S. and Gilligan, R. (1999) *Child Development for Child Care and Protection Workers.* London: Jessica Kingsley Publishers.

Davies, M. (1985) *The Essential Social Worker: A Guide to Positive Practice,* 2nd edn. Gower Addison Wesley.

Davies, M. (ed.) (2002) *The Blackwell Companion to Social Work,* 2nd edn. Oxford: Blackwell.

Davis, A. and Garrett, J.M. (2004) 'Progressive practice for tough times: social work, poverty and division in the twenty-first century', in M. Lymbery and S. Butler (eds), *Social Work Ideals and Practice Realities.* Basingstoke: Palgrave Macmillan.

De Jong, P. and Berg, I.K. (2001) 'Co-constructing cooperation with mandated clients', *Social Work,* 46(4): 361–74.

Department for Education and Skills (DfES) (2004) *Every Child Matters: Next Steps.* Annesley: DfES Publications.

Department for Education and Skills (DfES) (2005) *Youth Matters.* London: The Stationery Office.

Department for Education and Skills (DfES), Department of Health (DoH) and Home Office (2003) *Keeping Children Safe: The Government's Response to the Victoria Climbié Inquiry Report and Joint Chief Inspectors' Report Safeguarding Children.* Norwich: The Stationery Office.

Department of Health (DoH) (1989) *Caring For People: Community Care in the Next Decade and Beyond.* London: HMSO.

Department of Health (DoH) (1991a) *Care Management and Assessment: Managers' Guide.* London: HMSO.

Department of Health (DoH) (1991b) *Care Management and Assessment: Practitioners' Guide.* London: HMSO.

Department of Health (DoH) (1995) *Child Protection: Messages from Research.* London: HMSO.

Department of Health (DoH) (1998) *Modernizing Social Services: Promoting Independence, Improving Protection, Raising Standards.* London: HMSO.

Department of Health (DoH) (2000a) *Shaping the Future NHS: Long Term Planning for Hospitals and Related Services.* London: Department of Health.

Department of Health (DoH) (2000b) *The NHS Plan.* London: Department of Health.

Department of Health (DoH) (2000c) *A Quality Strategy for Social Care.* London: Department of Health.

Department of Health (DoH) (2000d) *Framework for the Assessment of Children in Need and Their Families.* London: The Stationery Office.

Department of Health (DoH) (2001a) *Valuing People: A New Strategy for Learning Disability for the 21st Century.* London: Department of Health.

Department of Health (DoH) (2001b) *National Service Framework for Older People.* London: Department of Health.

Department of Health (DoH) (2002a) *Requirements for Social Work Training.* London: Department of Health.

Department of Health (DoH) (2002b) 'Guidance on the single assessment process for older people', *Health Service Circular 2002/001; Local Authority Circular 2002(1).* London: Department of Health.

Department of Health (DoH) (2005) *Independence, Well-being and Choice: Our Vision for the Future of Social Care for Adults in England.* Norwich: The Stationery Office.

Department of Health (DoH) and Department for Education and Skills (DfES) (2004) *National Service Framework for Children, Young People and Maternity Services: Executive Summary.* London: Deapartment of Health.

Department for Work and Pensions (2003) *United Kingdom Employment Action Plan.* London: Department for Work and Pensions.

Diamond, J. (2004) 'Local regeneration initiatives and capacity building: whose "capacity" and "building" for what?', *Community Development Journal*, 39(2): 177–89.

Diorio, W. (1992) 'Parental perceptions of the authority of public child welfare caseworkers', *Families in Society: The Journal of Contemporary Human Services*, 73(4): 222–35.

Doel, M. and Marsh, P. (1992) *Task-centred Social Work.* Aldershot: Ashgate.

Doel, M. and Sawdon, C. (1999) *The Essential Groupworker: Teaching and Learning Creative Groupwork.* London: Jessica Kingsley Publishers.

Dominelli, L. (1996) 'Deprofessionalizing social work: anti-oppressive practice, competencies and postmodernism', *British Journal of Social Work*, 26: 153–75.

Dominelli, L. (1997) *Anti-racist Social Work: A Challenge for White Practitioners and Educators.* Basingstoke: BASW/Macmillan.

Dominelli, L. (2002) *Anti-oppressive Social Work: Theory and Practice.* Basingstoke: Palgrave Macmillan.

Driver, S. and Martell, L. (1997) 'New Labour's communitarianisms', *Critical Social Policy*, 17(3): 27–44.

Driver, S. and Martell, L. (2002) 'New Labour, work and the family', *Social Policy and Administration*, 36(1): 46–61.

Drury Hudson, J. (1997) 'A model of professional knowledge for social work practice', *Australian Social Work*, 50(3): 35–44.

Durrant, M. (1996) 'Foreword', in D. Scott and D. O'Neil, *Beyond Child Rescue: Developing Family-centred Practice at St Luke's.* St Leonards: Allen and Unwin.

Eades, D. (1992) *Aboriginal English and the Law.* Brisbane: Queensland Law Society.

Ellis, K., Davis, A. and Rummery, K. (1999) 'Needs assessment, street-level bureaucracy and the new community care', *Social Policy and Administration*, 33(3): 262–80.

Ellison, N. (1998) 'The changing politics of social policy', in N. Ellison and C. Pierson (eds), *Developments in British Social Policy.* Basingstoke: Macmillan.

Ellison, N. and Pierson, C. (1998) 'Conclusion', in N. Ellison and C. Pierson (eds), *Developments in British Social Policy.* Basingstoke: Macmillan.

Ellison, N. and Pierson, C. (eds) (2003) *Developments in British Social Policy*, 2nd edn. Basingstoke: Macmillan.

Epston, D. and White, M. (1992) *Experience, Contradiction, Narrative and Imagination: Selected Papers of David Epston and Michael White 1989–1991.* Adelaide: Dulwich Centre Publications.

Ernst, J. (1995) 'Privatisation and social work', *The West Australian Social Worker*, December: 1–4.

Etzioni, A. (1993) *The Spirit of Community: Rights, Responsibilities and the Communitarian Agenda.* London: Fontana Press.

Farrar, A. and Inglis, J. (eds) (1996) *Keeping It Together: State and Civil Society in Australia.* Sydney: Pluto Press and Australian Council of Social Service.

Fatout, M. and Rose, S. (1995) *Task Groups in the Social Services.* Thousand Oaks, CA: Sage.

Feinberg, J. (1980) *Rights, Justice and the Bounds of Liberty: Essays in Social Philosophy.* Princeton, NJ: Princeton University Press.

Finch, J. and Groves, D. (1983) *A Labour of Love: Women, Work and Caring.* London: Routledge and Kegan Paul.

Finn, D. (2003) 'The "employment-first" welfare state: lessons from the New Deal for Young People', *Social Policy and Administration*, 37(7): 709–24.

Fisher, B. and Tronto, J. (1990) 'Toward a feminist theory of caring', in E. Abel and M. Nelson (eds), *Circles of Care: Work and Identity in Women's Lives.* New York: State University of New York Press.

Fisher, M. (1992) 'Defining the practice content of care management', *Social Work and Social Sciences Review*, 2(3): 204–30.

Fitzgerald, G. (1992) *Community Profile, SW215 Assignment.* Brisbane: University of Queensland.

Foley, M. (1977) 'The hidden courts in Australia', *Legal Service Bulletin*, 2: 268.

Fook, J. (1986) 'Feminist contributions to casework practice', in H. Merchant and B. Wearing (eds), *Gender Reclaimed: Women in Social Work.* Sydney: Hale and Iremonger.

Fook, J. (1993) *Radical Casework: A Theory of Practice.* St Leonards: Allen and Unwin.

Freedberg, S. (1989) 'Self-determination: historical perspectives and effects on current practice', *Social Work*, 34: 1–96.

Fullmer, E.M., Shenk, D. and Eastland, L.J. (1999) 'Negating identity: a feminist analysis of the social invisibility of older lesbians', *Journal of Women and Aging*, 11(2/3): 131–48.

Gaha, J. (1996) 'A professional code of ethics: an imperfect regulator', *Third National Conference of the Australian Association for Professional and Applied Ethics.* Wagga Wagga: Charles Sturt University.

Gambrill, E. (2000) 'The role of critical thinking in evidence-based social work', in P. Allen-Meares and C. Garvin (eds), *The Handbook of Social Work Direct Practice.* Thousand Oaks, CA: Sage.

Gardiner, D. (1989) *The Anatomy of Supervision.* Milton Keynes: Society for Research into Higher Education and Oxford University Press.

Garrison, J. and Werfer, S. (1977) 'A network approach to clinical social work', *Clinical Social Work Journal*, 52(2): 108–17.

Geldard, M. (1989) *Basic Personal Counselling: A Manual for Counsellors.* Brookvale, NSW: Prentice Hall.

General Social Care Council (GSCC) (2003) *GSCC Arrangements for Monitoring Social Work Degree Courses: Information for Course Providers and External Examiners.* London: General Social Care Council.

George, J. and Davis, A. (1998) *States of Health: Health and Illness in Australia*, 3rd edn. Melbourne: Addison Wesley Longman.

Germain, C. and Gitterman, A. (1980) *The Life Model of Social Work Practice.* New York: Columbia University Press.

Gewirth, A. (1978) *Reason and Morality.* Chicago, IL: University of Chicago Press.

Gibbons, J. (1997) 'Relating outcomes to objectives in child protection policy', in N. Parton (ed.), *Child Protection and Family Support: Tensions, Contradictions and Possibilities.* London: Routledge.

Gibbs, A. (2001) 'Social work and empowerment-based research: possibilities, process and questions', *Australian Social Work*, 54(1): 29–39.

Gibbs, L. and Gambrill, E. (1999) *Critical Thinking for Social Workers: Exercises for Helping Professions*, 2nd edn. Thousand Oaks, CA: Pine Forge Press.

Giddens, A. (1998) *The Third Way: The Renewal of Social Democracy.* Cambridge: Polity Press.

Gilchrist, A. (2003) 'Community development in the UK – possibilities and paradoxes', *Community Development Journal*, 38(1): 16–25.

Gillies, V. (2005) 'Meeting parents' needs? Discourses of "support" and "inclusion" in family policy', *Critical Social Policy*, 25(1): 70–90.

Gilligan, C. (1982) *In a Different Voice: Psychological Theory and Women's Development.* Cambridge, MA: Howard University Press.

Goldson, B. (2002) 'New Labour, social justice and children: political calculation and the deserving–undeserving schism', *British Journal of Social Work*, 32: 683–95.

Goldstein, H. (1973) *Social Work Practice: A Unitary Approach.* Columbia: University of South Carolina Press.

Gould, N. (1996) 'Introduction: social work education and the crisis of the professionals', in N. Gould and I. Taylor (eds), *Reflective Learning for Social Work: Theory, Research and Practice.* Aldershot: Arena Ashgate Publishing, pp. 1–10.

Gould, N. and Taylor, I. (eds) (1996) *Reflective Learning for Social Work: Theory, Research and Practice*. Aldershot: Arena Ashgate Publishing.

Graham, M. (2004) 'Empowerment revisited – social work, resistance and agency in black communities', *European Journal of Social Work*, 7(1): 43–56.

Gray, M. (1995) 'The ethical implications of current theoretical developments in social work', *British Journal of Social Work*, 25: 55–70.

Graycar, A. and Jamrozik, A. (1993) *How Australians Live: Social Policy in Theory and Practice*, 2nd edn. Melbourne: Macmillan.

Griffiths, R. (1988) *Community Care: An Agenda for Action*. London: HMSO.

Gutierrez, L. and Lewis, E. (1999) 'Strengthening communities through groups: a multicultural perspective' in H. Bertcher, L. Kurtz and A. Lamont (eds), *Rebuilding Communities: Challenges for Group Work*. New York: Haworth Press.

Hall, S. (2001) 'Protests as Prague airport asylum screening resumes', *Guardian*, 28 August, p. 2.

Hall, S. and Nevin, B. (1999) 'Continuity and change: a review of English regeneration policy in the 1990s', *Regional Studies*, 33(5): 477–91.

Harbison, J. and Morrow, M. (1998) 'Re-examining the social construction of "elder abuse and neglect": a Canadian perspective', *Ageing and Society*, 18: 691–791.

Harris, T. (2000) 'The effects of taxes and benefits on household income, 1998–99', *Economic Trends: Office for National Statistics*, No. 557.

Health Advisory Service 2000 (1998) '*Not Because They Are Old': An Independent Inquiry into the Care of Older People on Acute Wards in General Hospitals*. London: Health Advisory Service 2000.

Healy, K. (1998) 'Participation and child protection: the importance of context', *British Journal of Social Work*, 28: 897–914.

Healy, K. (2005) *Social Work Theories in Context: Creating Frameworks for Practice*. Basingstoke: Palgrave Macmillan.

Henderson, P. and Thomas, D.N. (2001) *Skills in Neighbourhood Work*, 3rd edn. London: Routledge.

Hepworth, D., Rooney, R. and Larsen, J. (2002) *Direct Social Work Practice: Theory and Skills*, 6th edn. Pacific Grove, CA: Brooks/Cole Thompson Learning.

Heraud, B. (1979) *Sociology in the Professions*. London: Open Books.

Heumann, L., McCall, M. and Boldy, D. (eds) (2001) *Empowering Frail Elderly People: Opportunities and Impediments in Housing, Health, and Support Service Delivery*. Westport, CT: Praeger.

Hewitt, R. (1986) *White Talk, Black Talk: Interracial Friendship and Communication Amongst Adolescents*. Cambridge: Cambridge University Press.

Hill, M. (2002) 'Network assessments and diagrams', *Journal of Social Work*, 2(2): 223–54.

HM Government (2004) *Every Child Matters: Change for Children*. Annesley: DfES Publications.

Ho, K.M. and Chui, W.H. (2001) 'Client resistance in outreaching social work in Hong Kong', *Asia Pacific Journal of Social Work*, 1(1): 114–30.

Holman, B. (1993) *A New Deal for Social Welfare*. Oxford: Lion Publishing.

Home Office (2000) *Human Rights Act: A New Era of Rights and Responsibilities. Core Guidance for Public Authorities*. London: HMSO.

Honey, P. and Mumford, A. (1986) *The Manual of Learning Styles*. Maidenhead: Ardingly House.

Hornby, S. and Atkins, J. (2000) *Collaborative Care: Interprofessional, Interagency and Interpersonal*, 2nd edn. Oxford: Blackwell Science.

Horner, N. (2003) *What Is Social Work? Context and Perspectives*. Exeter: Learning Matters.

Hughes, B. (1993) 'A model for the comprehensive assessment of older people and their carers', *British Journal of Social Work*, 23: 345–64.

Hugman, R. (1991) *Power in Caring Professions*. London: Macmillan.

Hugman, R. and Smith, D. (eds) (1995) *Ethical Issues in Social Work*. London: Routledge.

Humphrey, J.C. (2003) 'New Labour and the regulatory reform of social care', *Critical Social Policy*, 23(1): 5–24.

Humphreys, J.C. and Thiara, R. (2003) 'Mental health and domestic violence: "I call it symptoms of abuse"', *British Journal of Social Work*, 33(2): 209–26.

Humphries, B. (2004) 'An unacceptable role for social work: implementing immigration policy', *British Journal of Social Work*, 34: 93–107.

Ife, J. (2002) *Community Development: Community-based Alternatives in an Age of Globalisation*, 2nd edn. Melbourne, Australia: Longman.

Ivanoff, A., Blythe, B. and Tripodi, T. (1994) *Involuntary Clients in Social Work Practice: A Research-based Approach*. New York: Aldine De Gruyter.

Jagger, A. (1983) *Feminist Politics and Human Nature*. New Jersey: Rowman and Allenheld.

Jamous, H. and Peloille, B. (1970) 'Professions or self-perpetuating systems? Changes in the French university hospital system', in J.A. Jackson (ed.), *Professions and Professionalization*. Cambridge: Cambridge University Press.

Johns, R. (2003) *Using the Law in Social Work*. Exeter: Learning Matters Ltd.

Jordan, B. (1970) *Client Worker Transactions*. London: Routledge and Kegan Paul.

Jordan, B. (1979) *Helping in Social Work*. London: Routledge and Kegan Paul.

Jordan, B. (1988) 'Poverty, social work and the state', in S. Becker and S. MacPherson (eds), *Public Issues, Private Pain: Poverty, Social Work and Social Policy*. London: Social Service Insight Books.

Jordan, B. (1990) *Social Work in an Unjust Society*. New York: Harvester Wheatsheaf.

Jordan, B. (1991) 'Competencies and values', *Social Work Education Reporter*, 10(1): 5–11.

Jordan, B. (1997) 'Social work and society', in M. Davies (ed.), *The Blackwell Companion to Social Work*. Oxford: Blackwell, pp. 8–24.

Jordan, B. (2000) *Social Work and the Third Way: Tough Love as Social Policy*. London: Sage.

Jordan, B. and Jones, M. (1995) 'Association and exclusion in the organisation of social care', *Social Work and Social Sciences Review*, 6(1): 5–18.

Kadushin, A. (1972) *The Social Work Interview*. New York: Columbia University Press.

Kahana, E. and Young, R. (1990) 'Clarifying the caregiving paradigm: challenges for the future', in D.E. Biegal and A. Blum (eds), *Ageing and Caregiving: Theory, Research and Policy*. Newbury Park, CA: Sage.

Kahn, S. (1970) *How People Get Power*. New York: McGraw-Hill.

Kearney, P. (2003) *A Framework for Supporting and Assessing Practice Learning. SCIE Position Paper No. 2*. London: Social Care Institute of Excellence.

Keating, N., Otfinowski, P., Wenger, C., Fast, J. and Derksen, L. (2003) 'Understanding the caring capacity of informal networks of frail seniors: a case for care networks', *Ageing and Society*, 23: 115–27.

Kelly, A. and Sewell, S. (1988) *With Head, Heart and Hand: Dimensions of Community Building*. Brisbane: Boolarong.

Kemshall, H. (2002) *Risk, Social Policy and Welfare*. Buckingham: Open University Press.

Kenny, S. (1999) *Developing Communities for the Future: Community Development in Australia*, 2nd edn. Melbourne: Nelson Australia.

Kernke, C. (1991) *Profile of C, SW215 Assignment*. Brisbane: University of Queensland.

Knowles, M.S. (1972) 'Innovations in teaching styles based upon adult learning', *Journal of Education for Social Work*, 8(2): 32–9.

Kolb, D. (1984) *Experiential Learning: Experience as the Source of Learning and Development*. Englewood Cliffs, NJ: Prentice Hall.

Laming, Lord (2003) *The Victoria Climbié Inquiry: Report of an Inquiry*. London: HMSO.

Lammy, D. (2003) 'Third anniversary of the Human Rights Act', speech given to *Audit Commission Conference*, 6 November.

Langan, M. (1998) 'The personal social services', in N. Ellison and C. Pierson (eds), *Developments in British Social Policy*. Basingstoke: Macmillan.

Langley, J. (2001) 'Developing anti-oppressive empowering practice with older lesbian women and gay men', *British Journal of Social Work*, 31(6): 917–32.

Lee, J. (2001) *The Empowerment Approach to Social Work Practice: Building the Beloved Community*. New York: Columbia University Press.

Lehmann, P. and Coady, N. (eds) (2001) *Theoretical Perspectives for Direct Social Work Practice: A Generalist-Eclectic Approach*. New York: Springer Publishing Co.

Levin, E. (2004) *Involving Service Users and Carers in Social Work Education. SCIE Resource Guide No. 2*. London: Social Care Institute of Excellence.

Lindow, V. (1993) 'A vision for the future', in P. Beresford and T. Harding (eds), *A Challenge to Change: Practical Experiences of Building User-led Services*. London: National Institute for Social Work.

Lister, R. (1997) *Citizenship: Feminist Perspectives*. Basingstoke: Macmillan.

Littlewood, R. and Lipsedge, M. (1982) *Aliens and Alienists: Ethnic Minorities and Psychiatry*. Harmondsworth: Penguin.

Loewenberg, F. and Dolgoff, R. (1992) *Ethical Decisions for Social Work Practice*. Itaska, NJ: F.E. Peacock.

Lord Chancellor's Department (2001) *Courts Matching up Well to Human Rights Act*. Media Release, 20 March.

Lynn, R. (2001) 'Learning from a "Murri Way"', *British Journal of Social Work*, 31(6): 903–16.

McCouat, M. (1988) 'Morality, non-judgement and faithfulness', in E. Chamberlain (ed.), *Change and Continuity in Australian Social Work*. Melbourne: Longman Cheshire.

McIntyre, E.C. (1986) 'Social networks', *Social Work*, 31: 421–6.

McMaster, K. (2001) 'Men and social work', in M. Connolly (ed.), *New Zealand Social Work: Contexts and Practice*. Auckland: Oxford University Press, pp. 110–21.

Mailick, M. and Ashley, A. (1981) 'Politics of inter-professional collaboration: challenges to advocacy', *Social Casework*, 62: 131–7.

Mandelstam, M. (1995) *Community Care Practice and the Law*. London: Jessica Kingsley Publishers.

Marshall, T.H. (1950) *Citizenship and Social Class*. Cambridge: Cambridge University Press.

Marx, K. (1963) *Early Writings*. London: Fontana.

Mattaini, M. (1995) 'Knowledge for practice', in C. Meyer and M. Mattaini (eds), *The Foundations of Social Work Practice*. Washington, DC: NASW Press.

Mayo, M. (1994) *Communities and Caring: The Mixed Economy of Welfare*. Basingstoke: Macmillan.

Mehta, K. and Vasoo, S. (2001) 'Editorial', *Asia Pacific Journal of Social Work*, 11(2): 1–5.

Mendes, P. (1997) 'The left, social workers and the welfare state: an old debate revisited', *25th AASW National Conference Social Work Influencing Outcomes* 21–24 September, Canberra, pp. 482–9.

Milner, J. and O'Byrne, P. (1998) *Assessment in Social Work*. London: Macmillan.

Mishra, R. (1998) 'Beyond the nation state: social policy in an age of globalization', *Social Policy and Administration*, 32(5): 481–500.

Monkman, M. (1991) 'Outcome objectives in social work practice', *Social Work*, 36(3): 253–58.

Mooney, G. and Poole, L. (2004) 'A land of milk and honey'? Social policy in Scotland after devolution', *Critical Social Policy*, 24(4): 458–83.

Morris, J. (1997) 'Care or empowerment? A disability rights perspective', *Social Policy and Administration* 31(1): 54–60.

Mullaly, R. (1997) *Structural Social Work: Ideology, Theory and Practice*, 2nd edn. Toronto: Oxford University Press.

Munford, R. and Nash, M. (eds) (1994) *Social Work in Action*. Palmerston: Dunmore Press Ltd.

Munro, E. (2002) *Effective Child Protection*. London: Sage.

Nash, M. (2001) 'Social work in Aotearoa New Zealand: its origins and traditions', in M. Connolly (ed.), *New Zealand Social Work: Contexts and Practice*. Oxford University Press, pp. 32–43.

Nelson, J. (1975) 'Dealing with resistance in social work practice', *Social Casework: The Journal of Contemporary Social Work*, 56: 587–92.

Northern Ireland Social Care Council (2003) *Practice Learning Requirements for the Degree in Social Work*. Belfast: Northern Ireland Social Care Council.

Nunnally, E. and Moy, C. (1989) *Communications Bases for Human Service Professionals*. Newbury Park, CA: Sage.

O'Connor, I. (1988) 'Social work and the law revisited', in E. Chamberlain (ed.), *Change and Continuity in Australian Social Work*. Melbourne: Longman Cheshire.

O'Connor, I. (1989) *Our Homeless Children: Their Experiences*. Sydney: Human Rights and Equal Opportunity Commission.

O'Connor, I. (1992) 'Violence and society: imperatives for social work education', *Advances in Social Work Education*, 1991: 121–40.

O'Connor, I. (1993) 'Aboriginal child welfare law, policy and practice in Queensland', *Australian Social Work*, 46(3): 11–22.

O'Connor, I. and Dalgleish, L. (1986) 'Cautionary tales from beginning practitioners: the fate of personal models of social work in beginning practice', *British Journal of Social Work*, 16: 431–47.

O'Connor, I. and Sweetapple, P. (1988) *Children in Justice*. Melbourne: Longman Cheshire.

O'Connor, I., Wilson, J. and Thomas, K. (1991) *Social Work and Welfare Practice*. Melbourne: Longman Cheshire.

Office for National Statistics (ONS) (2004) *Social Trends. No. 34. 2004 Edition*. London: HMSO.

O'Hagan, K. and Dillenberger, K. (1995) *The Abuse of Women within Childcare Work*. Buckingham: Open University Press.

Okin, S. (1994) 'Gender, inequality and cultural difference', *Political Theory*, 22: 5–24.

Oliver, M. (1996) *Understanding Disability*. London: Macmillan.

Orme, J. (2001) 'Regulation or fragmentation? Directions for social work under New Labour', *British Journal of Social Work*, 31: 611–24.

Ow, R. and Katz, D. (1999) 'Family secrets and the disclosure of distressful information in Chinese families', *Families in Society*, 80(6): 620–8.

Palmore, E. (1999) *Ageism: Negative and Positive*, 2nd edn. New York: Springer Publishing Co.

Papell, C. and Rothman, B. (1966) 'Social group work models: possession and heritage', *Journal of Education for Social Work*, 2: 2.

Parton, N. (1991) *Governing the Family: Child Care, Child Protection, and the State*. Basingstoke: Macmillan.

Payne, M. (1982) *Working in Teams*. London: Macmillan.

Payne, M. (1986) *Social Care in the Community*. London: Macmillan.

Payne, M. (1991) *Modern Social Work Theory: A Critical Introduction*. London: Macmillan.

Payne, M. (1995) *Social Work and Community Care*. Basingstoke: Palgrave Macmillan.

Payne, M. (1997) *Modern Social Work Theory: A Critical Introduction*, 2nd edn. London: Macmillan.

Payne, M. (2000) 'Team leadership/team management', in M. Davies (ed.), *The Blackwell Encyclopaedia of Social Work*. Oxford: Blackwell Publishers, pp. 345–7.

Pearson, G. (1975) 'Making social workers: bad promises and good omens', in R. Bailey and M. Brake (eds), *Radical Social Work*. London: Edward Arnold.

Peile, C. (1980) *Towards a Theory of Natural Helping*. Honours thesis. Brisbane: Department of Social Work, University of Queensland.

Perlman, H. (1957) *Social Casework: A Problem Solving Process*. Chicago, IL: University of Chicago Press.

Phillips, B. (2004) 'Regeneration games: the politics of childhood in urban renewal', *Community Development Journal*, 39(2): 166–76.

Phillipson, C. (1982) *Capitalism and the Construction of Old Age*. London: Macmillan.

Phillipson, C. (1994) 'Community care and the social construction of citizenship', *Journal of Social Work Practice*, 8(2): 103–12.

Piachaud, D. (2001) 'Child poverty, opportunities and quality of life', *The Political Quarterly*, 72(4): 446–53.

Pierson, C. (1998) 'Theory in British social policy', in N. Ellison and C. Pierson (eds), *Developments in British Social Policy*. Basingstoke: Macmillan.

Pipes, R. and Davenport, D. (1990) *Introduction to Psychotherapy: Common Clinical Wisdom*. Englewood Cliffs, NJ: Prentice Hall.

Plant, R. (1970) *Social and Moral Theory in Casework*. London: Routledge and Kegan Paul.

Plant, R. (1974) *Community and Ideology: An Essay in Applied Social Philosophy*. London: Routledge and Kegan Paul.

Polansky, N. (1971) *Ego Psychology and Communication*. Chicago, IL: Aldine Publishing Co.

Powell, M. (ed.) (1999) *New Labour, New Welfare State? The 'Third Way' in British Social Policy*. Bristol: Policy Press.

Practice Learning Taskforce (2003) *Practice Learning: "Everybody's Business": Summary of the Regional Development Projects*. London: Department of Health.

Prince, K. (1996) *Boring Records? Communication, Speech and Writing in Social Work*. London: Jessica Kingsley Publishers.

Pringle, K. (1998) 'Men and childcare: policy and practice', in J. Poppay, J. Hearn and J. Edwards (eds), *Men, Gender Divisions and Welfare*. Routledge: London.

Pugh, R. (1996) *Effective Language in Health and Social Work*. London: Chapman and Hall.

Quality Assurance Agency for Higher Education (2000) *Subject Benchmark Statement: Social Policy and Administration and Social Work*. Gloucester: Quality Assurance Agency for Higher Education.

Rack, P. (1982) *Race, Culture and Mental Disorder*. London: Tavistock Publications.

Ramsden, P. (1992) *Learning to Teach in Higher Education*. London: Routledge and Kegan Paul.

Rawls, J. (1973) *A Theory of Social Justice*. Oxford: Oxford University Press.

Reamer, F. (2001) *The Social Work Ethics Audit: A Risk Management Tool*. Washington, DC: NASW Press.

Reay, R. (1986) 'Bridging the gap: a model for integrating theory and practice', *British Journal of Social Work*, 16: 49–64.

Reder, P., Duncan, S. and Gray, M. (1993) *Beyond Blame: Child Abuse Tragedies Revisited*. London: Routledge.

Rees, S. (1991) *Achieving Power: Practice and Policy in Social Welfare*. Sydney: Allen and Unwin.

Rees, S. and Wallace, A. (1982) *Verdicts on Social Work*. London: Edward Arnold.

Reid, W. and Shyne, A. (1969) *Brief and Extended Casework*. New York: Columbia University Press.

Reigate, N. (1997) 'Networking', in M. Davies (ed.), *The Blackwell Companion to Social Work*. Oxford: Blackwell.

Reverby, S. (1987) *Ordered to Care: The Dilemma of American Nursing, 1850–1945*. Cambridge, MA: Cambridge University Press.

Rhodes, M.L. (1986) *Ethical Dilemmas in Social Work Practice*. Boston: Routledge and Kegan Paul.

Robinson, L. (1995) *Psychology for Social Workers: Black Perspectives*. London and New York: Routledge.

Rogers, G., Collins, D., Barlow, C. and Grinnell, R. (2000) *Guide to the Social Work Practicum: A Team Approach.* Itaska, IL: F.E. Peacock.

Room, G.J. (1999) 'Social exclusion, solidarity and the challenge of globalization', *International Journal of Social Welfare*, 8: 166–74.

Rothman, B. (1979) 'Three models of community organisation practice', in F. Cox, J. Erlich, J. Rothman and J. Tropman (eds), *Strategies of Community Organisation.* Itaska, IL: Peacock Press.

Rothman, B. (1992) *Guidelines for Case Management: Putting Research to Professional Use.* Itaska, IL: F.E. Peacock.

Rothman, B. (1998) *From the Front Lines: Student Cases in Social Work Ethic.* Needham Heights, MA: Allyn and Bacon.

Rowe, D. (1983) 'The meaning and intention of helping', in P. Pilgrim (ed.), *Psychology and Psychotherapy.* London: Routledge and Kegan Paul.

Rowe, D. (1988) *The Successful Self.* London: Fontana.

Roy, S. (1997) 'Globalisation, structural change and poverty: some conceptual and policy issues', *Economic and Political Weekly*, 16–23 August: 2117–35.

Royal Commission on Long Term Care (1999) *With Respect to Old Age: A Report by the Royal Commission on Long Term Care.* London: HMSO.

Rudowicz, E. and Au, E. (2001) 'Help-seeking experiences of Hong Kong social work students: implications for professional training', *International Social Work*, 44(1): 75–91.

Ryan, P., Ford, R., Beadsmoore, A. and Muijen, M. (1999) 'The enduring relevance of case management', *British Journal of Social Work*, 29: 97–125.

Saleeby, D. (ed.) (1997) *The Strengths Perspective in Social Work Practice.* New York: Longman.

Schiller, L. (1997) 'Rethinking stages of development in women's groups: implications for practice', *Social Work with Groups*, 20(3): 3–9.

Schon, D. (1995) *The Reflective Practitioner: How Professionals Think in Action.* London: Arena.

Scott, G., Campbell, J. and Brown, U. (2002) 'Child care, social inclusion and urban regeneration', *Critical Social Policy*, 22(2): 226–46.

Scottish Social Services Council (2003) *The Framework for Social Work Education in Scotland.* Edinburgh: Scottish Social Services Council.

Seden, J. (2005) *Counselling Skills in Social Work Practice.* Buckingham: Open University Press.

Sevenhuijsen, S. (1998) *Citizenship and the Ethics of Care: Feminist Considerations on Justice, Morality and Politics.* London: Routledge.

Shardlow, S. (1995) 'Confidentiality, accountability and the boundaries of client–worker relationships', in R. Hugman and D. Smith (eds), *Ethical Issues in Social Work.* London: Routledge.

Shardlow, S. and Doel, M. (1996) *Practice Learning and Teaching.* Houndmills: Macmillan.

Sheafor, B., Horejsi, C. and Horejsi, G. (2000) *Techniques and Guidelines for Social Work Practice*, 5th edn. Boston, MA: Allyn and Bacon.

Sheppard, M. (1995) *Care Management and the New Social Work: A Critical Analysis.* London: Whiting and Birch.

Social Services Inspectorate (SSI) (1997) *Better Management, Better Care, The Sixth Annual Report of the Chief Inspector of Social Services Inspectorate 1996/97.* London: HMSO.

Solomon, B. (1976) *Black Empowerment: Social Work in Oppressed Communities.* New York: Columbia University Press.

Sosin, M. and Caulum, S. (1983) 'Advocacy: a conceptualization for social work practice', *Social Work*, 28: 12–17.

Soysal, Y.N. (2001) 'Changing citizenship in Europe: remarks on postnational membership and the nation state', in J. Fink, G. Lewis and J. Clarke (eds), *Rethinking European Welfare.* London: Sage.

Statman, D. (1997) 'Introduction to virtue ethics', in D. Statman (ed.), *Virtue Ethics: A Critical Reader*. Edinburgh: Edinburgh University Press.

Sternbach, J. (2001) 'Men connecting and changing – stages of relational growth in men's groups', *Social Work with Groups*, 23(4): 59–69.

Stevenson, O. (1981) *Specialisation in Social Service Teams*. London: Allen and Unwin.

Stewart, J. and Rhoden, M. (2003) 'A review of social housing regeneration in the London Borough of Brent', *The Journal of the Royal Society for the Promotion of Health*, 123(1): 23–32.

Sullivan, M. (1996) *The Development of the British Welfare State*. London: Prentice Hall/Harvester Wheatsheaf.

Swain, J. and French, S. (2000) 'Towards an affirmation model of disability', *Disability and Society*, 15(4): 569–82.

Takei, N., Persaud, R., Woodruff, P., Brockington, I. and Murray, R.N. (1998) 'First episodes of psychosis in Afro-Caribbean and White people. An 18-year follow-up population-based study', *British Journal of Psychiatry*, 172: 147–53.

Tannen, D. (1990) *You Just Don't Understand: Men and Women in Conversation*. New York: Ballantine Books.

Thomas, M. and Pierson, J. (1995) *Dictionary of Social Work*. London: Collins Educational.

Thompson, N. (2001) *Anti-discriminatory Practice*, 3rd edn. Basingstoke: Palgrave Macmillan.

Thompson, N. (2005) *Understanding Social Work: Preparing for Practice*, 2nd edn. Houndmills: Palgrave.

Timms, N. (1972) *Recording in Social Work*. London: Routledge and Kegan Paul.

Titmuss, R. (1968) *Commitment to Welfare*. London: Allen and Unwin.

Tomm, K. (1988) 'Interventive interviewing: part III. Intending to ask lineal, circular, strategic or reflexive questions?', *Family Process*, 27(1): 1–15.

Towle, C. (1954) *The Learner in Education for the Professions*. Chicago, IL: University of Chicago Press.

Travis, A. (1999) 'Take on the criminals, Straw urges', *Guardian*, 19 February.

Trevithick, P. (2000) *Social Work Skills: A Practice Handbook*. Buckingham: Open University Press.

Trotter, C. (1999) *Working with Involuntary Clients: A Guide to Practice*. St Leonards: Allen and Unwin.

Twelvetrees, A. (2001) *Community Work*, 3rd edn. Basingstoke: Palgrave.

Twigg, J. (1997) 'Deconstructing the "social bath": help with bathing at home for older and disabled people', *Journal of Social Policy*, 26(2): 211–32.

United Kingdom Parliament (2004) *Hansard*.

Ungerson, C. (1997) 'Give them money: is cash a route to empowerment?', *Social Policy and Administration*, 31(1): 45–53.

Ungerson, C. (2000) 'Thinking about production and consumption of long-term care in Britain: does gender still matter?', *Journal of Social Policy*, 29(4): 623–43.

Utting, W. (1997) *People Like Us: The Report on the Review of Safeguards for Children Living Away from Home*. London: HMSO.

Vernon, A. (1999) 'The dialectics of multiple identities and the Disabled People's Movement', *Disability and Society*, 14(3): 385–98.

Victor, C.R. (1997) *Community Care and Older People*. Cheltenham: Stanley Thornes.

Warren, R. (1977) *Social Change and Human Purpose: Toward Understanding and Action*. Chicago, IL: Rand McNally.

Watzlawick, P., Beavin, A. and Jackson, D. (1967) *Pragmatics of Human Communication: A Study of Interactional Patterns, Pathologies and Paradoxes*. New York: W.W. Norton and Co.

Welsh Assembly Government (2005) *National Service Framework for Children, Young People and Maternity Services in Wales*. Cardiff: Welsh Assembly Government.

Wenger, G.C. (1994) *Support Networks of Older People: A Guide for Practitioners*. Bangor: Centre for Social Policy Research and Development, University of Wales.

Wenger, G.C. (1997) 'Review of findings on support networks of older Europeans', *Journal of Cross-Cultural Gerontology*, 12: 1–21.

Wenger, G.C. and Tucker, I. (2002) 'Using network variation in practice: identification of support network type', *Health and Social Care in the Community*, 10(1): 28–35.

Wijnberg, M. and Schwartz, M. (1977) 'Models of student supervision: the apprentice, growth and role systems models', *Journal of Education for Social Work*, 13(3): 107–13.

Williams, F. (2004) 'What matters is who works: why every child matters to New Labour. Commentary on the DfES Green Paper *Every Child Matters*', *Critical Social Policy*, 24: 406–27.

Willmott, P. (1989) *Community Initiatives: Patterns and Prospects*. London: Policy Studies Institute.

Wilson, J. (1984) 'Understanding network intervention', *Australian Social Work*, 37(2): 11–17.

Wilson, S. (1980) *Recording Guidelines for Social Workers*. New York: Free Press.

Woodcock, J. (1997) 'Groupwork with refugees and asylum seekers', in T. Mistry and A. Brown (eds), *Race and Groupwork*. London: Whiting and Birch.

Zarit, S.H., Reever, K.E. and Bach-Peterson, J. (1980) 'Relatives of the impaired elderly: correlates of feelings of burden', *Gerontologist*, 20: 649–55.

Zastrow, C. and Kirst-Ashman, K. (2001) *Understanding Human Behaviour and the Social Environment*, 5th edn. Pacific Grove, CA: Wadsworth/Thomson Learning.

INDEX